A TEA READER

A Tea READER

LIVING LIFE ONE CUP AT A TIME

*An anthology of readings
for tea lovers old and new*

KATRINA ÁVILA MUNICHIELLO

TUTTLE Publishing

Tokyo | Rutland, Vermont | Singapore

Published by Tuttle Publishing, an imprint of Periplus Editions (HK) Ltd.

www.tuttlepublishing.com

Library of Congress Cataloging-in-Publication Data

A tea reader : living life one cup at a time / [compiled by] Katrina Avila Munichiello.
  p. cm.
 Includes bibliographical references.
 ISBN 978-0-8048-4176-4 (hardcover)
1. Tea--Social aspects. 2. Tea--Miscellanea. I. Munichiello, Katrina Avila.
 GT2905.T44 2011
 394.1'2--dc23

                        2011014441

ISBN 978-0-8048-4176-4

Distributed by

North America, Latin America & Europe
Tuttle Publishing
364 Innovation Drive
North Clarendon, VT 05759-9436 U.S.A.
Tel: 1 (802) 773-8930; Fax: 1 (802) 773-6993
info@tuttlepublishing.com
www.tuttlepublishing.com

Japan
Tuttle Publishing
Yaekari Building, 3rd Floor
5-4-12 Osaki
Shinagawa-ku
Tokyo 141 0032
Tel: (81) 3 5437-0171
Fax: (81) 3 5437-0755
sales@tuttle.co.jp
www.tuttle.co.jp

Asia Pacific
Berkeley Books Pte. Ltd.
61 Tai Seng Avenue #02-12
Singapore 534167
Tel: (65) 6280-1330; Fax: (65) 6280-6290
inquiries@periplus.com.sg
www.periplus.com

First edition
15 14 13 12 11   10 9 8 7 6 5 4 3 2 1   1106TP

Printed in Singapore

DEDICATION

This book is dedicated to my husband Michael and my children.
You make me believe I can do anything.

Contents

THIRD STEEP

Tea Rituals

FOURTH STEEP

Tea Careers

FIFTH STEEP
Tea Travels

Falling in Love with Tea

BY KATRINA ÁVILA MUNICHIELLO

I was seemingly not destined to fall in love with tea.

I have very few childhood tea memories. Oddly, the most vivid remembrance is of lying on the living room couch after staying home from school, sick. I was probably nine or ten years old, and I hadn't eaten all day. I nibbled at a warm piece of cinnamon toast while my mom grabbed a dusty box of tea bags from the cupboard. She brewed up a cup of strong black tea and sweetened it with big spoonfuls of sugar and a generous pour of milk. This was the "cure" for an upset stomach. The milky sweetness soothed and warmed as I drifted to sleep.

The only other times I can recall drinking tea were scorching summer days—a fairly rare occurrence in my home state of Maine. My mom would put a glass jar filled with water and tea bags in the yard to steep in the summer sun. We would pour that sun tea into tall tumblers filled with ice. We clutched icy cups as we sat close to the box fan, gasping at any whisper of cool air. I don't think I particularly liked the tea, but I loved the ritual.

Since those early moments, my tea horizons have expanded dramatically. I have attended Korean and Japanese tea ceremonies where I watched tea masters whip up frothy cups of green tea. I have sampled tea cocktails at upscale hotels and traveled to London to study tea with experts. I've reveled in the ever-changing complexities of *oolongs*, the ethereal delicacy of white teas, and the rare and haunting memories of yellow tea. I've burned my fingers trying to master the *gaiwan*, and I've bravely faced my fear of *pu-erh*. Tea has become an important focus of my life, personally and professionally.

What is striking, however, is that no matter how far I travel from childhood days, the emotions evoked by those early tea moments remain visceral. The memory of that hot, milky tea is one of a mom's comfort, warm blankets, and listening to my favorite books being read to me. Remembering the iced tea gives way to thoughts of blue skies, newly cut grass, and running barefoot. The emotion I feel about these moments makes them as important as the other, more "elegant," experiences.

Tea has a remarkable power to spark such images and nostalgia. It is from this power that my tea journey, and the idea of *A Tea Reader*, evolved.

It was 1996 when I first fell deeply in love with tea after the chance discovery of a new local tea shop. I spent the next decade studying tea and consuming vast quantities of it. I finally took the leap and launched my *Tea Pages* blog. At first, I focused primarily on reviewing teas for my readers, sharing my opinions and mistakes. Over time, I expanded my mission, studying the various tea regions, the processes by which teas are made, and the operations of every tea shop that I encountered. I became more engaged in the subject of tea each day and greedily pursued new experiences. I soon realized the opportunities that having a blog could afford me, primarily in the form of access. I could call a vendor to ask for a tour or write to a publisher to request books to review. I began to e-mail my tea world idols seeking interviews. I became bold.

What amazed me in this experience was the generosity of tea people. They shared their knowledge, resources, and passion for tea. Personal relationships began to develop and stories flowed. Tea became an entry point for conversations that became very personal. I began to actively seek those moments when a story was filled with the emotional responses that had been created by tea.

About eighteen months into my blogging project, I formulated the concept for this book. I made it my mission to capture these personal stories. I wanted to include all types of tea people: not only those brought up in the tea tradition, but also those newly discovering it. Their stories would mix and mingle with those of people who were making tea their career: vendors, shop owners, authors, and tea masters, as well as classic writings by tea lovers from long ago. Together these tales would create a new image of a "tea drinker." They would show that tea is not simply something you drink, but it also provides quiet moments for making important decisions, a catalyst for conversation, and the energy we sometimes need to operate in our lives.

In *A Tea Reader*, you will find stories that cover the spectrum of life. People will develop new friendships, start new careers, and take journeys of which they'd only dreamed. They will share deep moments with their families. A tea shop owner will have his heart broken by Hurricane Katrina, and then find the strength to start again. A woman will share a last moment with her father. You will see reflections of yourself and those that you know.

Whether you are a tea lover or not, here you will discover stories that speak to you and inspire you. Sit down, grab a cup, and read on.

TEA REVERIES

Reverie

BY KATRINA ÁVILA MUNICHIELLO

Reverie(n.): The state of being lost in one's thoughts.

Six types of tea, hundreds of varieties, are all produced from a single plant, the *Camellia sinensis*. Consider that it is possible to drink a different tea every day for years on end. It is stunning to consider. For many tea lovers, this extraordinary diversity and complexity brings forth feelings of reverence for every step of the tea-making process.

A connoisseur stops to examine the dry leaf. Is it large or small, twisted tightly or flat, broken or full? A silver needle tea will have buds that are long like pine needles and covered with fine down. An *oolong* may be rolled into tight pea-sized balls that unfurl as hot water courses down, the "agony of the leaves." We smell. We touch. We admire. We pause. Each second is experienced as something memorable.

Those who have embraced tea may develop their own ways to make the "perfect cup." They have preferences for certain teapots or other brewing devices or the cups from which they sip. Some are adamant about weighing the leaf while others make their best guess on the amount. They think about their tea vendors, storage vessels, and even about the source of their water.

Some "collectors of experience" will spend the rest of their lives seeking that one, unforgettable tea moment that surpasses the rest. Others will embrace tea as practitioners of Japanese tea ceremony do—with the belief that each experience is unique and sacred and cannot be reproduced ever again.

While many details may differ, what is common among all who worship tea is the quest for that moment of reverie. We wish to dive deep into that cup and become mesmerized. Lost in our thoughts, we embrace this time of quiet inspiration.

The Spirit of Tea

BY FRANK HADLEY MURPHY

Tea flowers twice: Once on the bush and once in our hearts.

Just the idea of making tea for myself shifts my consciousness into a sort of dreamtime. Especially if I am alone, I know that I can now hang my mind up on a hook in the mud room and close the door behind me. The ritual has already begun.

Because I like to be intimately involved with every step of the process, I boil water in an open saucepan and I brew the leaves in a clear glass tumbler. This way I can watch everything that's going on. I then decant through a gourd strainer into simple porcelain.

With this first sip, there is another shift. We make tea in an empty vessel and then we become an empty vessel to receive it. The practice of maintaining this emptiness runs through all of the world's mystical traditions. In the West, there is a prayer that says, "Lord, make me decrease so that you might increase in me," but this "Lord" can be any "lord." The point is to get out of our own way and become a kind of receiver, a radar screen if you will, for whatever comes to us. We take that first sip and open to it, yield to it, and let it wash over us.

The ritual of making and tasting tea becomes what I call an "entry ritual," a doorway into other realms. My attention shifts to my pelvic floor, where the tea's warmth has settled. And this is where *Thea*, the goddess of light after whom tea was named, begins to illuminate my soul.

The sensation of light is that of mobilizing forces, the feeling that new synapses are being formed. As an image, it is one I liken to moonbeams shining out from inside me. Things are clearer.

The Chinese say that tea "brightens the eyes" but this, like all things Chinese, can have several meanings. Sometimes tea brightens my entire perspective on the universe and my place within it. That is why I write of tea as an "*entheogen*," because it is a plant that affects my consciousness and my heart in a beneficent manner.

So there are these opening, flowering sensations in my tummy, and then, as my body and the tea continue to shift and mobilize in union with each other, there are these opening, flowering sensations in my heart: broad, expansive feelings of pure, unadulterated joy.

So where do we go from here?

Do I make myself another cup of tea?

No.

I just sit.

Perhaps I am not done with my tea. Perhaps all this is the result of a single sip. It's happened before. I peer down into that porcelain cup and, lo and behold, it's still full.

Tea is such a sensual experience. There's the handling and holding of warm vessels as we brew. There's that initial fragrance when we moisten the dry leaves with a few drops of water and bring it to our nose. There's that first sip, when our lips break the surface of our brew and our whole body fills with the essence of the leaf. With the first taste we encounter the silken viscosity, the floral notes and fruity tones, the earthen depths, wooded bite and all of it bathing our tongues with waves of unfolding complexity before it slides down the back of our throats. I muse that it might be more accurate to say "waves of cascading epiphanies" for such is the way it feels when Thea shares with us her deepest mysteries and stirs us to our souls.

And so she stirs. And she mobilizes. Tea tastes good in my mouth and feels good in my body. It lifts my spirits and opens my heart. What more could we ask of a friend?

I have landed in my body. If I'm lucky, I can hang out here for a while in this peace and calm, for that is what it finally ends up being, and that is why tea has been grown on monastic properties for a thousand years. It brings us to a place of wakeful tranquility. I call it reverie.

Perhaps it is that tea pulls me back so far into myself that my senses become attuned to a different set of coordinates. Perhaps my senses align themselves with a subtle, more refined resonance. Someone once said that tea muffles strident noises. It certainly seems this way to me, but then, I have never been known for my powers of deductive reasoning. I would prefer to lay down under tea bushes on the green, terraced hills of Yunnan...and dream.

I Don't Drink Tea
BY STEPHANIE WRIGHT

I don't drink tea. I drink coffee. Black coffee for years until my first pregnancy sent me the route of decaffeinated. Don't believe them when they tell you the difference can't be tasted. It can, and I started using cream to offset the variation in flavor. Somehow, I never went back to black even after weaning that first daughter from the breast and reverting to "high octane." At some point, I picked up a taste for sweetener, too.

But I digress.

I don't drink tea. One shouldn't mistake the lack of indulgence for lack of acquired taste. I adore tea. I adore many teas. *Oolong* and Darjeeling. The simple delight of bergamot in an early morning cup of Earl Grey. One long winter, I took a fancy to Irish Breakfast. Hearty stuff, Irish Breakfast. For tea, I like sugar, not sweetener, and lots of cream. I even have three cups in which I take my tea. Two were gifts from my mother, delicate bone china cups with saucers. One has violets around its elongated form, while the other has a slender band of roses trailing just the outer rim. The third I purchased for myself. It's only a small cup, hardly large enough to hold a decent amount, but it's sweet in its simple shape and muted reds. Those three cups are part of the reason I eschew the brew. Look, a little rhyme. A bitty ditty, if you will, to keep me from my point. The point, of course, is that I don't drink tea.

Should you come upon me one day in the process of setting kettle to hob, you can safely assume rebellion is on the horizon. I'd run for cover were I you. Do not be kind and ask what troubles me. Do not offer to sit with me in my despair. If a china cup with violets or roses sits in readiness on the counter, if sugar and cream wait with tiny silver-plate tongs and spoon, back away slowly and don't look for the ground wire. There isn't one.

In fact, I'll probably wish I were you in that moment, for a pot of tea can only signify that a watershed moment in my life has been reached. Some have their tea as a matter of daily course, of routine, of comfort or relaxation. Tea has always been for me a fortification, a metaphorical battening down of the hatches as I prepare for momentous decisions and the rendering of judgments.

Take, for instance, one such pot prepared. The night in question was dressed in mist and accessorized by a flamboyant full moon. I fixed the pot, an African *rooibos* delicately flavored with vanilla, and sat at the kitchen window. Alone. I sipped, and as I did, I turned over the promises of fidelity and eternity I'd made, searching for fault-lines. Somewhere between finishing the second cup and pouring the third, the sentiment of "I love you" transformed into "I need to love me," and I rose to rinse the cup. I felt a bit ill and blamed the sensation on over-consumption.

The nausea dissipated. The resolve did not. Decaffeinated coffee and I have enjoyed three brief affairs, one per pregnancy, and each time we parted in amiability with no regrets. The same is never true of tea and me. Was it perhaps the subtle wildness of the *rooibos*? Was it something already set within me that needed nothing more than the quiet instilled only from sitting with a cup of tea, the customary making of which renders the drink more potent in its ability to bring clarity of thought? I do not know, and I shy away from looking too closely for the answer. Resolute, I moved forward. Alone.

These days, I keep a wary eye on my little cast iron teapot. Several months ago, my sister sent me a box of green tea with jasmine flowers inside each little mesh bag. When hot water is poured over the bag, the petals of the flowers open, and the sight is just beautiful. My daughter bought me a tin of lemongrass tea, its flavor nothing short of distilled peace. I steer clear of both—and the pot—lest my decision prove temporary. These days, I'm back to coffee, back to routine. Routine maintains my resolve. Tea seduces me into false judgement. I do not wish to revisit my decisions once made, and a pleasant cup of Lady Jane just might make me do that.

I don't drink tea. I drink coffee. Though bitter, addictive, and not terribly good at forging bonds or demolishing lines between social classes, coffee is safe. Perhaps the day will come when my hand won't automatically stray towards the handle of my teapot each time I reach for a coffee filter. That would be nice.

The Spectator on Tea

AUTHOR UNKNOWN

Excerpted from an essay in The Outlook *magazine,*
January 19, 1907.

[1]The Spectator confesses to an unmanly weakness for tea. Not the tea of the drawing-room, be it understood, that implies social amenities and an acrobatic style of chit-chat for which the Spectator has no sort of genius. What he wants when he is jaded, body, soul, and spirit—when the day is glowering into the unsympathetic twilight of early winter, and he has before him the long journey into Suburbia—is the soothing effect of the fragrant cup sipped solitary, or with only a good companion who knows the mercy of silence. If his office were only in London, now, he could despatch the office-boy to the nearest "A.B.C."[2] for a steaming pot, a plate of paper-thin bread and butter, jam, and perhaps a buttered scone. Imagine the result should he send the *Outlook*'s Billy, or James, or Jonathan on such an errand! What is there disgraceful about tea? The Spectator supposes that he could step out and get a cocktail without forfeiting the office-boy's respect. But he doesn't like cocktails. They fret him instead of soothing. Indeed, there are times when he fancies that the nervous tension of New York business life is founded upon the cocktail, and that if we could substitute the English teacup we should accomplish as much and wear out less rapidly.

---

1   [Certain British spellings have been amended. Ed.]
2   A.B.C. is Aerated Bread Company. In 1864, A.B.C. opened the U.K.'s first tearoom.

Perhaps the tea-table of the drawing room is the entering wedge. Mrs. Spectator reports a growing tendency among the men who drop in of an afternoon to look upon the tea she offers as something more than a compliment well meant but embarrassing. But we have by no means come to realize the full value of the Boon of the Orient. The Spectator had this forcibly borne in upon him not long ago when business called him to the little town of Peabody, Massachusetts, a suburb of Salem. The afternoon was chill and gloomy with fine rain. Trains are sixty minutes apart at the little Peabody station, and the Spectator's business detained him so that he caught just a glimpse of the departing four o'clock express. Fresh from an English summer, he at once bethought him of consolation to be found in some cozy tearoom where the hour might be idled away pleasantly enough. A glance up and down the dull little street banished abruptly his dream of consuming toothsome cakes by the glow of a leaping fire. This was not England. Still, the Spectator fancied the automobile might have developed some nice private refectory where he might stay the cravings of the inner man. He inquired, "A tearoom? Oh yes. There was Banning's, with the blue sign." The Spectator sought out Banning's. But alas for his comfortable anticipations! A fly specked window coldly warned him. Inside a dingy, two-by-twice shop, dense with the odors of untold successions of ill-cooked meals, was a bald lunch counter set forth with slabs of unspeakable leaden pie. A tearoom indeed!

The Spectator ultimately discovered little cakes of bakerish suggestion at a confectioner's, and beef-tea at a soda fountain. But as he sat bolt upright on a revolving stool and consumed the hot and so far comforting beverage, he could not help thinking how much the poetry of the exercise was dissipated by the surrounding drugs and nostrums, nor how cozily the kettle simmers, for native and stranger alike, in a thousand bright, clean little shops scattered through the tiniest villages of Old England.

For the matter of that, it's not in shops alone that you find the cheering cup. Does it not invite you, hot and fragrant, at the very door of your railway compartment every time the train stops? Do not the coaches upon the post-roads of Devon, Cornwall, and, for aught the

Spectator knows, the Lakes, draw up at tea time at some posting-house that the passengers may perform the graceful rite without which no English day is complete? The Spectator will not soon forget an October drive from Porlock over moor and forelands to Lynton. The hunt was out, the posting stations noisy with riders dashing in for fresh mounts, the whole countryside thrilling with the music of the horns. From all this heartening bustle the coach climbed up to the solitude of the moors. The sun dropped into a deep bank of cloud, a "nipping and eager air" awoke on the moor, and the Spectator began to find himself, as the guard said, "perishin' cold." It was after hours of brisk cantering over the long, red Devonshire road, when the Spectator's blood was congealing in his veins, that the coach drew up at a crossroads. And there, apparently miles from any house, sat a little old woman nursing a tea-tray! Off came a deep-padded cozy, and wreaths of beneficent steam began to rise on the frosty air. Nobody asked the Spectator whether he would have a cup of tea, and as he was perched on the highest seat of all, and the ladder was not forthcoming, he began to despair of getting any, when the guard came clambering up, dexterously balancing a full cup. And even now he did not ask if the Spectator would take it, merely demanding sixpence as if it were part of the road-fare. From his point of view it would have been as incomprehensible that a sane man should refuse tea as that he should profess to scorn bed and breakfast. Never shall the Spectator forget the genial glow that pervaded his whole being as he plied himself with bread and butter and piping-hot tea, nor the doze of dreamy contentment in which he passed the remainder of the drive until the lights of Lynton appeared, gleaming like a swarm of fireflies on the shoulder of the cliff. He thought then that he understood the cult of the tea leaf.

But he had still something to learn. A week or two later he and Mrs. Spectator attempted to travel to the little town of Broadway. At Evesham they were stayed by the absence of any sort of conveyance except a funereal-looking carrier's cart, the electric train having departed a few minutes before. They set out, therefore, to trudge the six miles afoot. The way was lovely enough, the placid Warwickshire country swimming in the golden afternoon light. But the way was long. Mrs.

Spectator's courage failed her when Broadway was yet three miles away, and down she sat her, with an air of hopeless exhaustion, on the long grass beside the road. "Mr. Spectator," she gasped, "I would sell my soul for a cup of tea!" The words were scarcely out of her mouth when her jaw fell. She looked as if she had seen a ghost. Then she began to laugh hysterically. "Is it"—she pointed with a shaky finger—"is it *real*?" The Spectator looked behind him. Tiptoeing across the road came two little English girls in pinafores, bearing—yes, it *was* real—bearing cups of smoking tea. "Mother said," began the elder, shyly, "would you like some tea? She was just pouring hers, and she thought you looked tired." Mrs. Spectator declares that hereafter, whenever the tea craving seizes her, she shall simply recline upon the landscape and tea will be brought to her. So much for the humanizing influence of the cult....

When the Spectator wants to dine out and enjoy the full luxury of the experience, it is rarely to an American hotel or restaurant that he goes. The little foreign cafés, these provide brisk service when service is wanted, and complete obliviousness when it is not. The Spectator knows a little French place in Boston where this principle is understood to perfection. You may dine at six and smoke till ten, and not a waiter will cast an envious eye upon your table. It is this that as a nation we must learn—the fine art of idleness. It is for this reason that he advocates the teakettle in the counting-room, and inscribes upon his banners those memorable words of Colley Cibber's:[3] "*Tea!* thou soft, thou sober, sage, and venerable liquid, smile-smoothing, heart-opening cordial, to whose glorious insipidity I owe the happiest moments of my life, let me fall prostrate!"

---

3   Colley Cibber (1671–1755) was an English playwright and Poet Laureate.

A Poem in Praise of Tea

BY PETER ANTHONY MOTTEUX

Excerpted from its namesake, originally published in London in 1712.[1]

Last Night my Hours on Friendship I bestow'd,
And Wine and Mirth a while profusely flow'd.
Soon as some Beauty's Health had walk'd the Round,
Another's Health succeeding Glasses crown'd.
But while these Arts to raise our Joys we use,
Our Mirth, our Friends, and ev'n ourselves we lose.
'Tis vain in Wine to seek a solid Joy;
All fierce Enjoyments soon themselves destroy,
Wine fires the Fancy to a dangerous height,
With smokey Flame, and with cloudy Light.
From its Excess ev'n Wisdom's self grows mad;
For an Excess of Good itself is bad.
All Reason's in a Storm, no Light, nor Skies,
But the Red Ocean rolls before our Eyes.
Unhappy State! the Chaos of the Brain,
The Soul's Eclipse, and Exile of the Man.
From boist'rous Wine I fled to gentle Tea;
For, Calms compose us after Storms at Sea.
In vain wou'd Coffee boast an equal Good;
The Crystal Stream transcends the flowing Mud.
Tea ev'n the Ills from Coffee sprung repairs,
Disclaims its Vices, and its Virtue shares.

---

1   [Certain British spellings have been amended. Ed.]

To bless me with the Juice two Foes conspire,
The clearest Water with the purest Fire....
...I drink, and lo the kindly Steams arise,
Wine's Vapor flags, and soon subsides and dies.
The friendly Spirits brighten mine again,
Repel the Brute, and re-inthrone the Man.
The rising Charmer with a pleasing Ray
Dawns on the Mind, and introduces Day.
So its bright Parent with prevailing Light,
Recalls Distinction, and displaces Night.
At other times the wakeful Leaf disdains
To leave the Mind entranc'd in drowsy Chains.
But now with all the Night's Fatigue opprest,
'Tis reconcil'd to Sleep, and yields me up to Rest.
Hail, Drink of Life! how justly shou'd our Lyres
Resound the Praises which thy Pow'r inspires!
Blest Juice, assist, while I the Vision draw
Which then in Sleep with inward Eyes I saw![2]
Thy Charms alone can equal Thoughts infuse:
Be thou my Theme, my Nectar, and my Muse.
I saw the Gods and Goddesses above,
Profusely feasting with Imperial *Jove*.
The Banquet done, swift round the Nectar flew,
All Heav'n was warm'd, and *Bacchus* boist'rous grew.
Fair *Hebe* then the grateful Tea prepares,
Which to the feasting Goddesses she bears.
The Heav'nly Guests advance with eager haste;
They gaze, they smell, they drink, and bless the Taste.
Refresh'd and Charm'd, while thus employ'd they fit,
More bright their Looks, and more Divine their Wit;
At large each Goddess pleasing Censures flung.

---

2 Motteux is about to describe a dream he had after drinking tea. It involves Jove, King of the gods and the god of thunder in Roman mythology; Hebe, the daughter of Zeus and Hera in Greek mythology who served as cupbearer on Mount Olympus; and "the drunken God" Bacchus.

For, ev'n above, the Sex will, right or wrong,
Enjoy their dear Prerogative of Tongue.
The drunken God, long courted, tastes at length:
Then swears the Liquor's damn'd for want of Strength.
How low, cried he, in quaffing are we sunk!
Will Stuff like this make Gods or Mortals drunk?
'Twixt this and Wine how mighty are the odds!
Wine makes us drunk, and something more than Gods.
Rais'd with that Nectar o'er the Skies I rove,
And only to be drunk is to be *Jove*.
Now raving *Bacchus*, reeling to his Place,
Crowns his Assertion with an ample Glass;
And *Hebe* then replies with modest Grace.
Immortal Pow'rs of Heav'n, and Earth, and Sea,
Permit Youth's Goddess to defend her Tea.
What Food, what Drink a Taste deprav'd can please,
Averse to Cure, and fond of its Disease!
The purest Air gross Mortals ne'er befriends,
And Heav'n itself cannot be Heav'n to Fiends.
Thus kindly Tea perhaps insipid seems
To Sense debauch'd by Wine's seducing Steams;
But sure, where-e'er these lov'd Abuses fail,
Tea, Temperance and Reason will prevail.
Wine proves most fatal when it most invites,
Tea most is healthful when it most delights.
Wine conquers Man with its pernicious Fumes,
Tea conquers Wine, tho' Wine the Man o'ercomes.
Wine but inflames the Brain it wou'd inspire,
Tea gives the Light, and yet excludes the Fire.
Relieve me, God of Physic, and of Lays,
And reach a Theme superior to my Praise.
Here *Hebe* ceas'd: The Thund'rer[3] with a Nod,
Bespeaks Assent of the Melodious God.

---

3 "The Thund'rer" refers again to Jove, the god of the sky and thunder, who takes up Hebe's defense of tea.

Tell, Muse, for sure no Mortal can rehearse
The hallow'd Utt'rance of the God of Verse;
Tell how of Tea the great Physician sung!
Words like his Theme flow'd sweetly from his Tongue.
At once the God two Attributes reveal'd,
His Sense enlighten'd, and his Numbers heal'd.
He sung of Rage, by Harmony controll'd,
And manly Clay with living Fire infoul'd.
Of Arts devis'd, of Plants for Wonders prais'd,
And Tea, whose Fame shoul'd o'er all Plants be rais'd.
None, says the God, shall with that Tree compare;
Health, Vigor, Pleasure bloom forever there;
Sense for the Learn'd, and Beauty for the Fair.
Tea both imparts: For, while it cheers the Mind,
Her Seat's refresh'd, and ev'ry Charm refin'd,
The Eyes, the Judgment with authentic Light
Receive their Objects, and distinguish right.
Bright are the Sallies of the rising Thought,
Sublime the Flights, yet regularly wrought.
Hence, then, ye Plants, that challeng'd once our Praise,
The Oak, the Vine, the Olive, and the Bays.
No more let Roses *Flora's* Brows adorn,
Nor *Ceres* boast her golden Ears of Corn.
The Queen of Love her Myrtles shall despise;
Tea claims at once the Beauteous and the Wise.
Think of the Rose, that inoffensive Sweet,
Of fragrant Gums, the Brain's luxurious Treat;
Or kinder Odors which in verdant Fields,
When newly cropped, the grassy Harvest yields.
Think ev'ry grateful Smell diffus'd in one,
And in Imperial Tea find all their Charms out-done.
Tea, Heav'ns Delight, and Nature's truest Wealth,
That pleasing Physic, and sure Pledge of Health:
The Statesman's Counselor, the Virgin's Love,
The Muse's *Nectar*, and the Drink of *Jove*....

*****

...Soon as the Day in Orient Climes is born,
The wife *Chinese* with Tea salute the Morn.
And as my Beams, their Vigor to renew,
Sport in the Waves, and drink their Morning Dew,
So there each rising Nymph with Tea supplies
The intermitted Luster of her Eyes.
Serene and lovely as the new-born Ray,
Afresh they dazzle, and augment the Day.
Tea first in China did all Arts improve,
And, like my Light, still Westward thence they move.
Well might all Nations be by those out-done
Who first enjoy'd that Nectar and the Sun....

*****

...There, Chemists, there your Grand Elixir see,
The *Panacea* you should boast is Tea.
There, Sons of Art, your Wishes doubled find,
Tea cures at once the Body and the Mind:
Chaste, yet not cold; and sprightly, yet not wild;
Tho' gentle, strong, and tho' compulsive, mild:
Fond Nature's Paradox, that cools and warms,
Cheers without Sleep, and, tho' a Med'cine, charms.
Ye Sages, who, with weighty Notions fraught,
Tho' doz'd with Study, would persist in Thought,
When the Lamp sickens, and the Moon-beams faint,
And trembling Sight obeys but with Constraint,
You know 'tis Tea whose Pow'r new Strength allows,
And drives the Slumbers from your yielding Brows;
Night's conquer'd, and the weary Stars retire,
Yet still the Mind preserves her active Fire....

*****

...Immortals, hear, said *Jove*, and cease to jar!
Tea must succeed to Wine, as Peace to War;
Nor by the Grape let Men be set at odds,
But share in Tea, the Nectar of the Gods.

Bi Luo Chun

BY ROY FONG

Bi Luo Chun has been prized since the Ming Dynasty and was selected as a tribute tea during the Qing Kang Xi era (1661–1722). The Kang Xi Emperor's grandson, Emperor Qian Long (1735–1795), was a great tea lover, and he reportedly enjoyed *Bi Luo Chun* very much during his visit to the area.

The ancient Chinese called the tea "Astonishingly Fragrant Tea" for obvious reasons. The name was later changed to *Bi Luo Chun*, "Green Conch Spring," as the tea was being selected as tribute to the emperor. "Astonishingly Fragrant Tea" was not a name deemed poetic enough for the Court. The Chinese have many words to describe the color green; "*Bi*" in this case means jade or sea color, algae green. "*Chun*" means spring, full of life, or young and tender. "*Luo*" means conch, describing the twisted spiral shape of the leaf. The word "*Luo*" can also refer to the beautiful lacy dress of an ancient Chinese beauty; the choice of this word was intended to add even more elegance to this ultra elegant tea.

It was not until after a few years in the tea business that I met this great tea close up. A trip to the *Bi Luo Chun* tea farm was arranged by my friend Chen Nong, whose sister-in-law was a city official from Shanghai. She arranged for me to meet with officials from Yixing and also to meet with some famous Yixing teapot artists. Since Yixing is very close to Lake Tai, where the best *Bi Luo Chun* are grown, I naturally asked to visit one of the most noted tea farms there.

I arrived at the farm in mid-afternoon and was greeted by the owner and offered a glass of tea from that morning's production. Hot water was poured into a tall glass and a handful of tiny dark green and twisted leaf sets were added to the water. The leaves slowly infused and gently spiraled to the bottom of the glass, opening up into small flower-like sets as they descended. The aroma of fresh sweet green filled the air. I waited until almost all the leaves settled in the bottom of the glass and took a sip. I still remember that silky soft and juicy mouth-feel without any hints of bitterness, the sweetness that slowly but surely filled my mouth and seemed to fill my whole being. All I could say to myself at that time was a big inward "*wow*!"

Seduced by a Leaf

BY BABETTE DONALDSON

"How did you become interested in tea?"

I'm often asked this very general question for which there are many different answers, just as there are many different aspects to tea. A more appropriate question would be: "When did tea become important to you?"

And to that I must confess that I was seduced by the leaf.

The specific tea and moment came in a small tea shop in Chinatown, San Francisco. Seated on a short stool at the tasting table, the owner of the shop suggested I sample their high-mountain *Bi Luo Chun*. He pulled a large canister from the shelf and tipped the lid to release the sweet, green fragrance trapped and intensified within. He poured some of the dry leaf—thin, twisted threads in a spectrum of green—into a small dish. As he measured the tea and prepared the water, he *talked* tea. He had been to the garden where this tea had grown. The women who picked and the men who processed the green leaf are people he had known for many years. His family had been buying this tea since they opened the shop here in the U.S. And he had been preparing and serving tea in this way since he was a child. It felt as if I was watching performance art and learning a new language.

The tea, *Bi Luo Chun*, grows in the high mountains of Jiangsu Province of southern China. The tea gardens are planted close to peach, plum and apricot orchards drawing the sweet fragrance of the fruit blossoms into the tea leaves. The tiny shoots are picked in the early morning before the newest leaves open, when they are still covered with a soft, white down. The green leaves are then pan fried and dried quickly, shrinking the leaf into little twisted bits, trapping the flavor and sealing the lovely variations of color into the prepared leaf.

It was in the second steeping that the sweet, fruitiness came through.

"Can you taste the plums?" the tea man asked.

"Yes. And something else," I answered.

"The creaminess. The way it makes your mouth feel."

"Yes. That too," I said. "And something more."

He continued telling me about the tea. It has many names. It may be called *Bi Luo Chun*, *Pi Lo Chun*, Green Snail Spring, or Green Conch Spring. Other times it is referred to by fragrance: *Xia Sha Ren Xiang* (Scary Fragrance.)

"Like Halloween?" I asked.

"Like awesome," he answered.

The legend of this tea is that one young tea picker had filled her basket but wanted to carry more. She filled her bodice with what must have been several thousand more shoots, enough to make another pound of dry, processed tea. The warmth of her body released the surprisingly strong aroma.

It was the third infusion and the story that sucked me into this new world. It was the first time I tasted tea with awareness and intention. I tasted more than I could describe. I tasted more than just the fruitiness carried from the breezes blowing over surrounding orchards. I tasted the land, the soil, the processing and something of the people who had created my tea.

The leaf was fully reconstituted after the third infusion. We compared the wet leaf with the original dry, all the leaves about 1/2 inch long, most of them a single bud or still attached in tiny sets of two leaves.

"How much per pound?" I asked.

"Sixty-nine dollars," he answered.

I spread some of the wet, spent leaf in the palm of my hand.

"How many leaves per pound?"

"More than 7,000."

The math was easy and staggering. Approximately $0.01 was the price for each leaf picked by that young girl, who then carried it back in her basket, for processing at the tea plant where the male work-ers dried it in several stages, including stirring it in a large wok over an open fire. It also included the packing, shipping, taxes, fees, and a profit for the retailer. The owner of the tea shop completed the equa-tion for me.

"That's less than $0.50 per cup."

He thought I was complaining about the price. Quite the opposite. The tea seemed rare and precious. I felt that the sense of value was not being fully appreciated.

I couldn't afford to buy an entire pound but I walked out of the shop with a small package and my head filled with images of a world of tea. I felt the connection to the people who had grown the tea and wanted them to feel my deep gratitude, to know that their labor was valued for more than the pennies per pound they had been paid. But how?

The little sealed pouch of tea was difficult to open without scissors. But even the few minutes that had elapsed from the time I left the shop seemed to have intensified the aroma. I took a pinch and put it in my own bodice and finished my shopping, still tasting the third cuppa and feeling a bit naughty with my little secret.

"Nice perfume," said the woman who sat next to me on the cable car.

"Thank you." But I didn't explain.

That was several years ago and the price for a good *Bi Luo Chun* is now a bit higher, but not by much. I order some of the new harvest every year. It is one of the flavors I crave about the same time the new crop arrives.

Is it my favorite tea? No. But it always touches my heart like a first love; the tea that seduced me. It is the tea that helped me understand the *something else* I taste in tea.

Over the years, I've had the blessing of being seduced by more teas, each with its own story: a legend, a history, a bit of geography. Every cup of whole leaf tea makes me feel that I am coming to know the world in a more intimate and tangible way. I am coming to think of tea as the taste of peace on Earth.

Song of Tea *or* Writing Thanks to Imperial Grand Master of Remonstrance Meng for Sending New Tea

BY LU T'UNG, AS TRANSLATED BY STEVEN D. OWYOUNG FOR *CHA DAO*[1]

The sun is as high as a ten-foot measure and five; I am deep asleep.

The general bangs at the gate loud enough to scare the Duke of Chou![2]

He announces that the Grand Master sends a letter; the white silk cover is triple-stamped.

Breaking the vermilion seals, I imagine the Grand Master himself inspecting these three hundred moon-shaped tea cakes.

He heard that within the tea mountain a path was cut at the New Year, sending insects rising excitedly on the spring wind.

As the emperor waits to taste Yang-hsien tea, the one hundred plants dare not bloom.

Benevolent breezes intimately embrace pearly tea sprouts, the early spring coaxing out buds of golden yellow.

Picked fresh, fired till fragrant, then packed and sealed: tea's essence and goodness is preserved.

---

1 chadao.blogspot.com
2 The Duke of Chou was also known as the "God of Dreams." "Dreaming of Zhou (or Chou)" meant you were sleeping.

Such venerable tea is meant for princes and nobles; how did it reach the hut of this mountain hermit?

The brushwood gate is closed against vulgar visitors; all alone, I don my gauze cap, brewing and tasting the tea.

Clouds of green yielding; unceasingly, the wind blows; radiantly white, floating tea froth congeals against the bowl.

The first bowl moistens my lips and throat.

The second bowl banishes my loneliness and melancholy.

The third bowl penetrates my withered entrails, finding nothing except a literary core of five thousand scrolls.

The fourth bowl raises a light perspiration, casting life's inequities out through my pores.

The fifth bowl purifies my flesh and bones.

The sixth bowl makes me one with the immortal, feathered spirits.

The seventh bowl I need not drink, feeling only a pure wind rushing beneath my wings.

Where are the immortal isles of Mount P'englai? I, Master Jade Stream, wish instead to ride this pure wind back to the tea mountain where other immortals gather to oversee the land, protecting the pure, high places from wind and rain.

Yet, how can I bear knowing the bitter fate of the myriad peasants toiling beneath the tumbled tea cliffs!

I have but to ask Grand Master Meng about them; whether they can ever regain some peace.

Reprinted with permission from Stephen D. Owyoung and Cha Dao. *Originally published in the April 2008 issue of* Cha Dao *as part of "Lu T'ung and the 'Song of Tea': The Taoist Origins of the Seven Bowls."*

Ode on Tea

BY KIEN-LONG, EMPEROR OF CHINA AND TARTARY FROM 1735–1796

Written in 1746. Translated/published in the Public Advertiser,
March 9, 1772.[1]

How tenderly striking to the Eye, is the Flower *Mey-hoa*![2]
How sweet the Scent exhaled from the delicate Plant of *Fo-tchow*![3]
How aromatic the Flavor of the invitingly odorous Fruit of the Pine[4]
Song-tchow!
Three admirable Gifts of Nature these,
For Pleasure to the Sight, the Smell, and Taste!
   With these at hand; let there upon a moderate Fire,
Stand placed a tripod Boiler,
Well fashion'd, and whose Color shall attest its seasoning for Service:
Filled with the limpid Water of melted Snow
When it shall have boil'd just to the Heat,
That serves to whiten the Flakes of the finny Tribes[5]
Or redden the black Shell of the coated Kind;[6]
Then, into a Cup of the rare Porcelain of *Yvay,*[7]

---

1   [Certain British spellings have been amended. Ed.]
2   May refer to plum blossoms (*Mei Hua*). It is the national flower of the Taiwan. Translated elsewhere as *Mei-hoa* and *M-i-hoa*.
3   Possible reference to *Fo Shou* tea, aka Buddha's Hand, a Wuyi *oolong* tea. Also translated as *Fo-choea*, *Fo-ch ou*, and *Fo-cheou*.
4   "Fruit of the pine" are, perhaps, pine nuts.
5   Hot enough to cook a fish, turning its meat to white.
6   Other translations say "reddening the crustaceous kind." Hot enough to cook a lobster, turning its shell from black to red.
7   Yué in other translations. Refers to the Yue Kiln of Zhejiang Province, one of the most

Pour it on the fragrant Leaves of the Tea tree;

Let it stand 'till the fervent Steam

That will, at first, have risen, like a thick Cloud,

Shall have evaporated to a thin Mist:

Then may you, leisurely, sip the fine-flavor'd Liquor;

Nothing more powerful to dispel any of those Uneasinesses,

That may have proceeded from their five Causes;

Then may you regale your Smell and Taste;

But inexpressible is the placid Calm,

That steals upon the Senses, from that virtuous Infusion.

    Deliver'd, for a while, from the Tumult of Affairs,

I find myself, at length, alone in my Tent;

Restor'd to the Power of enjoying myself, at Liberty.

    In one Hand, I take the Fruit of the *Fo-tchow*,

Just by Way of Relish;

In the other, I hold the Cup,

From the Contents of which, the vaporous Mist sent up,

Invitingly hovers on the Surface;

As I sip the Tea,

I now and then cast a delighted Eye,

On the Flower *Mey-hoa*.

Then it is that I give a Loose to my Thoughts;

They naturally, of themselves, and without Effort,

Turn to the Sages of Antiquity.[8]

    I love to represent to myself the famous *Oot-fu-eng*

Whose sole Food was the Fruit of the Pine *Song-tchow*,

In the midst of this primitive Frugality

He enjoy'd himself in Peace;

In Emulation of him,

I put some Kernels in my Mouth,

And find them delicious.

---

important sites for the creation of celadon porcelain in China.

8   In the next parts of the ode, Kien-Long imagines how various Chinese "Sages of Antiquity," philosophers of the past, would experience his current setting. He discusses *Oot-fu-eng* (also written as *Ou-tfuen*), *Lin-foo* (also *Lin-fou*), *Ttchao-Tcheoo* (also *Tchao-tcheon*), and *Yu-tchuang* (also *Yu-tchou* or *Yu-tchouan*).

With Imagination's Eye,
Then next I see the virtuous *Lin-foo*,
Pruning and trimming up the Leaves,
Of the flower *Mey-hoa*;
Thus it was, say I to myself, that that great Man,
Indulg'd his Mind with some Relaxation;
A Mind fatigu'd with intense Meditation,
On the most important Objects;
I apply myself then to the Flower *Mey-hoa*,
And fancy myself, with *Lin-foo*, arranging the Leaves,
And giving to the Plant the most pleasing Form.
     From *Lin-foo* I, mentally, make Transition
To *Ttchao-tcheoo*, and *Yu-tchuang*,
I think I see the *first* having before him,
Various Cups with various teas,
Affectedly sipping and tasting of each:
The *other* I figure to myself drinking churlishly,
The most exquisitely fine Tea,
Without any Distinction of its Flavor,
From that of the coarsest Sort
Be neither of these Extremes mine.
     But, hark!—I hear the Martial Music
Already announce the Evening.
The reviving Freshness of the Night is coming on
Already the Moonshine entering at the Windows of my Tent
Throws a pleasing Light,
On the Military Simplicity of its Furniture.
I feel myself free from Fatigue, free from Uneasiness,
My stomach relieve'd and unoppress'd;
With my Spirits clear, I may then
Deliver myself up to sweet Repose.
In this Mood it was, that, with but a small Talent for Poetry
I wrote these Lines, in the First of the Spring
Of the tenth Month of the *Ping-yu* Year of my Reign.

Tea to Last Lifetimes

BY AARON FISHER

"It is obvious that the life of action will be shallow indeed if it does not go hand in hand with an interior spiritual life wherefrom the strength and vision needed for action are drawn."
—Alan Watts

One of the most amazing experiences of my life happened when my whole family, including my very aged grandfather and great uncle, came to visit me in Taiwan. I took the whole group to see a tea master. The eight of them sat around the table chit-chatting about how exotic the tea room was, with its walls and walls of tea, waterfalls, and bonsai trees. Eventually, my teacher passed me a sly grin and reached behind him to a jar of very old *pu-erh* tea. Brewing the deep and dark liquor—leaves ancient and wise, connected to the spirit of Nature—changed the entire atmosphere of the room. Within minutes, it was enshrouded in a deep and peaceful silence, only the waterfall singing in the background. For the next two hours, I sat with my family in complete quiet, connected to one another as never before: Never in my entire life before that day had my family and I ever sat in quiet; never had we been so close.

My mother wept with joy; my grandfather cried too, saying later that he felt the presence of my then recently departed grandmother. The power that tea can have—the life-changing presence and connection that it may offer when prepared in the right environment—became clearer to me than ever before. I share this experience, so personal, to show that one need not be a saint, a meditator, or even a tea lover to experience the profundity of what a tea ceremony steeped in the Tao can offer.

In this day and age, loud and cluttered, a drop or two of quiet emptiness is forceful enough to make the average person weep. Nothing is needed more. When we study the history of tea, we find such sweeping statements as "for thousands of years tea was medicine to Chinese people," as if this somehow even approximated a description of the largest part of man's relationship with this majestic plant. Authors often begin where the brush first touches paper, feeling more comfortable standing on historically verifiable ground. It takes a greater affinity with the Leaf to approach the much larger substrata of prehistory. Sure, it's true that tea was "medicine" for thousands of years before it was ever a commodity, social pleasure, or hobby. But that word, at least in English, is a bit misleading. It was "medicine" in the way that Native Americans use that word: "healing" or "with spiritual presence/power."

In the beginning, tea was eaten and steeped by aboriginal shamans who used it to heal, to inspire meditation and to commune with divinities. Some of the earliest references to tea are as offerings to spirits and as a part of rituals to communicate with them. Slowly, over time, the steeped leaf became an essential brew in the life of Taoist mendicants. These hermits sought out wild bushes, claiming that tea was an ingredient in the "Morning Dew," which was the elixir of life and key to immortality. They drank tea for health, to clarify the mind, and to promote meditation as well as transmission from master to student.

From martial arts to mathematics, the tradition of student and teacher sharing tea continues even today. If the student brews the tea and the master accepts, it is also an acceptance of the student into the lineage. More poignantly, when the master brews tea and presents it to the student there is a direct transmission of what Eastern mystics believe to be an ineffable wisdom, only available to experience. What could be more symbolic than the master brewing his mind into a bowl, which the student then consumes, taking that wisdom into himself?

When Buddhism came to China, it was heavily influenced by indigenous shamanism and Taoism. Anthropologists call such blending of beliefs "syncretism," suggesting that newfound systems never completely replace the old ways, but rather blend, forming new traditions. No doubt, the first Buddhists arriving from India and Tibet were served tea by the local Taoist masters, and found much concordance in their mutual appreciation for quiet, meditation, and completion through Nature. Very soon after, tea was incorporated into the lives of the burgeoning monasteries. In fact, every single tea mountain in China is also home to a famous monastery. Sometimes the monks brought the trees, for they were indeed the first farmers; but more often, they built their monasteries on mountains where wild tea bushes grew. Tea drinking, offerings, and ceremonies were recorded as part of their monastic code, and such an essential part of the Buddhist life that when Japanese monks first came to the mainland to study and carry Buddhism back to their homeland, they couldn't do so without also bringing knowledge of tea—production, preparation, and even seeds and saplings to plant. They said, "The taste of tea is the taste of Zen, and there is no understanding of one without the other."

Primarily it was in the Tang dynasty that the royalty and literati were first introduced to tea during their visits to monasteries. They wished to take tea home and perhaps recapture the quietude that had transformed them on the mountain. Slowly, tea was commoditized, heralding new farming techniques, trades and eventually tea houses, private brewing for pleasure and all the other well-documented migrations of tea throughout Asia and beyond to the West. No matter what reason you've found a love for tea, it is important to remember tea's heritage, which is ultimately Nature itself; passing beyond the Buddhist to the Taoist and their steaming bowls, past the early shamans, we come at last to eons and eons of simple trees in the forests of southern China, silent and undisturbed by man.

To many it may seem almost like a fairy tale that those Taoist mystics cloudwalking around ancient China were able to find a sense of oneness, transcendence and connection to the universal energy when today people all over the world drink tea all the time and never get close to those sensations. My experience with my family that day proved to me that it doesn't take much for us to find a sense of tranquility and completion through tea: just provide a quiet space with a bit of respect for tea and people can change. I'd say it was strange if I hadn't seen it happen so many times. In an age of flurrying activity, some ancient stillness is needed more than ever. Rather than sweeping your tea into the hustle and bustle of your normal workday, why not try taking the time to slow down and have a cup of quiet? Aren't you a part of the same world those sages dwelt in? When asked to share a tea memory, I found myself passing through the experience I had with my family to the realization that I was connected to the same world all those who have ever practiced *Cha Dao* were connected to. Sharing in an ancient tradition of *Cha Dao*, I share all my elders' tea memories as my own. As you drink your tea, are you too feeling as they felt? Do the forests not soothe your soul in the same way? Perhaps we need not ask. A sip is enough. Our breath warmed, we return to the mountain hermitage of the heart.

TEA CONNECTIONS

Connections

BY KATRINA ÁVILA MUNICHIELLO

While genetic ties play a role in defining family, it is my belief that what truly unites us is shared experiences. Common DNA provides one link, but what often feels more important in our relationships are the moments when big brother comes to the rescue or little sister keeps you company while you cry. There are the memories of family car trips that were both magical and maddening. You are bonded by the birthday parties, late night phone calls, and those times as kids when you didn't "get caught."

These moments, the ones you stay up late remembering, are the unbreakable bonds. They are the ones that make sisters into best friends and best friends into sisters. They are your life's connections.

For me, food has always been an important component of these shared memories. The flavors, the aromas, the visual impact all serve as emotional triggers. The taste of lobster helps me recall nights at the lake with my family, eating and laughing on a hot summer night. The smell of dough frying brings thoughts of Sunday mornings at my grandmother's with a houseful of aunts, uncles, and cousins. The sound of beef stew bubbling on the stove returns me to snowy winter days in my childhood home in Maine.

For many of us, tea is a particularly important part of these food memories. Grandparents shared tea and "the old ways" with grandchildren. Parents used tea time as a chance to slow children down, to really talk. Friends shared quiet moments, baring their souls and daring their feelings.

Tea memories involve the sights, sounds, scents, and tastes of the moment. These shared experiences are links that are not easily disentangled. Tea inspires real and lasting connections.

Afternoon Tea under the African Sun

by Jodi-Anne Williams-Rogers

At the time of day when the afternoon draws close to twilight, my memory floats back to the pristine days of my childhood in the early 1980s. Nostalgia washes over me with feelings of enchantment while I reminisce about the treasured moments spent with my grandparents when I was a little girl growing up. During these late afternoons, the hot South African sun tinted the day with an ochre hue, as if to hint that the lounge was now sufficiently warmed for us to enjoy a leisurely afternoon in it. It signaled the start of my favorite family ritual. My cousin Justin and I would gather in the lounge where our grandparents would take a break from their active day to enjoy a cup of tea and eat sandwiches.

As we settled on the mustard cushioning that lined the white and gray mock-leather settees, the conversation would usually start off with my grandmother talking of the housework or gardening that she had managed to get done that day. I particularly remember the delight she took in christening the start of her daily relaxation with the first few sips of tea. Most days my grandparents would enjoy just plain old black or Earl Grey tea taken with milk; other days the scents of black tea with lemon filled the room with a warm citrus aroma. My grandfather always did something strange which amused Justin and me. He would pour his tea into his saucer and then drink it. When we asked why he did that, he explained that it was a means to cool the tea faster before drinking it. Apparently this is an age-old and long-forgotten English tradition that found its way to South Africa during colonialism.

What I most enjoyed about these afternoon tea sessions was that it was a time when my grandfather would engage our inquisitive young minds in discussions about everything under the sun. Being a natural-born philosopher, he loved educating us as well as picking our brains about what we knew. Our topics for discussion included dinosaurs, the formation of the earth, articles he read to us in the newspapers, historical events, the latest scientific discoveries, and even UFOs. When he brought up the subject of the existence of a higher deity or whether or not there was any point in confessing your sins to a priest, my grandmother would become infuriated. Being a devout Catholic she would make the sign of the cross, frown in dismay, and say to my grandfather, the instigator of such conversations, "I will pray for Thomas!" Nevertheless, discovering the fascinating facts, possibilities, and complexities of the world through these discussions filled me with excitement. I loved the feeling of learning and seeing the world expand with what I learned each day.

At some stage, *rooibos* tea was introduced to the afternoon tea ritual. *Rooibos* translates to "red bush" tea. It is endemic to South Africa and is believed to have been discovered by the ancient Khoisan people. The Khoisan were the first people to populate Southern Africa. They used the *rooibos* leaves to brew tea. South Africa's Cederberg area holds the richest concentrations of *rooibos*. Coincidently this is also one of the regions rich in Khoisan rock art. Some people believe that *rooibos* was the source of inspiration for the Khoisan rock art. *Rooibos* tea was made popular again in the 1970s and 1980s when its numerous health benefits came to light. Naturally the arrival of this new tea to our afternoon tradition sparked lengthy conversations of its origins, as well as its healing and anti-aging properties.

In the summer months, on days when the heat inside the house was too unbearable, we would sit out in the shade on the veranda and watch the African sun drift closer and closer to the horizon. The intense shades of the green rolling hills that defined the rural setting of Eshowe, the place where my grandparents lived, always provided a breathtaking scene as the blue skies turned to crimson.

Visiting these parts of the world often makes me wonder what the experience must have been like for the early British colonialists such as my grandmother's great-grandfather, John Dunn, an infamous trader and hunter in the late 1800s, or the likes of the wild and free-spirited explorer and writer, Lady Florence Dixie. When they traveled through these lands more than a century before my time, did they boil some water on the coals to brew a fresh cup of tea in the late afternoon? Did they view the land with the same appreciation that I do? The romantic in me conjures up images of Lady Dixie at her camp, sitting in the open *bushveld* wearing brown leather boots and hunting gear, taking in the surrounds as herds of plentiful buck danced in the distance, while she sipped tea and wrote in her journal.

When twilight was born, the afternoon ritual would come to an end. Soon the sounds of neighborhood children playing outside would begin to subside. Parents would start returning home, exhausted from their day's work; kitchens in the homes that lined the street where my grandparents lived would be a hub of activity as hands, pots, stoves and ovens got to work preparing the night's meal.

Years on, a blissful cup of tea or two a day is still very much a part of my life. The variety of tea selections that we now have access to is tremendous. Nothing beats a refreshing cup of mint tea to help increase my concentration at work during the later afternoons, or the sweet and playful aroma of mango and berry tea in summer. To keep the flu and colds at bay, lemon, ginger and honey tea is my favorite winter warmer. Chai or chamomile tea helps me unwind and beat the day's stress, while fennel or peppermint tea works wonders for digestive problems. Beyond that, although something as simple as a cup of tea is easy to take for granted, it is very much a part of my heritage. It is something that laces my childhood memories to the various stages of my life. The afternoon tea tradition is something I hope to carry forward with my own children and perhaps my grandchildren someday.

The *Mistri-Sahib*

AUTHOR UNKNOWN

Excerpted from Rings from a Chota Sahib's Pipe, *1901.*[1]

Ay! The *Mistri-Sahib*![2] Was it not Shakespeare who said "What's in a name?" But of course I hardly think Willy knew much about *Mistris* when he wrote that, or he might have thought fit to modify it—but to the point.

Mac and I are great friends and he confides in me "a wee bit;" yet there are lots of things I should like to ask him about himself but dare not, for he is very "touchy."

For instance he wears huge solid double-soled "tackety" English boots, for which, I know, he pays a great price. These monstrosities are made in his *busti*[3] in Scotland, and he gets a pair "out" at regular intervals. He is proud of his boots, and keeps telling you they simply *can't* wear out. If this is so, why does he get so many pairs? His bungalow is not more than thirty yards from the tea house, and as his work is entirely inside and round about that beastly structure, there is absolutely no necessity for him to wear boots at all. He would be comfortable in a pair of loose slippers which would do admirably for his work; but, no, he goes thumping round with these heavy "beetle crushers" to the detriment of the tea house floor, and the annoyance of all lovers of peace. Thud, thud, thud!

---

1   [Certain British spellings have been amended. Ed.]
2   "*Mistri*" refers to a carpenter or other craftsman. "*Sahib*" is a term of respect used in colonial India for respected white Europeans.
3   "*Busti*" is a Hindi term for a small village or settlement.

Well, well! at the same time it is hardly fair to criticize his boots and not his clothes, which are beautifully clean and neat every morning. Mac looks the reverse of "at home" in 'em so long as they *are* clean; five minutes in the tea house and he is himself again. His first action is to peel off his coat and hang it on a nail, along with numerous wrenches, in the engine house. To get to the engine house he has to pass through the office where there is a neat little hat-rack, and why the deuce he doesn't hang his coat there, instead of going out of his way to make it the neighbor of dirty, greasy tools, passes my comprehension.

Rid of his coat, he gives a sigh of contentment and rolls up his shirt-sleeves, exposing to view a forearm of massive proportions hardened by years of "work at the file in the shops at home." He then proceeds to poke his hand into every part of the engine, which he addresses familiarly in this way; "An' hoo are ye feelin' this mornin', ye auld Rechabite, ye?"

He has no fear; he chucks her under the chin here, he tickles her there, he wrestles with the great piston, he climbs over the flywheel, he opens and shuts every handle she's got; he dives under her, he slides along her, he slaps her, and after risking every limb he possesses, he emerges from the conflict, smeared with dirt and oil, but with the flush of victory on his face.

"She's daein' fine, man!" he says, stepping back to look at the little clock on the top of the boiler. Ah!—another handle attracts his attention; he can't resist; without a word of warning he jerks it round and "ph-r-r—r—br-r-r—oof"—"What the devil?" you yell, as you leap into space, thinking the boiler is burst! But Mac has now got the furnace door open and the fierce red glow lights up his grim face and gives it a weird, uncanny look, as he peers in.

Now what in creation does he want to look into the furnace for? It beats me hollow. Bang goes the great door, and a heated—bound to be so!—discussion arises between the *kalwallah* and himself. Neither can hear one word that the other says, from the noise of the machinery, but they shout and gesticulate for all they're worth, till Mac eventually clears out having evidently had the worst of the argument. The *kalwallah* tugs nonchalantly at the whistle cord, the answering *poof-poof* of the whistle signaling his triumph and Mac's discomfiture and retreat.

From the engine house Mac makes his way through the tea house, leaving behind him a trail of badly-treated and loudly-grumbling rollers, firing machines, sifters, etc. Not one escapes; he pulls every one of them about most mercilessly and, if it should happen that there is no handle, cock or lever by which he can annoy any machine, then he relieves himself by abusing in most opprobrious terms the dead relations of the poor devil in charge of it.

Finished with the machinery, he wipes his brow, throws away the end of his Burma,[4] and begins to sidle towards the tasting-table. His bullying manner is now quite gone; he knows there are no handles or wheels *here*, and besides, it is a serious matter this tasting. At his invitation, I gingerly lift the cup pointed out, and suck up a mouthful of its contents noisily, throwing back my head, and gargling away beautifully, with Mac's eyes fixed on my face. And now I spit, and I can see he is satisfied; for, though my gargle is not much to boast about, I can *spit* with anyone.

Next the leaf houses come in for a share of his attention, and it is a sight to see Mac chase the leaf-boys from end to end of the different houses. Yes! it's quite worth anyone's while to go round the tea house with Mac.

A funny thing about the *mistri-sahib* is, that it is next to impossible to catch him, if you should drop into the teahouse for a minute. As you stroll in you see him at the other end of the rolling room bending over the last "roll." You start along towards him, but by the time you have got round all the litter in your way, behold! he is gone. Oh, there he is, smelling the *mal* at the Victoria,[5] but when you circumvent the *kutcha*[6] sifter, he is gone again. "Confound the man!" you say as he again reappears, this time on his way to the withering-loft; "got him now" you think, and you nip up the stairs after him; "gone away, tally ho!" as you hear him thundering down the outside gangway, for he has outwitted you once more. But he is heavily handicapped, carrying all the

---

4   "Burma" likely refers to a clipped cigar type called a cheroot which was common in Burma and India and was popular with the British in this time period.
5   "Victoria" likely refers to a piece of equipment built by Victoria Machine Tools.
6   "*Kutcha*" means makeshift or second-rate.

weight he does on his feet, and you bless his *busti mochi*, as, pumped and blown, you pursue your quarry to the three-decked leaf-house. The scent is now strong, and you hear he has just left, by the south door. Hurrah—! *View holloa!*[7] for there he is sauntering back into the tea house; a good spurt and you run him "to earth" in the fermenting room—a grand finish! I've often thought that, if you wanted to see Mac for a minute during the day, it would be best to start with him in the morning and stay by him all day. Then when you wanted to speak to him, why there he is at your side! How's that for Political—or should I say "Domestic"?—Economy?

Mac takes his "leave" on Monday as there is always manufacture on Sunday—our "leave day." On Sunday evenings I generally dine with Mac, unless I go visiting; and sometimes Hamilton, the junior assistant brings the party up to three, but I know he only stays by invitation, while it is an understood thing that I dine with Mac whenever I can. We always ask him—Mac—if he is going out anywhere on Monday. The joke is, that Mac never goes out. Nevertheless he mentions every Sunday night that he is thinking of "takkin' a rin ower to Kalybeti (our next garden)—the morn's morn," but we know he'll never "tak that rin." It's like his trip down the river; he has been threatening to "gæ doon the watter" for the last six years, but always puts it off till the next cold weather. When I come in to breakfast on Mondays, I regularly find Mac stretched on a long chair in my verandah with a peg[8] and a Burma cheroot of much potency. A clean shave, clean clothes, a pair of highly polished boots, if anything heavier than usual, and this breakfasting with me, comprises his idea of a holiday. I remark casually as I toil up the steps, "You didn't go over to Kalybeti then?" "Ah well, you see," he says "A' jist thocht a'd better get at the guts o' that infernal drier as long as she's cauld, an' by the time a' wis threw wi' the waster, an' haud a bathe and a clean sark, a' seen it wisna worthwhile orderin' the pony."

The *Burra-Sahib*[9] says he often used to see Mac take a ride round the garden on his leave days, but I've never seen him out "on the field."

---

7   "*View holloa!*" is the fox hunter's cry when the prey leaves cover.
8   A "peg" is an alcoholic beverage.
9   "*Burra-Sahib*" is a term of respect for a manager.

I rather think he despises the outside work; I know he does what he calls "that dawmned muttie scrapin," by which elegant term he means the "hoe." However, in some mysterious way, Mac always knows where and how the outside work is being carried on, and I have always found that, should he by any chance ever pass an opinion on any work, what he says shows an amount of knowledge and judgment hardly to be expected in a man whose entire time is spent in the tea house. He is acknowledged by the district to be one of the best engineers, whose abilities have been thrown away on tea; for thrown away they are, most certainly. One Monday night, when we had more pegs than usual, Mac produced, from deep down in one of his boxes, letters and certificates which testified to my belief that the "old country" had lost one of its best engineers when Mac sailed in the City of Glasgow for India. Little Scotland, lumpy and swollen as its top end is, should feel proud that it can produce men of such caliber as "Our Mac."

In some documents this text is classified as fiction, but it is unclear how much is based in fact. In any event, this text provides an interesting description of some of the relationships that occurred within the confines of Indian tea gardens.

Five O'Clock Tea

BY ANNE THACKERAY RITCHIE

Excerpted from From an Island: A Story and Some Essays, *1877.*[1]

> *"For lo! the board with cups and spoons is crowned!*
> *On shining Altars of Japan they raise*
> *The silver lamp; the fiery spirits blaze;*
> *From silver spouts the grateful liquors glide,*
> *While China's earth receives the smoking tide.*
> *At once they gratify their scent, and taste,*
> *And frequent cups prolong the rich repast."*
>
> —Alexander Pope, *Rape of the Lock*

Five o'clock tea is rarely good. It is either strongly flavored with that peculiar bitter taste which shows that the tea has been kept waiting and neglected too long, or else it is cold, weak, and vapid. These remarks apply strictly to the tea itself; for, as a general rule, it is the pleasantest hostess who provides the worst tea, and it would almost seem, notwithstanding a few noticeable exceptions, that a lively conversation and a pleasant wit are incompatible with boiling water, and a sufficient supply of cream, and sugar, and *souchong*. But, fortunately, the popularity of five o'clock tea does not depend upon its intrinsic merits. Five o'clock friendship, five o'clock gossip, five o'clock confidence and pleasant confabulation, are what people look for in these harmless

---

1   [Certain British spellings have been amended. Ed.]

cups; a little sugar dexterously dropped in, a little human kindness, and just enough pungency to give a flavor to the whole concoction, is what we all like sometimes to stir up together for an hour or so, and to enjoy, with the addition of a little buttered muffin, from five to six o'clock, when the day's work is over, and a pleasant, useless, comfortable hour comes round.

Everybody must have observed that there are certain propitious hours in the day when life appears under its best and most hopeful aspects. Five o'clock is to a great many their golden time, when the cares which haunt the early rising have been faced and surmounted; when the mid-day sun is no longer blazing down and exhibiting all the cracks and worn places which we would fain not see; when the labors of the day are over for many, and their vigils have not yet begun; and when a sense of soon-coming rest and refreshment has its unconscious effect upon our spirits. Whether for work or for play, five o'clock is one of the hours that could be the least spared out of the twenty-four we have to choose from. Two o'clock might be sacrificed; and I doubt whether from ten o'clock to eleven is not a difficult pass to surmount for many: neither work nor play comes congenially just after breakfast, but both are welcome at this special five o'clock tea-time. A painter told me once that just a little before sunset, at the close of a long day's toil, there comes a certain light which is more beautiful and more clear and still than any other, and in which he can do better work than at any other time during the day. It is so, I believe, with some people who make writing their profession, and who often find that after wrestling and struggling with intractable ideas and sentences all through a long and wearisome task, at the close, just as they are giving up in despair, a sudden inspiration comes to them, thoughts and suggestions rush upon them, words fall into their places, and the pen flies along the paper. Miss Martineau[2] says in one of her essays that after writing for seven hours, the eighth hour is often worth all the others put together.

---

2   Harriet Martineau (1802–1876), a noted writer and sociologist.

There is no comparison, to my mind, between the merits of luncheons and breakfasts and five o'clock tea, in a social point of view. People sometimes experimentalize upon the practicabilities of the minor meals, but pleasant as luncheons or breakfasts may be at the time, a sense of remorse and desolation when the entertainment is over generally prevents anything like an agreeable reminiscence. One has wasted one's morning; one has begun at the wrong end of the day; what is to be the next step on one's downward career? Is one to go backwards all through one's usual avocations, and wind up at last by ordering dinner just before going to bed? The writer can call to mind several such meetings, where persons were present whom it was an honor and a delight to associate with, and where the talk was better worth listening to than commonly happens when several remarkable people are brought together; and yet, when all was over, and one came away into the mid-day sunshine, an uncomfortable feeling of remorse and general dissatisfaction, of not knowing exactly what to do next or how to get through the rest of the day, seemed almost to overpower any pleasant remembrances. It was like the afternoon of a wedding-breakfast, without even a wedding. No such subtle Nemesis attends the little gathering round the three-legged five o'clock tea-tables. You know exactly the precise right thing to do when the tea party is over. You go home a little late, you hurriedly dress for dinner with the anticipation of an agreeable evening, to which your own spirits, which have been cheered and enlivened already, may possibly contribute; and the knowledge that each other member of the party is also hurrying away with a definite object, instead of straggling out into the world all uncertain and undecided, must unconsciously add to your comfort.

Two o'clock is much more the hour of friendship than of sentiment. Sentimental scenes take place (it would seem) more frequently in the morning and evening, or out of doors in the afternoon. One can quite imagine that after breakfasts or luncheons the stranded guests might fly to sentiment to fill up the ensuing blank vacancy. But although one has never heard of an offer being made at five o'clock tea, the story of the engagement—more or less interesting—and all the delightful particulars of the trousseau, and settlements, and wedding presents, are more fully discussed then than at any other time. What is *not* discussed at five o'clock tea, besides the usual gossip and chatter of the day? How much of sympathy, confidence, wise and kindly warning and encouragement it has brought to us, as well as the pleasure of companionship in one of its simplest forms! It is now the fashion in some houses to play at whist[3] at five o'clock, but this seems a horrible innovation and interruption to confidence and friendship. If the secret which Belinda has to impart is that she happens to hold four trumps in her hand, if the advice required is whether she shall play diamonds or hearts; if Florio is only counting his points, and speculating on his partner's lead, then, indeed, all this is a much ado about nothing. Let us pull down the little three-legged altars, upset the cream jugs and sugar-basins, and extinguish the sacred flames of spirits of wine with all the water in the tea kettle.

I do not know whether to give the preference to summer or winter for these entertainments. At this time of the year one comes out of the chill tempests without to bright hearths, warmth, comfort, and kindly welcome. The silver kettle boils and bubbles, the tea table is ready spread, your frozen soul melts within you, you sink into a warm fireside corner, and perhaps one of the friends that you love best begins with a familiar voice to tell you of things which mutually concern and interest you both, until the door opens and one or two more come in, and the talk becomes more general. In summer time Lady de Coverley has her tea-table placed under the shade of the elm trees on the lawn. There is a great fragrance of flowering azaleas and rhododendrons all about; there are the low seats and the muslin dresses in a semicircle under the bright green branches; shadows come flickering, and gusts of summer sweetness; insects buzzing and sailing away, silver and china wrought in bright array, and perhaps a few vine-leaves and strawberries to give color to the faint tints of the equipage. You may almost see the summer day spreading over the fields and slopes, where the buttercups blaze like a cloth of gold, and the beautiful cattle are browsing.

---

3 "Whist" is a classic English card game.

Five o'clock is also the nursery tea-time, when a little round-eyed company, perched up in tall chairs, struggles with mugs, and pinafores, and large slices of bread and butter. I must confess that the nursery arrangements have always seemed to me capable of improvement, and I have never been able to understand why good boys and girls should be rewarded with such ugly mugs, or why the bread and butter should always pervade the whole atmosphere as it does nowhere else. It is curious to note what very small things have an unconscious influence upon our comfort at times, and I could quite understand what a friend meant the other day when she told me that whenever anybody came to see her with whom she wished to have a comfortable talk, she was accustomed to move to a certain corner in her drawing-room, where there was a snug place for herself and an easy chair which her guest was certain to take. Those who have been so fortunate as to occupy that easy chair can certify to the complete success of the little precaution.

Of the sadder aspect of my subject, of the tea parties over and dispersed for ever, of old familiar houses now closed upon us, of friends parted and estranged, who no longer clink their cups together, I do not care to write.

The readers of *Pendennis* may remember Mrs. Shandon and little Mary at their five o'clock tea, and the extract with which I conclude:

"So Mrs. Shandon went to the cupboard, and in lieu of a dinner made herself some tea. And in those varieties of pain of which we spoke anon, what a part of confidante has that poor teapot played ever since the kindly plant was introduced among us! What myriads of women have cried over it, to be sure! what sick-beds it has smoked by! what fevered lips have received refreshment from out of it! Nature meant very gently by women when she made that tea plant; and with a little thought, what a series of pictures and groups the fancy may conjure up, and assemble round the teapot and cup."

Easy on the Ice

by Julie L. Carney

I first noticed my dad putting lemon juice in his iced tea about two months ago. I'm 45 years old and I see my parents every day. I heard the telltale sound of a long-handled spoon stirring something in a tall glass and wondered, "What could he be stirring?"

My dad is a creature of habit. With some people, "creature of habit" would be a quaint expression to describe someone who tends to wear poplin or who has a regular coffee klatch in the mornings. With my dad, his habits are more like rituals, hard and fast rules, compulsions. Though never officially diagnosed, he's been known to joke with people about his "obsessive-compulsive" tendencies. My siblings and I talk about his "o.c." behavior.

That's why I was so struck by the simple stirring sound; it was an anomaly. My mom was at work and the dog, who at age 15 has become a nearly full-time patient, was asleep. I wandered into the kitchen and watched the stirring. I can't remember if I asked him about it or not, but sure enough, the next time we were at a restaurant, his drink order, which had been the same for 70-plus years, had changed. It used to be, "Do you have brewed iced tea, not made from a mix or powder? Unsweetened?" And if they did: "Easy on the ice." Or, if it's a "regular" joint, like Morey's, the family-owned diner my parents eat at every Friday, simply, "Iced tea, easy on the ice." He doesn't really want any ice, just cold tea, but the phrase sticks. Suddenly, lemon has been added to the order.

For as long as I can remember, our house has had brewed, un-sweetened, iced tea available in the fridge year-round. The sound of a tea kettle roaring to a boil and finally working up to a whistle is a near-daily experience. My dad has his own glass—a tall, yellowed, mildly patterned glass filled with cold tea—which accompanies him around the house. Sometimes in the summer, I have iced tea at my parents' house. Sometimes my sister will visit and have cold tea with lemon juice. My dad eschewed both ice and lemon, at least until recently.

As kids, we realized the tea thing was different from the habits of other parents who drank coffee, water, milk, or even wine with their dinner. Our dad never drank any of those things, just tea, morning to evening. The big old teapot was a fixture by the stove from year to year. Four tea bags (five if the tea was a weak one that someone had given as a gift) or sometimes loose tea carefully measured into a large tea ball, sat in the pot awaiting the boiling water. After the tea steeped—How many American kids grow up knowing that word?—it was poured into the one-gallon clear glass jug which always resided in the refrigerator. With a metal lid and no label, this jug may have contained orange juice in its previous life, but has now held tea longer than it ever held anything else.

My dad was a professor at our local state university for most of his career. For reasons we never understood, all of his classes were in the mornings, so he would be home when we returned from school. But he would still be "at work" in his office. Long before homes were built with "home offices" for people to stow their PCs, in fact, long before PCs, our dad had an office that was exclusively his work zone. Found off our parents' bedroom, accessed from the dining room, dad's office holds a huge wooden desk, multiple file cabinets, and bookshelves on every wall loaded to the ceiling with books. And always on the desk, at the upper left hand corner of the blotter, is what I always thought of as his tea-holder: a shallow, round ceramic piece, the likes of which I have never seen anywhere else, which perfectly cups the bottom of my dad's regular tea glass, keeping the sweat off his papers. The office doesn't get much use these days, my dad having retired 20 years ago. The blotter rarely sees the light of day, papers piled atop it, forgotten.

In the afternoons of our childhood, until dinnertime, my dad worked at his desk, grading papers, writing letters, reading. Occasionally rising to go to the bathroom or to make tea or refill his tea glass, he was otherwise ensconced there, not to be disturbed. At dinnertime, the tea glass accompanied him to his spot at the table; after dinner, it went to his spot on the couch. Sometime during our teenage years, the dining area changed from the dining room to the living room, as Americans learned to watch TV during all activities, even meals. The tea didn't change, however: brewed, unsweetened, cold but un-iced, unadorned tea.

As we grew up, we were sometimes asked to refill the tea glass. Occasionally we'd be asked to go in search of the glass if my dad had worked in the garden and left the tea glass out back, for instance. We had to be tall and strong enough to be allowed to pour the boiling water from the kettle into the pot. We had to be coordinated enough to be allowed to pour the cooled, steeped tea into the refrigerator jug.

Birthdays, Father's Day, Christmas, we always knew we could gift my dad some tea—though we eventually figured out he preferred the strong classic flavors of Irish or English breakfast teas. Teapots also became an easy gift and began to accumulate around the house; not ones he would use, mind you, they were just interesting specimens of the art of the drink he drank. When his teapot collection became unruly, he hired a local carpenter to build him shallow shelves around the dining room wall, near the ceiling, to display his pots. Later, when his collection reached into the hundreds, shelves were added around the perimeter of the kitchen too. Some homes have plate rails; ours has teapot shelves. The pots themselves were made in England, Ireland, China, Germany, even "Occupied Japan." They range from functional pots that look like standard-issue, restaurant serving-ware to whimsical pots that appeared to be made by artists with no interest in tea to a pot shaped like the classic teapot, only apparently made of grass.

Of the four kids, I am the only one who returned to our hometown, eventually buying a house a block away from our parents who still lived in our old family home. As our parents have entered their 70s, I find myself spending more and more time at their house, helping with daily tasks. I helped clean out our grandfather's house when he died. I walk our old dog every day, help my dad unload the groceries from the car, and help my mom file her taxes electronically. Sometimes it frightens me when they don't recognize one of their old friends or seem not to be their old selves. The constants are reassuring: teapots keep accumulating and tea keeps getting brewed and consumed. But the lemon has me worried.

A Tea Cup of Friends

BY STEPHANIE LEMMONS WILSON

It was Halloween and a pregnant moon hung in the sky. We were entering the dreary time of year, and the hubby and I were moving back to the Midwest where the weather was even drearier. I wanted to make this move, but the wanting didn't make it any easier. I was leaving behind an incredibly strong network of friends. Two of these friends shared my passionate love for tea. I realized what a treasure I was leaving. I knew our friendships would persist, but it would be a tough break. As the hubby and I drove off in the wee morning hours, heading east under a full moon, I held a tender heart full of excitement and loss. It was a mixed blessing, this move.

In the new town, I was fortunate to continue my corporate job while working from my home office. This situation held many advantages, like working in my running clothes. (That is, until we began using webcams.) Still, I discovered that working from home was harder than expected. While I loved not having to be in the office each day, I was sorely lacking companionship, especially from women. I had never realized how much of my daily social needs were met from work-related social interactions. I was isolated in my own lovely little home office. Once I began to feel settled, I tried connecting with a few women. I even held a tea party. Unfortunately, none of the participants seemed to share my spark for tea and I was growing lonelier. Fortunately, my tea-loving friends in the west were ever-faithful. We regularly chatted on the phone, wrote letters, and held virtual tea parties to keep in touch. These little and big things kept me going as I slowly made my way in a new community.

I looked for ways to get involved and meet people. I made some collegial connections, but it seemed the union of women's deep friendship continued to evade me. By chance, I happened to be in a social-service committee meeting when a woman brought in a homemade cake for a birthday celebration. Through the course of the conversation (and a heavenly slice of cake), I discovered her interest in tea. In fact, she hosted an annual and elaborate tea party for her girlfriends. It was a month away. Would I be interested in speaking at it? Yes! I jumped at this opportunity to connect with another tea lover and share my passion.

Over the next several weeks, my heart sang as I grew to know this fellow tea lover (and baker extraordinaire). We planned the tea party foods, the teas to accompany the foods, the party favors and the program. She introduced me to another creative soul and the three of us formed our own tea adventure trio. Over several cups of tea (and a few tea trips), these new friends introduced me to the gems in my community. The sense of being new to town slipped away, while the sense of being home blossomed.

Now, nearly five years later, I continue to feel very blessed. I've maintained close ties with my western-U.S. friends, feeling just as connected as ever. We hold virtual tea parties, which are fun, creative and connecting. We explore using Skype for video calls. We practice the age-old arts of letter-writing and postcard-sending. In my new home town, I revel in my circle of woman-kinship. I enjoy hosting friends for a simple cup of tea on the porch or a more elaborate tea party in my "parlor" (my living room). These two circles have even cross-mingled, and I look forward to more of that in the future. The tea cup of friends is beautiful.

A full moon, a heavy heart
A tea quilt set in blues
Boxes full, set to depart
Goodbyes and tears from you.
A new home, so much to see

Delight in treasures found
A lonely time, a test for me
A tea friend to be found?
Fates prevail, our paths criss-cross
Tea and cake, the theme is set
A lighter load, and still a loss
With new hope now we've met.
On the phone, the voice is sweet
And letters in the mail
A visit soon, an airplane seat
Then antiques; find the sale!

The finest cup, the kettle start
My two worlds now proclaim
A cup of tea, a friend's dear heart
And tea, my cheer sustain.

After Anna's Marriage

BY LOUISA MAY ALCOTT

Excerpted from Louisa May Alcott: Her Life, Letters, and Journals, *1899.*

Sunday Morn, 1860.

Mrs. Pratt:

My Dear Madam,

The news of the town is as follows, and I present it in the usual jour-nalesque style of correspondence. After the bridal train had departed, the mourners withdrew to their respective homes; and the bereaved family solaced their woe by washing dishes for two hours and bolting the remains of the funeral baked meats.[1] At four, having got settled down, we were all routed up by the appearance of a long procession of children filing down our lane, headed by the Misses H. and R. Father rushed into the cellar, and appeared with a large basket of apples, which went the rounds with much effect. The light infantry formed in a semi-circle, and was watered by the matron and maids. It was really a pretty sight, these seventy children loaded with wreaths and flowers, standing under the elm in the sunshine, singing in full chorus the song I wrote for them. It was a neat little compliment to the superintendent and his daughter, who was glad to find that her "pome" was a favorite among the "lads and lasses" who sang it "with cheery voices, like robins on the tree."

---

1   It seems that this is Alcott's facetious way of talking about how they all felt at "losing" her sister Anna.

Father put the finishing stroke to the spectacle by going off at full speed, hoppity-skip, and all the babes followed in a whirl of rapture at the idea. He led them up and down and round and round till they were tired; then they fell into order, and with a farewell song marched away, seventy of the happiest little ones I ever wish to see. We subsided, and fell into our beds with the new thought "Annie is married and gone" for a lullaby, which was not very effective in its results with all parties.

Thursday we set our house in order, and at two the rush began. It had gone abroad that Mr. M. and Mrs. Captain Brown were to adorn the scene,[2] so many people coolly came who were not invited, and who had no business here. People sewed and jabbered till Mrs. Brown, with Watson Brown's widow[3] and baby came; then a levee took place. The two pale women sat silent and serene through the clatter; and the bright-eyed, handsome baby received the homage of the multitude like a little king, bearing the kisses and praises with the utmost dignity. He is named Frederick Watson Brown, after his murdered uncle and father,[4] and is a fair, heroic-looking baby, with a fine head, and serious eyes that look about him as if saying, "I am a Brown! Are these friends or enemies?" I wanted to cry once at the little scene the unconscious baby made. Someone caught and kissed him rudely; he didn't cry, but looked troubled, and rolled his great eyes anxiously about for some familiar face to reassure him with its smile. His mother was not there; but though many hands were stretched to him, he turned to Grandma Bridge, and putting out his little arms to her as if she was a refuge, laughed and crowed as he had not done before when she danced him on her knee. The old lady looked delighted; and Freddy patted the kind face, and cooed like a lawful descendant of that pair of ancient turtledoves.

---

2 Captain John Brown and his family were friends of Louisa's father Bronson Alcott. Brown was an abolitionist who organized and led a raid on an armory in Harpers Ferry, Virginia (now West Virginia) in 1859. He was trying to begin an uprising that would liberate Virginian slaves, and later slaves throughout the south. Brown and his men were captured. Brown was tried and hanged for treason. Here, in 1860, Brown's widow has come to stay with the Alcotts.

3 Watson Brown was John Brown's son. He was shot during the raid.

4 Frederick Brown was killed in 1856 when the Browns were trying to defend the Kansas from a group of pro-slavery Missourians.

When he was safe back in the study, playing alone at his mother's feet, C. and I went and worshipped in our own way at the shrine of John Brown's grandson, kissing him as if he were a little saint, and feeling highly honored when he sucked our fingers, or walked on us with his honest little red shoes, much the worse for wear.

Well, the baby fascinated me so that I forgot a raging headache and forty gabbling women all in full clack. Mrs. Brown, Sen., is a tall, stout woman, plain, but with a strong, good face, and a natural dignity that showed she was something better than a "lady," though she *did* drink out of her saucer and used the plainest speech.

The younger woman had such a patient, heart-broken face, it was a whole Harper's Ferry tragedy in a look. When we got your letter, Mother and I ran into the study to read it. Mother read aloud; for there were only C., A., I, and Mrs. Brown, Jr., in the room. As she read the words that were a poem in their simplicity and happiness, the poor young widow sat with tears rolling down her face; for I suppose it brought back her own wedding-day, not two years ago, and all the while she cried the baby laughed and crowed at her feet as if there was no trouble in the world.

The preparations had been made for twenty at the utmost; so when forty souls with the usual complement of bodies appeared, we grew desperate, and our neat little supper turned out a regular "tea fight." A., C., B., and I rushed like comets to and fro trying to fill the multitude that would eat fast and drink like sponges. I filled a big plate with all I could lay hands on, and with two cups of tea, strong enough for a dozen, charged upon Mr. E. and Uncle S., telling them to eat, drink, and be merry, for a famine was at hand. They cuddled into a corner; and then, feeling that my mission was accomplished, I let the hungry *wait* and the thirsty *moan* for tea, while I picked out and helped the regular Antislavery set.

We got through it; but it was an awful hour; and Mother wandered in her mind, utterly lost in a grove of teapots; while B. pervaded the neighborhood demanding hot water, and we girls sowed cake broadcast through the land.

When the plates were empty and the teapots dry, people wiped their mouths and confessed at last that they had done. A conversation followed, in which Grandpa B. and E. P. P. held forth, and Uncle and Father mildly upset the world, and made a new one in which everyone desired to take a place. Dr. B., Mr. B., T., etc., appeared, and the rattle continued till nine, when some Solomon[5] suggested that the Alcotts must be tired, and every one departed but C. and S. We had a polka by Mother and Uncle, the lancers by C. and B., and an *ètude* by S., after which scrabblings of feast appeared, and we "drained the dregs of every cup," all cakes and pies we gobbled up, etc.; then peace fell upon us and our remains were interred decently.

---

5   This is a reference to Solomon, the son of David and King of Israel in the Hebrew Bible. He was known for great wisdom.

Midnight Tea

BY SIR WILLIAM ROBERTSON NICOLL (AKA CLAUDIUS CLEAR)

Excerpted from Letters on Life, *1902.*[1]

There were four of us round a dinner table one Thursday evening. Our kind hostess had arranged her guests as in a restaurant. The four were two celebrated lady novelists, one gentleman novelist, and your correspondent. We will call the ladies Miss A. and Miss B., and the gentleman Mr. C. The conversation turned, as it often does in these days, on the question whether people are on the whole happy or unhappy. Miss A. resolutely argued that unhappiness was the rule. She said that, if you watched a number of travelers coming out of a railway train, the question was settled forever. Their general aspect was one of unmistakable discontent and weariness. Mr. C. took up the opposite side. He maintained that life was full of small comforts which were all the time making for happiness, and that we did not sufficiently appreciate them. For instance, it was a happiness to waken in the morning and look back on a night of sound sleep. It was a great happiness to have a cup of tea, not too strong, and yet not weak—a nice, refreshing, homely liquor, not the pale, straw-colored infusion of Lady Dedlock, nor the washerwoman's rasping *bohea*.[2] Then there came the newspaper, with something to interest and to talk about. A kind or encouraging word in speech, or in writing, or in print, revived the heart. A good book, old or new, need never be wanting. There were for many domes-

---

1 [Certain British spellings have been amended. Ed.]
2 "*Bohea*" is an inferior grade of black tea.

tic solaces, and others deprived of these were not less happy in their friendships, friendships usually more intimate and unreserved than in the case of those whose first thoughts and feelings were claimed by those who belonged to them. Miss B. expressed her agreement with this view of the case, but Miss A. was unconvinced. At last Miss A. declared that she believed that the great reason why people were not happy was because they had lost the power of falling in love....

...After coming home I began to think of our conversation, and especially of pain as an antagonist to happiness, and I remembered an essay written twenty years ago by a great sufferer, with the strange title which I have borrowed today, "Midnight Tea." The essayist confessed this title was practically a misnomer. She was thinking of two, three, or four in the morning. She suffered from one of those forms of illness which eat the sweet kernel out of sleep....Well, then, there are two friends, let us say, or a man and wife, or a mother and daughter, who pass the night together in order that one of the two who suffers may receive the help which only one hand can give. The immediate pain suddenly ceases. Then springs up a sudden thought out of the new, sweet peace: "Let us have a cup of tea." It can be managed at once. The tea is forthcoming, the spoons tinkle in the cups, the sweet incense goes up, and there is for a time calm and cheer, a soothed feeling, a quiet triumph in human resources, a genial gleam of light in the long tract of the dark hours. There may be no conversation, save that highest form of conversation which passes between two who, through the love and intimacy of long years, understand what each is thinking, and interchange ideas without words.... There is hardly any such tie between human beings as "Do you remember?" and "Do you remember when we had midnight tea?" brings back many softening, hopeful thoughts.

After Twenty-Two Years

by Russell Hires

I hadn't seen her in twenty-two years. She was my first girlfriend and, as we had been young and inexperienced, I ended up hurt. Now, after all these years, I was about to meet her, at a tearoom of all places.

We had talked about getting coffee, because that feels like the default place for getting together. Except that she doesn't drink coffee. That actually made me happy, because now I had a good excuse for taking her for tea instead. Interestingly, this was a new thing for her.

I've found that women don't know what to make of a guy who wants to go for tea. It's considered to be a "girly" thing and many of the tearooms do little to disabuse people of this notion. We went anyway.

Our meeting was set for a Friday at 1:30 P.M., the day after Christmas. The tearoom was packed. I was the only man there, except for the waiter. My friend called to tell me she was going to be late, which worked out perfectly because there was still a wait for a table. I browsed around the shop out front, enjoying the various items for sale: teapots, infusers, and some kitchen-type decorations. It was all so beautiful.

I kept one eye on the window as I browsed. And then I saw her. The store and restaurant is a converted house and because of its design, she had to park in the front and then walk around to the back. I watched and waited in anticipation. As she entered, she said, "I've driven by here a thousand times and never seen the place before."

She looked about the same as I'd known her. She had a more mature look about her and she seemed more settled and sure of herself. I wasn't sure how to greet her: A hug? A kiss? A handshake? I went with a token hug, which worked. I couldn't believe that I was looking upon the face of a woman who had so deeply influenced me and my life.

We were shown to our table. We had previously discussed, through Facebook, some details of our lives. But now, it was time to do more, to say more. And we did. We talked, and shared things with each other. She'd been suspicious of me and my motives. Things hadn't ended well with us the first time, but now I was there, telling her that it didn't matter what had happened before, because here we were, laughing and talking about our lives, our children, and anything else we could think of.

I was growing impatient with the unresponsive service, so I excused myself to get the waiter's attention. He was still slow to arrive at our table, though. I had wanted for this experience to be perfect, and it wasn't. I felt very protective of her, wanting to do what I could to make it wonderful. I'm glad she was such good company. At the table next to us, a tea party was in progress. Even though we had been seated first, I watched in the background as the party was seated and served.

The owner brought menus, and apologized for the slow service. We asked about the different varieties of tea. My friend asked about a particular tea. The owner strongly recommended against it. We wondered to ourselves why it was on the menu if the owner didn't like it so much.

The waiter finally came and took our order. I ordered a black tea with cranberry; my tablemate ordered the green tea from which she'd been warned away. I got a sandwich and we both ordered the soup.

The sluggish service turned out to be a benefit, as it gave us the chance to really talk. The conversation was light and easy. We got our tea and our soup. The soup was hot! She laughed at me for almost burning my tongue, but it was okay, as it broke the tension a little. Eventually, I got my sandwich, too. After that, I think the staff forgot us.

We took advantage of our privacy, and the lack of interference from the staff, to look at each other through twenty-two years' worth of experiences, turning off the outside world as we chatted, increasingly involved in our own bubble. What had been happening in her life? What had been happening in mine? As we sipped tea, the world continued to slip away from us, our lives becoming more and more intertwined. This wasn't a simple reunion, not anymore.

We were still dealing with the pain of our past selves, trying to understand the transformations that we were seeing in each other. She was kind, understanding, easy going, and pleasingly feminine. I'd grown stronger, more mature, and better able to handle life's challenges. I'd been through so much. I found myself surprised by her warmth and openness. And she was beautiful. This was turning into something interesting.

At one point, I caught her looking at me with that look. She has a look. It says she's feeling something, deeply. Enjoying the conversation? I called her on it: "I know that look. I've seen it before. I know what it means." She quickly changed her expression. I felt something stir in me.

I began to wonder what was really going on. I felt that pull, and I know she did, too.

But we weren't there yet. There was still too much mystery, too much hesitation about what we both wanted, what we were both thinking. After talking for two hours, it was time to go. But we didn't want to go. And yet there was mystery about whether we would continue our conversation.

We paid the check. I walked her to her car. We made no plans for seeing each other again. Our future was left undefined. Maybe I could have tea with her again? We'll have to see....

Three Cups of Tea for Peace

BY KIRSTEN KRISTENSEN

One School at a Time

March 8, 2006 changed my life. I had the television tuned to ABC's Morning News when I heard Diane Sawyer mention something about tea before going to a commercial break. As a tea enthusiast, I prepared to listen. A few minutes later I saw her sitting with a big, tall man with a shy smile whom she introduced as humanitarian Greg Mortenson. The talk was not about tea at all but about building schools in Pakistan and Afghanistan, helping children get a basic education in an area of the world where education—especially for girls—is a curse word for the fundamentalists who harmfully influence their daily lives. Greg Mortenson's work is described in his book *Three Cups of Tea* that was released that day and which has now become a bestseller in countries all over the world.

So what has tea got to do with building schools in Central Asia? After getting the book, I soon found out. In mountainous regions that are covered by snow a significant part of the year, tea has a cultural importance—not only for its nutritional benefits, which are in high demand in this terrain, but also for the ritual that "three cups of tea" represents. When you are offered the first cup, you are a stranger; getting the second, you become a friend; and when you enjoy the third cup, you become family. For family, one is willing to do anything—even die. The tea they drink is called "*paiyu cha*"—green tea they cook in a tin pot with salt, baking soda, goat's milk, and a slice of their treasured "*mar*"—rancid yak butter.

In his book, Mortenson describes a mountain climbing expedition to K2 in the Karakoram Mountain Range during which he encountered the village of Korphe, Pakistan. He noticed a group of children gathered on a hill, writing with sticks in the sand. When he asked them what they were doing, they explained that they were in school. Greg resolved to raise money in the U.S. and return to build them a real school.

With unbelievable challenges, including selling all he owned and sleeping in his car, Greg managed to raise $15,000 and return to Korphe in 1995 where the first school was built. Seeing the impact this school had, Greg decided to make it his mission in life to build schools for these children in the Karakoram Range region. He has built many secular schools with his nonprofit organization, Central Asia Institute. The schools are built in the name of peace in the belief that with a balanced view, people have an alternative to the Taliban fundamentalist *madrasas*.

As I said earlier, March 8, 2006 changed my life. When I listened to Greg Mortenson talking passionately about his book and work, I knew I had to meet this man. Together with my local college we set a two-year goal to raise $35,000 to build a school in the name of Brookdale Community College. In January 2007, nearly a year into our challenge, our college advisor, a few students, alumni members and I drove from Lincroft, New Jersey to Philadelphia where we had learned that Greg Mortenson was the speaker at a business meeting. Seeing this tall, humble man in person was an incredible experience. After his speech, we lined up to have our books signed. (Of the 300 people present we were among the very few who had actually read the book and knew who he was.) When he saw us he stood up and said, "You are the Brookdale people." He gave us a real bear hug and asked if he could come to our school to meet with us! Now we were in awe! This busy man, who spends half of his year in Central Asia and the rest of his time promoting his book, wanted to spend a day with us!

May 10, 2007 became the official "Greg Mortenson Day" in Monmouth County with resolutions from the County Freeholders, the board of trustees and the alumni association. Greg was interviewed by our college president live on "Brookdale Views," our local TV station and was the guest of honor at a colloquium held that evening for a full house of professors, students, and the community.

As an inspirational feature between the day's interviews and meetings, I had volunteered to do a presentation on "The World of Tea," relating the significance of the Central Asian ceremony of "three cups of tea" to other tea ceremonies in the world. After the presentation a smiling Greg came up to me and mentioned that he had never thought of tea in connection to his work! "Three Cups of Tea?"

We shared three cups of tea (Green Spice Chai) that afternoon and later in a quiet corner of the Student Life Center, after all the scheduled events were over. Greg had no intention of leaving us even though his driver had waited outside for hours. We shared such a connection between his ideals and what we could do to help him promote the cause. An important part of our fundraising was done that day, but our awareness campaign continued and has been an inspiration for many organizations, clubs, and individuals who are true supporters of Greg and his work. Through my company, Tea 4 U, we are dedicated to supporting Greg's schools through frequent fundraisers serving plenty of sets of "three cups of tea." Our goal of raising $35,000 was reached in June 2008.

At the graduation ceremony for Brookdale Community College in May 2009 we were very proud to have this prominent friend in tea, Nobel Peace Prize nominee and recipient of a Brookdale Honorary Degree, on the program as our keynote speaker. Being a friend of Greg Mortenson, the most humble man I have ever met with the most significant cause—to promote peace in our world one school at a time— gives me the conviction that *anything is possible* if you do it from your heart and drink tea with it.

Asalaam Alaikum—Peace be with you.

A Chat over a Cup of Tea

BY JEHIEL KEELER HOYT

Excerpted from The Romance of the Table, *1872.*[1]

> *"Conceive them sitting tete-a-tete,*
> *Two cups—hot muffins on a plate—*
> *With 'Anna's Urn' to hold hot water;*
> *The brazen vessel for a while*
> *Had lectured in an easy song,*
> *Like Abernethy—on the bile—*
> *The scalded herb was getting strong;*
> *All seemed as smooth as smooth could be,*
> *To have a cozy cup of tea."*
> —Richard Harris Barham, "The Ingoldsby Legends"

I have had occasion to note the fact that the English (I include our-selves) differ from all the rest of the world in the customs of the table, as well as in what is on the table, and the method of cooking. The tea table is with us a special institution. The effect of tea upon the nerves is undoubted, and we meet at the tea table to talk under its influence as much as the Chinese meet to gabble in their heathen fashion, while under the delicious influence of opium. Without people dine at a very early hour, they do not assemble at the evening meal to be fed, but merely to drink the celestial fluid, and talk; and, where late dining is

---

1   [Certain archaic spellings have been amended. Ed.]

the rule, as it is in England, the tea table is spread immediately after the dinner—generally in the drawing-room. There are hot muffins and a bit of cake; but to pour tea is the business and to drink it the pastime.

I inhale the smoke of a prime Havana with delight, and the odor of a pure tea comes to me like incense; yet I neither smoke nor drink. Tea puts my nerves in motions like the telegraph wires in a gale, and I toss on a sleepless pillow, while my brain whirls and spins with ceaseless and not pleasurable anxiety. I think I should make a capital subject on whom to try the effects of new medicines, so quick does my system respond to every innovation; but I should require a larger remuneration to induce me to drink tea in large quantities than to take mineral poisons in small. This fact proves either that the systems of the race are differently constituted, or that we can, by habit and practice, become accustomed to almost anything. I hope tea is harmless, for people enjoy it so much, and I like to see them happy.

But, although Americans and English make a feature of the tea-table proper, they by no means equal other nations in the amount consumed, or in their devotion to the article itself.

Russia, next to China, stands at the head of tea-drinking nations; and Russia has her pick of the crop before any other nation is allowed to come in. Russians take a natural pride in the fact that their tea is brought across the Ural Mountains and the steppes of Tartary, and that it does not lose its flavor in transportation, as does that which foreigners carry across the salt water. And the tea of Russia is delicious. Its aroma comes to meet you in a fragrant cloud, as you enter the room where it is. The Russian Bear is hardly a symbol of the people of those luxurious climes, who drive the fastest horses in the world, who clothe themselves in the furs of princes, and who monopolize all the champagne of the Widow Cliquot. Of course, they drink the best tea in the world, and they drink their fill. Russia would have been the Paradise of Dr. Johnson, whose allowance was twelve cups, although in that country they do not serve you out tea by the cup, but bring you a teapot of generous capacity. In supping his tea, the Russian gourmand will sometimes put lumps of sugar in his mouth, and filter his tea through that saccharine medium. *Tchai,* as the Russians call it, is the staple drink to offer a stranger. In the restaurants and refreshment rooms, of course, it is to be had quicker than anything else, while in private houses it is a mark of politeness to offer the caller a cup of the beverage that "cheers, but not inebriates." In an eating house, or exchange, called the *tratker,* an organ is the instrument which makes melody for the Russian while he is partaking of his beloved drink, and with the ability to call for tea—*stock au tchai*—the visitor may rest himself, and enjoy the organ as much as he pleases. The tea is drank from glass, and it requires some dexterity to handle a tumbler full of hot liquid, without being burned. The Russian does not like cold tea. He puts hot water into his glass, lets it stand a moment, then pours it out, and fills with tea. He weakens it, if too strong, and adds a slice of lemon. The pot of tea is to him an inspiration, and he knows well how to make it go as far as possible; and then, when it will possibly go no further, his next great luxury is taken up—the earthen pipe, with its long cherry stem.

I am almost inclined to think that there is some occult mystery hidden from us; some spiritual phenomenon which determines the natural likes and dislikes of mankind. Why should the Russians be tea drinkers above all others? They do not cultivate it; in fact, they could not.[2] It is brought by fatiguing journeys, and at great expense. Russia, too, is a cold and rather forlorn country, and one would suppose they would run into the use of spirits and drinks possessing much carbon— chocolate, for instance; but, while they do partake of all the luxuries of other nations, their passion is for tea. Now, if we go to the land of Hafiz and Abdallah,[3] we find that in Arabia they drink coffee, and in Persia, tea. In Spain they thirst for sugared water; in France, for heavy chocolate. The Frenchman sits for an hour lazily sipping his chocolate with a spoon, at a season of the year when it would seem the most improper beverage he could call for.

One thing, we can certainly vouch for—the love of tea drinkers for each other, when they are *at* the tea-table. It is asserted that scandal

---

2   Actually, Georgia, at that time part of the Russian Empire, was already growing tea and it became a significant tea growing region, at least for domestic use, by the 1800s.

3   "The land of Hafiz and Abdallah" refers to the Middle East.

is the predominant intellectual entertainment on such occasions and that, if the tea imbibers love themselves, they do not love anybody else. I am not prepared to accept this as a truth; but, were it so, it would open a wide field for philosophical inquiry. The study of the relationship between what we drink and the development of our mental and moral nature would be worthy of a Dr. Porson.[4]

Perhaps, as with other drinks, quantity has something to do with its action. People under the moderate influence of wine are full of fraternal kindness, and as happy as larks; beyond a certain quantity they grow quarrelsome, revengeful, and ready for any crime. I have seen people very happy at the tea-table, full of sparkling wit and ready repartee; but Mrs. Caudle, I believe, went very deep in her potations, and drank her tea very strong. I will not further recall that harrowing story. Let me bring up Dr. Johnson once more, and give an anecdote of his method of tea drinking:

Sir Joshua Reynolds reminded him that he had drank eleven cups. He replied: "Sir, I did not count your glasses of wine—why should you number my cups of tea? I should have released this lady from any further trouble, if it had not been for your remark; but you have reminded me that I want one of my dozen, and I must request Mrs. C. to round up my number. Madam, I must tell you, you have escaped much better than a certain lady did a while ago, upon whose patience I have intruded more than I have on yours; but the lady asked me for no other purpose than to make a zany of me, and set me gabbling to a set of people I knew nothing of. So, madam, I had my revenge, for I swallowed five and twenty cups of tea, and did not treat her to so many words."

Can anyone decide what the effect of tea is from such an illustration?

But there is one thing quite certain: that there is hardly a more beautiful object to be seen than a tea-table well set out, with the surroundings of proper furniture, pictures and curtains. The damask cloth, the silver service, the fragile, ethereal china, ready for the celestial nectar; the biscuit, preserves, and all the varied adjuncts of a well arranged household, fill the heart with a glow of enthusiasm. We

---

4   Dr. Porson was an English classical scholar who lived from 1759–1808.

know that this meal, at least, comes under the particular care of the lady of the mansion and her daughter, if she is so blessed; that fairy white fingers have beaten the eggs and the sugar, and brought into harmonious combination the cake and the jelly; that it was an eye for beauty and order which brought the bread to the table so nicely cut, and that only a soul which could soar above the prose of life could have put the peaches and the plums into a shape worthy of a Longfellow's poetic muse. The tea-table, thus arranged, *is* a poem; and, could I—dared I—take but one little cup, I can almost fancy I should immortalize myself, and take my proper position among the literary deities of Mount Parnassus.

*****

"Oh! Mr. Williams," exclaimed Florence, as that gentleman laid down the paper. "It is lucky for you that you are a married man. With such ideas you would find little favor with the ladies, I fear."

"I dare say you are right," rejoined that gentleman. "Temperance societies are easily formed, because the ladies have a horror of intemperance, but an anti-tea society would have up-hill work to perform."

"But tea does not affect everyone unpleasantly," said Dr. Lorton. "I have drank tea for forty years, and do not see but what I am as well off with it, as without it."

"Possibly," said Mr. Williams, "but that only proves the old adage, that what is one man's meat, is another man's poison. It is possibly true that those who are rendered nervous by tea drinking are the exceptions, and not the rule. What do you think, Dr. Sollinger?"

"I think," replied the Doctor, "that many, yes, most people, become habituated to both food and drink, and escape the evil consequences; they do not know that the poison works so slow as to escape positive detection. I can hardly believe that strict temperance in all things will not give us a longer average of life than we have at present. People use tobacco without apparent injury; yet, once in a while, a man is cut off with cancer, or some other horrible disease, which may be directly traceable to that noxious plant."

"There is a soothing effect about tea," said Thomas, "which lulls the mind into a false security. When the brain is fevered and anxious, people run to some opiate, and tea may be better than either alcohol, tobacco, or opium."

"We will agree, then, to consider it the least of many evils," said Mr. Williams. "We can never eradicate a habit so firmly fixed; all we can do is in some measure to control it."

"And tell what is a good and innocent substitute, if one can be found," continued Florence.

This second reunion passed as did the first—with much pleasant conversation, but with no particular subject which would interest the reader. It seemed almost impossible, in that pleasant abode, and with so many beautiful surroundings, to settle down to the consideration of any recondite question in philosophy.

A Cup of Comfort

BY DOROTHY ZIEMANN

My father was diagnosed with lung cancer in October 1997. He was a lifelong smoker who had suddenly quit several months before due to a tentative diagnosis of emphysema based on a routine x-ray done at his annual physical. Turns out that what the doctor thought was emphysema was actually a tumor. Because of the location of the tumor, surgery was not an option and the only treatments offered were chemotherapy and radiation. My father took this in stride and entered this last battle of his life with the good grace and quiet optimism he had always shown when faced with adversity. So my mother and siblings did likewise. I, however, did not. I am a nurse by profession and knew how deadly lung cancer can be and how fast it can take a life.

My father was not an outwardly demonstrative man. I knew he loved me and he knew I loved him, but we didn't say it much. Since I knew our time together was limited, I wanted to spend as much time as possible with him. This was a challenge because I worked part-time and was busy raising a family. But it was something I needed to do.

The office where he received chemo was located about forty-five minutes from my parents' home. Each treatment lasted four hours and he received it three times a week, one week a month. I decided to take him to the appointments and stay with him. I brought my knitting with me and Dad brought a book, although much of the time he just slept. I was knitting him a sweater for Christmas even though I knew he would probably not get much wear out of it. He asked about the knitting but never realized it was for him.

One of the joys in my dad's life was fine food and beverages. This was something we had always shared. We had many of the same tastes; the only big difference was that he was a coffee drinker while I only drank tea. I love the way coffee smells but don't like the taste. My dad thought tea was a woman's drink. It was so sad that chemo had changed his tastes for food. I tried to entice him to eat by making some of his favorites. One night I got all the ingredients to make Maryland-style crab cakes. This was somewhat difficult, since landlocked Atlanta is not known for its blue crab. He ate them but I could tell he didn't really enjoy them. He just had no appetite at all. So I was surprised when he asked for a cup of tea one day while he was receiving chemo. I asked the nurse if she had any tea bags. She didn't. She also only had paper cups, not really conducive for making hot beverages. So I told my dad I was going to the store and would be back shortly. I bought decaffein-ated tea bags because any caffeine kept him up at night and he was having a hard time sleeping anyway; I didn't want to make it worse. I bought two mugs and hurried back to the office. I made two cups of decaffeinated Lipton tea in the microwave and handed one to my fa-ther. He took a sip and sighed with a peaceful look on his face. "Doro-thy," he said, "I never knew tea was so soothing. I've really missed out, haven't I?" We talked and talked over that cup of tea. He talked about how proud he was of me and what I had accomplished so far in my life. He talked about how much he loved his granddaughters, my two girls, and his hopes and dreams for them. I told him how much I loved him and how much I appreciated everything he had done for me. I wouldn't be who I am without him. I said everything I had wanted to say out loud and I have no regrets about anything left unsaid.

I was used to drinking loose leaf tea brewed properly in a teapot. I was something of a "tea snob" and wouldn't normally drink tea bag tea, let alone tea bags obtained from a grocery store. But that tea I shared with my father on that dreary day in a chemotherapy office was the best tea I can remember drinking in my life. It tasted like ambrosia. I know I will never taste anything as sweet ever again.

That was the last afternoon my father and I spent alone together. He passed away shortly after and some of the light went out of my life. Now, every time I drink tea, I smile and think of my father and that cup we shared. We were not only sharing a beverage, we were finally sharing our feelings, our love, and our hopes and dreams. The memory of sharing tea with my father eases the pain of losing him. My father was right—tea *is* soothing. It has helped me grieve and it is still helping me heal these many years later. I look forward to sharing another cuppa with my father when we meet again.

THIRD STEEP

TEA RITUALS

Ceremony and Tradition

BY KATRINA ÁVILA MUNICHIELLO

The words "tea" and "ceremony" are frequently intertwined. When they come together, images of *tatami* mats, kimonos, delicate bamboo whisks, and small cups of *matcha* leap to mind.

The Japanese Tea Ceremony is a strikingly beautiful and peaceful experience. It combines reverence for art, nature, tea, and mindfulness with elegance and grace. This experience, also called *Chanoyu*, is not, however, the only tea ceremony. There is an equally lovely Korean tea ceremony, as well as Chinese *gongfu* and English afternoon tea.

In as many countries as tea is consumed, there are ceremonies and traditions that have taken root. Within these countries and regions, household traditions have also been established.

In a world where so much changes and feels out of our control, we cling to our traditions. We seek to perfect them, to experience them more fully, and to hand them down to future generations. It is our way of ensuring the unbroken link between the parents of our parents' parents and the children of our children's children. Tea can be that link.

Saké and Tea

BY SIR EDWIN ARNOLD

Excerpted from Seas and Lands, *1897.*[1]

Ariosto has, in his great poem, a canto commencing *"Donne! e voi ch'avete le donne in pregio,"* whereby he begs that no lady will read the severe reflections which follow upon the foibles of her sex. I, on the contrary, venture most respectfully to invite all ladies to read this present letter, that they may know how distinguished is the origin of the teacup and the tea-tray, what immense social and historical effects their favorite beverage has produced, and with how much grace and ceremony the simple act of tea drinking may be, and is, in this gentle land of Japan, constantly invested. For my own part, a perfectly new sentiment has been kindled in my breast towards the whole mystery of the teapot since I had the honor of being entertained at the *Cha-no-yu,* in the "Hall of Clouds." Over the spirit of everyone who arrives as a stranger in Japan, whether or not, by habit or by taste, a votary of the tea leaf, a change in this respect slowly and surely steals. The importance and dignity of tea reveal themselves in an entirely new light when he finds a whole population of some forty millions concentrated, so to speak, round the teapot, and all the dwelling-houses, all the habits, all the tastes, the very language, the meals, the diurnal duties and associations of town and country folk alike, circling, as it were, about the tiny cup. Insensibly you also fall into the gentle passion. You learn

---

1   [Certain British spellings and archaic references have been amended. Ed.]

on your road while journeying, or when arriving at its end, or in entering a friend's house, or while shopping in the "Ginza,"[2] to expect and
to accept with pleasure the proffered draught of pale yellow, fragrant
liquid; which at first you only tolerate, appearing as it does without
milk or sugar, but afterwards begin to like, and lastly to find indis-
pensable. Insensibly the little porcelain cup becomes pleasantly linked
in the mind with the snow-pure mats, the pretty, prostrate *musumës*,[3]
the spotless joinery of the lowly walls, the exquisite proprieties of the
latticed *shojis,* adding to all these a charm, a refinement, a delicate
sobriety and distinguished simplicity found alike amid high and low,
emanating, as it were, from the inner spirit of the glossy green leaf and
silvery blossom of the tea plant—in one word, belonging essentially to
and half constituting beautiful, wonderful, quiet, and sweet Japan.

All this arises from the entertainment with which I was honored
(with a) Japanese banquet in the "Hall of Clouds" and the *Cha-no-yu*
(or "Tea of Honor") which followed it for myself and a select few. Dinners in the native fashion have now become so familiar, by my happy
fortune in making friends among the native gentlemen, that I am
conscious of having lost those first impressions which enable one to
paint accurately a novel scene. But I have not lost my early admiration
of them, and still continue to regard a well-appointed and properly-
served Japanese dinner as one of the most elegant and agreeable, as
well as satisfying, forms of "dining-out" which the genius of hospitality ever invented. Like the dwellings, the apartments, and the appointments of Japan, one of these entertainments closely resembles another
in the methods and the *menus.* I sat—or rather kneeled—lately at a
large banquet given by Mr. Okura, a very wealthy merchant, at his
country seat in Mukojima, a suburb of Tokyo. The ride thither took
us clear through the vast city into a rural quarter upon the bank of
the chief river. The guests, including many of the present Ministers
of the Emperor's Cabinet, assembled first of all in a smoking pavilion, overlooking the stream, richly adorned with carvings and chased
brass ornaments, and warmed by a huge *hibachi,* or fire-box. Here we

---

2   "Ginza" is a shopping district in Tokyo.
3   "*Musumës*" means girls.

were served by kneeling *musumës* with tea, vermouths, and little balls of sweetened millet; and then proceeded through many passages glistening with polished pine and cherrywood to the *shuko-do,* or dining chamber. Sitting here on little square cushions—every guest having his fire-box beside him—a girl in flowing embroidered robes and bright satin *obi* appears before each, and places the first tray within his reach. There will be upon it a little lacquered bowl of soup, a saucer of *légumes,* a tiny dish of cutlet, or ragoût, a bowl of snowy boiled rice, a saké-cup, and a pair of new chopsticks. The guest of the evening gives the signal to start by beginning to wield these latter, and then all is festivity and joyous chat *sans gêne.*[4] Your pretty *musumë,* having well started you, kneels in front of your tray, armed with a porcelain flask of rice-wine, warmed; and if she can help it she will not allow your little red saucer to remain unbrimmed.

My fortunate cushion was placed between the American Minister's and that of Count Saigon, the President of the Imperial Marine Department, whose brother headed the Satsuma rebellion many years ago and lost his head. The Count was loyal, and has risen to high office—a frank, hearty, English-looking statesman, whose merry conversation made one often neglect the choice dishes which followed the first service in lavish variety. At perhaps the third tray—when the second soup and the thin slices of raw fish, the *daikon*[5] and the vermicelli with almonds, have appeared, and many a cup of saké has warmed the "honorable insides" of the convives—the sound is heard, behind the screen at the end of the room, of the *samisen*[6] and the *koto,*[7] and, being pushed back, it reveals the musicians and the dancers. These last—the geishas—wear always very festive apparel, and are extremely well trained in their graceful *odori.*[8] But you would be wrong to think that any Japanese woman may put on the splendid and showy *kimonos* borne by the *Maiko.*[9] There is a very strict social rule in Japan that

---

4 "*Sans gêne*" means without embarrassment.
5 A "*daikon*" is a large white radish. "*Dai*" means large and "*kon*" means root.
6 A "*samisen*" is a musical instrument with three strings, a square body, and a long neck.
7 A "*koto*" is Japan's national instrument and is six feet long and 14 inches wide. It has 13 strings, each on a bridge that can be moved. It is plucked with three fingers.
8 "*Odori*" is a traditional Japanese dance.
9 "*Maiko*" is a girl who dances and is training to be a geisha.

after the twenty-first year of her age a girl must no longer don bright colors; she then assumes the sober tints of gray, dark-blue, dove-color, and brown; so that, practically, only the quite young female people assume the gorgeous garments in question. When the geishas have finished one or two well-known dances, and have been applauded with words of approval and clapping of hands, one comes back to the little trays, now encircling each guest as boats surround a ship in harbor, and plays again with the chopsticks among the *entremets,* the cakes, the candied fruits, and perfumed "kickshaws" which complete the service. Or one lights a cigarette, or *kiseru;*[10] or rises from his cushion to go, first to the host, and afterwards to every well-known friend in the circle, kneeling down before him, and saying, "*Ippai Kudasai,*" "Permit me to drink with you in my own cup." The person thus invited rinses his saké-cup in the hot-water bowl, and hands it to you; you raise it to your forehead, and presenting it to the *musumë* to be filled, quaff it, rinse it anew, and hand it to your friend, who lifts it to his head, has it replenished, and drinks, bowing low, adding such a sentence as, "*O me ni kakaru kara taksan o tanoshimi gozaimas*"—i.e., "I am very happy to have hung in your honorable eyes." By this time the conversation has grown animated; the companions of the banquet are gathered in friendly groups; the gaily-clad *musumës* flit about with vases of rice-wine, or converse lightly and prettily with the guests, who may offer them a cup of saké, and flirt a little. If you have known how to select the most satisfactory dishes, and have not made the mistake of swallowing whole what looked like a sugared chestnut, and turned out, too late, to be a lump of fiery mustard, cayenne, and soy, the entertainment has abundantly satisfied the appetite, besides gratifying the sight, the hearing, and the spirit generally. When, amid a buzz of joyous farewell talk, your *musumë* wraps you in your fur coat, and, while you slip again into your shoes on the threshold, knocks her pretty brow upon the matting, murmuring, *Sayonara! mata o ide nasare* ("Goodbye! be pleased to come again"), you enter your *jinrikisha*[11] and roll

---

10 A "*kiseru*" is a type of pipe that was often intricately decorated.
11 "*Jinrikisha*" is the origin for the word rickshaw. "*Jin*" means human. "*Riki*" means power. "*Sha*" means vehicle. It is a carriage pulled by one to two people.

off through the streets glittering with paper lanterns and lively with thousands of clattering feet, repeating to yourself, "Fate cannot harm me. I have dined today!"

Such was, in slightest outline, our dinner at Mukojima, where I left the Minister of Marine deep in a cheerful discussion with two geishas and a *musumë*, as to the proper words of a celebrated song. The banquet at the "Hall of Clouds" being in connection with the University, and largely attended by imperial professors, wore somewhat graver aspects, and there were present, besides, some distinguished Buddhist abbots, as well as the youthful head of one of their sects. The chief priest, by the way, though he went through the friendly ceremony of drinking from my cup, raised it simply to his forehead; either he did not touch what the Buddha forbade, or would not let me see him do it. There were also no dancing and no music, for the *Cha-no-yu* was to follow, and nothing in the least frivolous must mingle with that. Duly, when the dinner was finished, the chief guests, six or seven in number out of the forty or fifty present, repaired to the little room set apart for the ceremony. Approaching its entrance we all washed our hands with water from a small wooden ladle, out of a white wooden tub. Above the door were written characters which meant "Hospitality, courtesy, purity, tranquility!" We passed into a tiny apartment, of spotless appearance, provided with mats, cushions, an antique tea equipage, a glowing hearth sunk in the floor, and one hanging picture, very old, which we were directed to admire and criticize. Our places are prescribed round the floor, with careful politeness, by the aged servitor. Sitting thus quietly but gaily in the little snow-clean alcove, the talk turns upon the origin of the *Cha-no-yu*, and what it has done, not only for Japanese art, manners, and national life, but, if anybody reflects rightly, for the whole civilized world. It is really to Buddhism that civilization owes the tea leaf, and its immense place at the present day in the affections and the commerce of mankind. The plant is indigenous to Japan, but the "calm brethren of the yellow robe" brought with them into Japan, along with their gentle religion, the art of using it. Up to the time of our Wars of the Roses,[12] tea in Japan was

---

12 The Wars of the Roses were a series of wars over the English crown that took place from 1455 to 1485.

still so rare that soldiers received small pots of it as gifts of honor, and infused it in special feasts among their friends as a precious beverage.

The great Regent Yoshi-tsunè, retiring from power, personally established its universal use in Japan, and indirectly gave, by his far-off foresight and refined taste, five o'clock tea to the Duchess in Belgravia; and also to the student, the washerwoman, and the seamstress "the cup that cheers." He and his friend Shuko, a Buddhist priest, invented the tea pavilion, and drew up the first rules of the *Cha-no-yu*. But though these great minds so early popularized tea drinking in Japan, and doubtless intended to simplify it, the fashion long remained aristocratic. The nobles were wont to sit over their teacups gambling for gilded armor, and even for precious sword-blades, which the winner would often lightly give away to the pretty flowery-robed geishas, who danced, sang, and waited for them. It was reserved for the low-born but powerful and accomplished tycoon, Hidéyoshi, "the Augustus of Japanese History," to stamp the cult of the tea leaf with that enduring grace, simplicity, and charm which have made tea drinking the central act of Japanese life, and even built all their houses and apartments on the same undeviating pattern. Hidéyoshi had for his Maecenas Sen-no-rikiu, another Buddhist priest, and the two together reformed the *Cha-Seki* by making it before all things intensely simple. Ostentation was ostracized.

The four great qualities which the *Seikasha*—the Tea Drinker— was to celebrate and cultivate over the sacred cup were hospitality, courtesy, purity, and tranquillity. The apartment must be plain, but elegant, with spotless mats and simple joinery; the utensils must be uncostly, but exquisite in shape and fitness. Temperance must be absolute; if food and wine mingled with the little feast nobody must exceed one bowl of rice and three saucers of saké. Nor was it solely for love of grace and the four chief virtues of the tearoom, *Ka-kei-sei-jaku*,[13] that the famous tycoon inaugurated the cult of the tea leaf. His great mind saw that if he could give Japan a national and tranquil habit, easy of practice for the poor and attractive to the rich, he

---

13 These are the four great qualities mentioned above: hospitality, courtesy, purity, and tranquility.

would do much to sheathe the sword and humanize his people; and so it has turned out. Never, in truth, had a statesman's subtle device such grand success. The teacup, as I have said, is today the central fact of this fair and gentle land. It decides the architecture, binds together the societies, refreshes the fatigue, and rewards the day's work of high and low in Japan. The perspiring *jinrikisha* man is satisfied with the warm infusion; the Minister and the Mikado himself are only happy when the "honorable tea" exhales its delicate fragrance from the hands of the kneeling *musumë*. And there are little gracious ceremonies even about the most ordinary tea drinking in humblest houses, which everywhere elevate it above a mere beverage. Good manners in Japan prescribe a sort of soft solemnity whenever the little cup is being filled, and no hut is so lowly but its kettle, its teapot, and its tea equipage display something about them of distinction, taste, and the love of a chaste and perfect art.

But the *Cha-no-yu,* as Hidéyoshi and Sen-no-rikiu settled it for ever, carries these ceremonials to a grave perfection. To be quite orthodox the tearoom must be very small, one of but four and a half mats, roofed, if possible, with a single finely grained plank, or else thatched with bamboo grass. The few honored guests should be called to the pavilion by wooden clappers, washing their hands first in pure water. No discontented person must be present, nor any scandal, or flattery, or unkind words be heard. The host himself should mend the fire, light the incense, brush the mats, fill the white-pine ewer, and lay the ladle of red-pine; as well as see that the single picture is hung and the single flower-pot fairly set in its place. The tea should be of the finest green powder, from a beautiful but common little jar; placed in a cup of ancient design holding, perhaps, half a pint. The "honorable" hot water is poured upon it, and then stirred in with a small bamboo whisk, which article itself, like the tiny spoon of the same material used for taking out the tea powder, must be of a certain form, and, if possible, ancient, and famous for its artistic origin.

Even about the boiling of the water there is orthodox tradition, there is solemnity, I had almost said there is religion. The *sumi*[14] in the brazier must be piled up in the outline of a glowing Fuji-San. The kettle of beaten iron must have no touch of modern vulgarity in its shape, the water must be drawn from the purest source, and—at the moment of use—in the third state of boiling. The first state is known by its low murmuring, and the appearance on the surface of the large slow bubbles distinguished as "fish eyes," *gyo-moku;* the second is when steam comes with quickly rising foam; the third is when the steam disappears in a tranquil, steady simmer, and the fluid is now "honorable old hot water." This is the propitious moment for the admixture, which being compounded appears in the guise of a light-green frothy compound, delicately fragrant and invigoratingly hot, contained in the antique cup, which, neatly folded in a fair cloth, should be handed now to the principal guest. Drinking reverently from it, he should tenderly wipe the rim at the spot where he has quaffed, but the next guest must drink at the very same place, for such is the "Kiss of brotherhood," in harmony with the friendly inspirations of this ceremony. The last guest must be heedful to drain the bowl to its dregs; then he passes it round to be examined, criticized, and made the subject of pleasant talk about the old days, the canons of true art in pottery, or any other topic lightly arising from the graceful moment, as the tender fragrance of the tea leaf wafts itself about the air of the little spotless chamber and among the kneeling, happy, tranquil companions of the occasion.

At a glance it will be seen how imperiously these elegant ceremonies, once established and received, have dictated to Japan the pure simplicity of her ceramic and metal work, and how they have passed down into all ranks of the people, constituting a standard of sweet and simple manners and of high-bred tastes which they were quicker to accept than any other nation. Perhaps nowhere except in Japan would it have been possible even for the great Hidéyoshi and the astute Sen-no-rikiu to have indoctrinated a whole people with so pure and refined a passion. But the commonest Japanese have this charm-

14 "*Sumi*" is charcoal.

ing tendency to a delicate sobriety of appetite and taste; they love the touch of art which elevates, the glimpse of grace which dignifies. They have the nature rather of birds or butterflies than of ordinary human beings, and when you send out to your Kurumaya a cup of tea and a saucer of boiled rice, and hear afterwards his grateful words, you wonder whether he is of the same race as that which you left quaffing half-and-half and eating rump-steaks on the banks of the Thames. Of course the austere etiquette of the *Cha-no-yu* is special; but its spirit, as the central ceremony of tea drinking, has palpably passed through all Japan, where everything begins and ends with the *tetsubin* and the teacup. Nor is it too much to declare that to Buddhism, which brought in her religious ideas and the tea leaf, and to Hidéyoshi, who taught her how to honor, enjoy, and infuse it, is due much, if not most, of the existing aspect of social and civic Japan.

Tokyo, Japan, Dec. 19, 1889

Immersion

BY VIRGINIA WRIGHT

I wasn't born into a family or a culture with any sort of tea traditions. I never felt much of a pull toward the lace doilies, pink rose-patterned cups, and delicate formality of the strictly-mannered Western tradition of afternoon tea; although I could certainly appreciate the exuberant logic-puzzle tea parties of the maddest of hatters. But my concepts of tea were mostly contaminated by awareness of the legacy of colonial oppression or written off as the silliness that little girls completely unlike my younger self served to dolls in suburban backyards.

So, unsurprisingly, it was not a Darjeeling, sugared, milked, and delicately sipped from a Limoges tea cup that caused me to become completely enamored with tea and tea traditions. With little foreknowledge and few preconceptions, my immersion into the tea world required falling accidentally and headlong into it through the doorway of a Chinese tea shop one bright summer Saturday a few years ago.

I'm sure that I had passed this particular tea shop in previous wanderings through the Chinese section of Seattle's International District, but I'd never noticed it or felt compelled to venture into it before. But on this day my friend and I had framed an indulgent day with tea drinking, starting out with an aromatic and evocative pot of jasmine pearls earlier in the day at a teahouse a short distance away. So we walked into the tea seller's shop to see what else we could find out about tea. I liked the place right away because of its unwaveringly clear identity. The furniture, the teas, and everything else in the store had a cultural coherence to them, clearly and distinctly Chinese. We did not feel like intruders, but it was clear that we were out of our element, in a place that was not fashioned to cater to us or to other non-Chinese-Americans. This is a shop where local Chinese-Americans buy Chinese tea. I find that it is often places with this type of cultural consistency that become frequent haunts for me, whether they're restaurants, shops, or other institutions. In the tea shop I was immediately fascinated, looking at all of the wonderful teaware, and the bricks and packages of tea arrayed on the varied and decorative shelves. It was a paradise of tools and vessels, mostly items that I had little to no familiarity with, but I was immediately captivated by their evident specificity and the range in styles and types and materials. I couldn't guess what each item was for, but I could tell that I had entered an environment full of rules and protocols, where the accoutrements of brewing and serving tea had undergone centuries of tradition and refinement.

Shortly after we entered, the woman running the shop asked us if we wanted to sit down and try some tea. My innate distrust of salespersons made me hesitate, but I agreed. We then sat down at the long wooden tea table and watched as she prepared tea for us in the traditional Chinese method called *Gongfu Cha*. "*Gongfu*" is one Anglicization of the same words as "kung fu" and "gung fu" and means the same thing: in essence, "skill" or "art." The term's use in reference to tea instead of a form of martial art had been previously unknown to me. Additionally, the only traditional tea ceremony I had ever been exposed to was *Chanoyu*, the Japanese Tea Ceremony—a practice of formidable precision and refined beauty that requires years of devoted study. This Chinese tea ceremony was something altogether different. It had formulas and correct practices, but was more casual, even in the approach of the server to the guests and the amount of casual dialog encouraged throughout. It was attainable, and right off I found myself wanting to learn more about it. Something in the nature of it resonated deeply with my sensibilities.

One of the essential aspects of this formative *Gongfu Cha* experience was that as the woman brewed and served the tea she gave us information about it, and about the procedures and how to perform them. First we watched as she poured clean, clear hot water over the teaware, warming and rinsing the cups, the serving pitcher, and the pot and allowing the hot water to run down the table's special draining system. The first tea she served us that day was a *pu-erh*, and she discarded the initial infusion after just a couple of seconds of steeping, explaining to us that this is a step that needs to be taken to ensure the cleanliness and best taste of the *pu-erh* tea. Some of this initial rinsing infusion was poured over the top of a clay sculpture in the form of a mythical creature that occupied a corner of the tea table. She called him a "five kind animal" and said that his frequent baptism in tea played some part in encouraging good fortune. This creature was similar to the commonly seen three-legged money frogs that often occupy the same role in *Gongfu Cha*, but I found the five-kind animal considerably more charming and elegant, with his flashy brush of a tail, spiky horns and tiny black bead eyes.

Then the brewing began in earnest with the first drinkable infusion of the *pu-erh*. She used a small, classically designed, dark reddish Yixing clay teapot for steeping and then decanted the tea through a strainer into a sharing pitcher; from this she poured tea into each of our tiny porcelain tasting cups in turn. She explained about the tea absorption of the Yixing pot and how it would become more valuable in time as it acquired a rich patina of tea outside and in, also explaining why this same absorbent quality meant that the same teapot should not be used for unlike varieties of teas. Tea liquor itself is almost always a beautiful thing, ranging from the barely shaded pales of white teas through the darkest chestnut liquors of black teas; the deep, rich reds of the *pu-erh* we were sampling were particularly dramatic in appearance. This first round of the tea was followed by at least five additional infusions, with the *pu-erh* leaf continuing to yield a lively, invigorating brew. She, of course, drank tea along with us as we asked questions and I began to formulate a desire to absorb as much of Chinese tea culture as I could.

Of course, none of this ceremony and fixation on process is of the slightest value if the physical, sensory experience of drinking the tea is not enjoyable. The milieu surrounding tea culture—the tools, the vessels, the history—are all secondary to the *Camellia sinensis* plant itself. The tea must provide a wonderful drinking experience; otherwise there's no point to any of the rest of it. Each tea should deserve the beauty of its vessel. But we were in a tea shop that specialized in high-quality, traditional Chinese teas, so we were in the right place to discover teas that not only looked good and were prepared attractively, but that also exhibited a wide range of wondrous flavors and characters. The teas we tasted that day were wonderful, rich in flavor and appearance. Some of that *pu-erh* that we tasted first was purchased to come home with us, although I really can't remember precisely what it was—something mid-grade and loose leaf. Subsequent visits to the shop introduced me to some exquisite *oolong*s and fabulous *pu-erh* teas, including the high-grade, lightly oxidized *Tie Guan Yin* that it's probably fair to call my favorite of all teas. Initiated alongside this newfound desire for acquiring good tea was a need for accumulating appropriate teawares to use in preparing and drinking them.

This first experience with *Gongfu Cha* pointed me down many more paths towards uncovering other forms of tea cultures and traditions. I've always been interested in learning about specific rituals and cultural traditions, and studying tea encompasses this basic interest and expands upon it into other realms of inquiry. The variety and the specificity of tea traditions in almost every country in the world is astonishing, and it provides me with rich fields of exploration—a seemingly inexhaustible source of topics for reading, writing and discovery. I find that the diverse elements involved in the inquiries into tea culture involve a great deal of what I'm generally interested in: cultural history, political history, aesthetics, art history, religion, craftsmanship, the science of materials, and at the core of it all lies the purest form of epicurean adventure: drinking delicious tea.

After the Walk

by George Robert Gissing

Excerpted from The Private Papers of Henry Ryecroft,
a semi-fictional memoir, 1903.[1]

One of the shining moments of my day is that when, having returned a little weary from an afternoon walk, I exchange boots for slippers, out-of-doors coat for easy, familiar, shabby jacket, and, in my deep, soft-elbowed chair, await the tea-tray. Perhaps it is while drinking tea that I most of all enjoy the sense of leisure. In days gone by, I could but gulp down the refreshment, hurried, often harassed, by the thought of the work I had before me; often I was quite insensible of the aroma, the flavor, of what I drank. Now, how delicious is the soft yet penetrating odor which floats into my study, with the appearance of the teapot! What solace in the first cup, what deliberate sipping of that which follows! What a glow does it bring after a walk in chilly rain! The while, I look around at my books and pictures, tasting the happiness of their tranquil possession. I cast an eye towards my pipe; perhaps I prepare it, with seeming thoughtfulness, for the reception of tobacco. And never, surely, is tobacco more soothing, more suggestive of humane thoughts, than when it comes just after tea—itself a bland inspirer.

In nothing is the English genius for domesticity more notably declared than in the institution of this festival—almost one may call it so—of afternoon tea. Beneath simple roofs, the hour of tea has some-

---

1 [Certain British spellings have been amended. Ed.]

thing in it of sacred; for it marks the end of domestic work and worry, the beginning of restful, sociable evening. The mere chink of cups and saucers tunes the mind to happy repose. I care nothing for your five o'clock tea of modish drawing-rooms, idle and wearisome like all else in which that world has part; I speak of tea where one is *at home* in quite another than the worldly sense. To admit mere strangers to your tea-table is profanation; on the other hand, English hospitality has here its kindliest aspect; never is friend more welcome than when he drops in for a cup of tea. Where tea is really a meal, with nothing between it and nine o'clock supper, it is—again in the true sense—the *homeliest* meal of the day. Is it believable that the Chinese, in who knows how many centuries, have derived from tea a millionth part of the pleasure or the good which it has brought to England in the past one hundred years?

I like to look at my housekeeper when she carries in the tray. Her mien is festal, yet in her smile there is a certain gravity, as though she performed an office which honored her. She has dressed for the evening; that is to say, her clean and seemly attire of working hours is exchanged for garments suitable to fireside leisure; her cheeks are warm, for she has been making fragrant toast. Quickly her eye glances about my room, but only to have the pleasure of noting that all is in order; inconceivable that anything serious should need doing at this hour of the day. She brings the little table within the glow of the hearth, so that I can help myself without changing my easy position. If she speaks, it will only be a pleasant word or two; should she have anything important to say, the moment will be *after* tea, not before it; this she knows by instinct. Perchance she may just stoop to sweep back a cinder which has fallen since, in my absence, she looked after the fire; it is done quickly and silently. Then, still smiling, she withdraws, and I know that she is going to enjoy her own tea, her own toast, in the warm, comfortable, sweet-smelling kitchen.

In a Teahouse with O-Toyo

BY JOSEPH RUDYARD KIPLING

Excerpted from Kipling's From Sea to Sea: Letters from Travel, *1899.*[1]
*This essay was part of a collection of letters and essays he originally
wrote for the* Civil and Military Gazette *and* Pioneer *between 1887–
1889 and then compiled into book form.*

This morning, after the sorrows of the rolling night, my cabin port-
hole showed me two great gray rocks studded and streaked with green
and crowned by two stunted blue-black pines. Below the rocks a boat,
that might have been carved sandalwood for color and delicacy, was
shaking out an ivory-white frilled sail to the wind of the morning. An
indigo-blue boy with an old ivory face hauled on a rope. Rock and tree
and boat made a panel from a Japanese screen, and I saw that the land
was not a lie. This "good brown earth" of ours has many pleasures to
offer her children, but there be few in her gift comparable to the joy of
touching a new country, a completely strange race, and manners contrary. Though libraries may have been written aforetime, each new be-
holder is to himself another Cortez. And I was in Japan—the Japan of
cabinets and joinery, gracious folk and fair manners. Japan, whence the
camphor and the lacquer and the shark-skin swords come: among what
was it the books said?—a nation of artists. To be sure, we should only
stop at Nagasaki for twelve hours ere going on to Kobé, but in twelve
hours one can pack away a very fair collection of new experiences....

---

1   [Certain British spellings and archaic references have been amended. Ed.]

...We entered a courtyard where an evil-looking bronze horse stared at two stone lions, and a company of children babbled among themselves. There is a legend connected with the bronze horse, which may be found in the guide-books. But the real true story of the creature is, that he was made long ago out of the fossil ivory of Siberia by a Japanese Prometheus, and got life and many foals, whose descendants closely resemble their father. Long years have almost eliminated the ivory in the blood, but it crops out in creamy mane and tail; and the pot-belly and marvelous feet of the bronze horse may be found to this day among the pack-ponies of Nagasaki, who carry pack-saddles adorned with velvet and red cloth, who wear grass shoes on their hind feet, and who are made like to horses in a pantomime.

We could not go beyond this courtyard because a label said, "No admittance," and thus all we saw of the temple was rich-brown high roofs of blackened thatch, breaking back and back in wave and undulation till they were lost in the foliage. The Japanese can play with thatch as men play with modeling clay, but how their light underpinnings can carry the weight of the roof is a mystery to the lay eye.

We went down the steps to tiffin,[2] and a half-formed resolve was shaping itself in my heart the while. Burma was a very nice place, but they eat *gnapi*[3] there, and there were smells, and after all, the girls weren't so pretty as some others—

"You must take off your boots," said Y-Tokai.

I assure you there is no dignity in sitting down on the steps of a teahouse and struggling with muddy boots. And it is impossible to be polite in your stockinged feet when the floor under you is as smooth as glass and a pretty girl wants to know where you would like tiffin. Take at least one pair of beautiful socks with you when you come this way. Get them made of embroidered *sambhur*[4] skin, of silk if you like, but do not stand as I did in cheap striped brown things with a darn at the heel, and try to talk to a tea-girl.

---

2   "Tiffin" is a light meal or lunch.
3   "*Gnapi*" is fish paste.
4   A "*sambhur*" is a type of deer with large antlers.

They led us—three of them, and all fresh and pretty—into a room furnished with a golden-brown bearskin. The *tokonoma*,[5] recess afore-mentioned, held one scroll picture of bats wheeling in the twilight, a bamboo flower-holder, and yellow flowers. The ceiling was of paneled wood, with the exception of one strip at the side nearest the window, and this was made of plaited shavings of cedar-wood, marked off from the rest of the ceiling by a wine-brown bamboo so polished that it might have been lacquered. A touch of the hand sent one side of the room flying back, and we entered a really large room with another *tokonoma* framed on one side by eight or ten feet of an unknown wood, bearing the same grain as a Penang lawyer,[6] and above by a stick of unbarked tree set there purely because it was curiously mottled. In this second *tokonoma* was a pearl-gray vase, and that was all. Two sides of the room were of oiled paper, and the joints of the beams were covered by the brazen images of crabs, half life-size. Save for the sill of the *tokonoma,* which was black lacquer, every inch of wood in the place was natural grain without flaw. Outside was the garden, fringed with a hedge of dwarf-pines and adorned with a tiny pond, water-smoothed stones sunk in the soil, and a blossoming cherry tree.

They left us alone in this paradise of cleanliness and beauty, and being only a shameless Englishman without his boots—a white man is always degraded when he goes barefoot—I wandered round the wall, trying all the screens. It was only when I stooped to examine the sunk catch of a screen that I saw it was a plaque of inlay work representing two white cranes feeding on fish. The whole was about three inches square and in the ordinary course of events would never be looked at. The screens are a cupboard in which all the lamps and candlesticks and pillows and sleeping-bags of the household seemed to be stored. An Asian nation that can fill a cupboard tidily is a nation to bow down to. Upstairs I went by a staircase of grained wood and lacquer, into rooms of rarest device with circular windows that opened on nothing, and so were filled with bamboo tracery for the delight of the eye. The passages floored with dark wood shone like ice, and I was ashamed.

---

5   A "*tokonoma*" is an alcove in a reception area where art or other objects are displayed.
6   A "Penang lawyer" is a type of walking stick.

"Professor," said I, "they don't spit; they don't eat like pigs; they can't quarrel, and a drunken man would reel straight through every portion in the house and roll down the hill into Nagasaki. They can't have any children." Here I stopped. Downstairs was full of babies.

The maidens came in with tea in blue china and cake in a red lacquered bowl—such cake as one gets at one or two houses in Simla. We sprawled ungracefully on red rugs over the mats, and they gave us chopsticks to separate the cake with. It was a long task.

"Is that all?" growled the Professor. "I'm hungry, and cake and tea oughtn't to come till four o'clock." Here he took a wedge of cake furtively with his hands.

They returned—five of them this time—with black lacquer stands a foot square and four inches high. Those were our tables. They bore a red lacquered bowlful of fish boiled in brine, and sea-anemones. At least they were not mushrooms. A paper napkin tied with gold thread enclosed our chopsticks; and in a little flat saucer lay a smoked crayfish, a slice of a compromise that looked like Yorkshire pudding and tasted like sweet omelette, and a twisted fragment of some translucent thing that had once been alive but was now pickled. They went away, but not empty handed, for thou, oh, O-Toyo, didst take away my heart—same which I gave to the Burmese girl in the Shway Dagon pagoda!

The Professor opened his eyes a little, but said no word. The chopsticks demanded all his attention, and the return of the girls took up the rest. O-Toyo, ebon-haired, rosy-cheeked, and made throughout of delicate porcelain, laughed at me because I devoured all the mustard sauce that had been served with my raw fish, and wept copiously till she gave me saké from a lordly bottle about four inches high. If you took some very thin hock,[7] and tried to mull it and forgot all about the brew till it was half cold, you would get *saké*. I had mine in a saucer so tiny that I was bold to have it filled eight or ten times and loved O-Toyo none the less at the end.

After raw fish and mustard sauce came some other sort of fish cooked with pickled radishes, and very slippery on the chopsticks.

---

7 "Hock" is white wine.

The girls knelt in a semicircle and shrieked with delight at the Professor's clumsiness, for indeed it was not I that nearly upset the dinner table in a vain attempt to recline gracefully. After the bamboo shoots came a basin of white beans in sweet sauce—very tasty indeed. Try to convey beans to your mouth with a pair of wooden knitting-needles and see what happens. Some chicken cunningly boiled with turnips, and a bowlful of snow-white boneless fish and a pile of rice, concluded the meal. I have forgotten one or two of the courses, but when O-Toyo handed me the tiny lacquered Japanese pipe full of hay-like tobacco, I counted nine dishes in the lacquer stand—each dish representing a course. Then O-Toyo and I smoked by alternate pipefuls.

My very respectable friends at all the clubs and messes, have you ever after a good tiffin lolled on cushions and smoked, with one pretty girl to fill your pipe and four to admire you in an unknown tongue? You do not know what life is. I looked round me at that faultless room, at the dwarf pines and creamy cherry blossoms without, at O-Toyo bubbling with laughter because I blew smoke through my nose, and at the ring of *Mikado* maidens over against the golden-brown bearskin rug. Here was color, form, food, comfort, and beauty enough for half a year's contemplation. I would not be a Burman any more. I would be a Japanese—always with O-Toyo *bien entendu*[8]—in a cabinet work-house on a camphor-scented hillside.

"Heigho!" said the Professor. "There are worse places than this to live and die in. D'you know our steamer goes at four? Let's ask for the bill and get away."

Now I have left my heart with O-Toyo under the pines. Perhaps I shall get it back at Kobé.

---

8   "*Bien entendu*" is French for "of course" or "well understood."

A Valuable Moment of Life

BY KATE FINNEGAN

Tea Ceremony with Mr. Kaji Aso

When I was studying fine arts at Tufts University and the School of the Museum of Fine Arts in Boston in the late 1970s, my professor was Mr. Kaji Aso. After I graduated in 1980 I began taking classes at his studio in Boston. Soon I discovered that Mr. Aso held Japanese tea ceremony every Sunday afternoon at the studio and I made a reservation to attend tea.

Kaji Aso Studio is located in a brownstone townhouse near Symphony Hall and, back then, tea ceremony was held in the art gallery. (Later, in 1987, Mr. Aso extended the studio by building a tea house and, in 1997, a tea garden). I had attended exhibitions, concerts, and poetry readings in the delightful gallery and was surprised on the day of tea ceremony to find the space magically transformed into a Japanese setting. An entrance screen shielded the doorway and *tatami* mats were carefully laid out on the floor. Hanging nearby was an art piece: a calligraphy character in which the black ink flowed on the page, thick to thin, dark to light, each stroke demonstrating flowing direction and movement. Later I would learn this character meant "dance" in Japanese. Just below this was an earthen-colored vase in which leaves with the first splashes of autumn colors were arranged.

Mr. Aso was sitting *seiza* (on his knees) in a steel-blue-colored kimono of fine material and, as always, there was an ambiance of calmness and focused positive energy emanating from him. A group of six people entered and sat across from each other on the *tatami* mats. There was a subtle scent of incense and an ancient kettle that made a pleasant sound. Mr. Aso placed a lacquer plate in front of him that held a ceramic bowl and other mysterious tea implements.

He bowed and said, "Good afternoon and welcome to tea."

We all bowed back and said, "Good afternoon."

In that moment and every moment that followed I was transported from my everyday world to a place of *exquisite*.

We were perfectly quiet as the tea assistant passed a small plate of sweets around so we could each take one. As we enjoyed the delicate taste, Mr. Aso began to prepare tea. His movements were mesmerizing—flowing and stopping and flowing again. They intertwined with other sounds and sights—the steam rising from the kettle, the tap of the bamboo spoon on the ceramic bowl, the scooping and pouring of water, the blur of the whisk followed by the smell of green tea, something akin to spring.

Mr. Aso picked up the tea bowl and turned it carefully: once... twice...a little more. He paused with a slight bow and then placed the tea bowl down. His assistant passed it to the first guest.

I watched as the guest bowed, carefully picked up the bowl, turned it and then took a sip. A satisfied smile came over her face. "Delicious," she said and she took two more sips. Then she took her napkin and wiped the bowl where her lips had touched and turned it back before setting it down for the next guest.

I was the third guest in line and when the bowl reached me I saw clearly for the first time the emerald green—so very green! The whisked up foam was like a shimmering green sea. I tried to imitate the movements I had seen the other guests do. Mr. Aso talked me through them. When I picked the bowl up, there was a painting of a crane facing me. I enjoyed the painting a moment and Mr. Aso said that I should not touch my lips to the painting, but turn the bowl two and a half times to the back and drink from there.

My first sip of tea was so different from anything I ever had. The smooth, rich, slightly bitter and fresh taste mingled with the lingering taste of the sweets in an enjoyable way.

"Delicious!" I said.

"Please finish it," Mr. Aso replied. "One bowl is for three people."

He mentioned that it was all right to make a sound on the last sip because the foam is the most delicious part. I slurped the last bit of tea and everyone smiled. Carefully I wiped the bowl where I drank, returned it back to the crane painting and placed it down. I said, "Thank you," and passed the bowl back to Mr. Aso. He carefully washed it and began preparing a second bowl for the remaining guests with the same consistent intent and focus. Nothing was rushed. Every movement mattered.

After everyone had tea, we had conversation. Mr. Aso passed the bowl and utensils around for closer viewing. We enjoyed the feel of the lacquer tea caddie, the sight of bright green tea powder, the intricacy of the bamboo whisk. Mr. Aso explained the crane bowl was from Korea from the Li Dynasty, fifteenth century. He said that many beautiful ceramics, as well as Buddhism, came to Japan through Korea.

When we were done, Mr. Aso put everything back and asked us to have a short meditation. We sat quietly and at the end he bowed and thanked us for coming. We bowed in return. At that moment I felt utterly calm and peaceful.

Mr. Aso encouraged the new guests to come again to tea. He said that the first time we are nervous and not sure what to do and the next time we would be more comfortable and discover another level of tea.

I did come back again and again and tea ceremony has become a lifelong pursuit. One tea has become a thousand teas, each one unique, specific to that day, that moment, and that group of people. All come with a desire to share a valuable moment of life, some more deeply calm and connected than others, but always reaching a moment of serenity.

Mr. Aso often presented a haiku poem at tea. He said that haiku and tea ceremony are very much related because each focuses on a moment. An eighteenth-century poet named Buson wrote one haiku in particular that Mr. Aso said expressed the essence of tea.

Kagiri aru
inochi no himaya
aki no kure

Life is short
Autumn evening is shorter than life
Yet there is a moment of luxury

Tea ceremony is the place for people to come together to enjoy tea, absorb the beauty of the world around them and share a complete moment of peace. With each tea I discover something new and valuable that stays in my heart and grows.

Mr. Kaji Aso had various experiences of tea ceremony school in Japan. He sought the most original and ancient form of tea ceremony to discover the true enjoyment of tea and true enjoyment of friendship through sharing a sip of tea. This vision of tea provides a wide understanding of life and nature.

Tea at 77 Guthrie Avenue
by Debbra Summers

A china tea cup perched on a matching saucer waits for me at my place at the table. Real china dishes are everyday dishes here. Mismatched teaspoons stand face up at the ready in a cut glass spooner.[1] Real silver spoons are polished and patient. A robin's egg-blue ceramic teapot is a perfect match with the glossy painted kitchen cupboards. Only the spout and handle are visible, poking out from under the insulated armor of tea-stained felt cloth and aluminum, as the tea steeps. It won't steep too long, otherwise it will be bitter and "fit only for the African violets to drink."

"One lump or two?" she asks me.

A tiny rectangular tray holds a small lidded dish of sugar cubes. "Flies like sugar too," she reminds me. There is just enough room on the tray for the made-for-two-cups milk pitcher, full and cold from the refrigerator. The milk is always poured in the cup first. This was something done during the Depression by those well off enough that they didn't need to worry about things like how much of this precious commodity they used. "They could use as much as they wanted. None of this 'just enough to lighten their tea' baloney. They did it then. We're doing it now." I still do it today.

A plate of tiny crustless triangles of egg salad sandwiches covered with clingy plastic wrap is taken out of the fridge at the last moment.

---

1   A "spooner" was part of a four-piece breakfast set that also included a creamer, sugar bowl, and butter dish. It held the spoons, which were the most-used utensils, and stayed in the center of the table.

"You can't be too careful with mayonnaise." The egg has been mixed with just the right amount of green onion from the garden and lots of black pepper and spread on low-calorie *Hollywood* bread. Mixed pickles with white baby onions and yellow cauliflower pieces are served; there are never enough of those. An oval ice-water-filled crystal dish offers radishes cut like lily pad flowers, curled carrot slivers and celery sticks.

A well-loved—"It sounds better than 'old'"—starched tablecloth, red, blue and yellow with fruit and flowers at each corner, is too long for the gray marbled Formica and chrome kitchen table. I have to pay extra special attention when I climb up onto my chair to make sure that everything on the table doesn't end up there with me. The vinyl upholstered chairs match the table perfectly. The tablecloth's home-made patches are hidden by our placemats, although you wouldn't notice them unless you knew they were there. "And that's what matters," I'm told. One of the long sides of the table is pushed right up against the ledge of the painted sash window between the kitchen and the back porch. From every seat at the table you can see the green velvet lawn in the backyard, beyond the two pine trees where Puddles the dog is buried, all the way back to the vegetable patch.

The salt and pepper shakers—today's choice from a collection of over 100 pairs—are the pale pink pigs with red china rosebuds tucked behind their ears and black, hand-painted snowflake eyes. A chipped juice glass shows off fragrant lillies-of-the-valley from the garden next to the gravel driveway. "A thing is always useful for something." A cheerful lemon yellow plastic teapot-motif napkin holder stuffed with white embossed napkins is the last piece to claim its place at the table.

It is twelve o'clock noon, exactly. The cuckoo clock just said so. It has been a very long day already. We have been up since 6 o'clock. After a breakfast of red grapefruit halves—sprinkled with sugar, dotted in the middle with a whole maraschino cherry, and left in the refrigerator to soak up the sweetness overnight, a bowl of Special K cereal, and tea, we "got right to it." Dishes first. I dry because the washer has to wear the yellow Playtex gloves and they don't fit me. The water, as hot as our tea, with a splash of vinegar—"It makes the dishes squeaky clean"—fills the second sink where the dishes are rinsed before they make their way into the drying rack. This makes my job easy. The dishes are almost dry by the time they get to me. Chores never seem like work here. Last night's white cotton bedding is fighting the wind's persistent attempts to wrap it around the pulley clothesline. I had done my part, helping the pillow cases and sheets through the rollers of the wringer washer. Then, "Do you think you can stand still long enough?" she asked as I balanced on the top step of the back stoop holding one end of each sheet, slowly letting it go as she pinned it on the line. We are done in no time. "Many hands make light work." She wipes her hands on her apron with the satisfaction of a job well done. "There. They shouldn't take long to dry today."

Back inside, strawberry-red rhubarb stalks, picked earlier from the patch behind the garage, stew in a copper-bottomed pot over a short blue flame on one of the back burners of the small gas stove. It will be dessert; warm and tart over a scoop of French Vanilla ice cream.

The delicious smell of early summer meets my nose. "Mmmmm. Can we have dessert first?"

It is the perfect time for tea. We are hungry. "That's the best time to eat," she announces.

"One lump or two?" she asks again.

I think about it for a minute.

"One" I say.

"One it is...Not that you need any," she says, with a bear hug from behind and a kiss on my cheek. "You're sweet enough." She smells like Noxzema cream and her house. I breathe her in.

Two long, tissue-paper-skin fingers pluck one of the sweet white cubes from the dish. There is no chance that any germ would dare remain after the scrubbing those hands just had. Plop, splash, fizzle; the sugar gets busy sweetening my tea.

I took sugar in my tea only when I was there with her. Even today, I still don't take sugar in my tea. Neither my Gran nor 77 Guthrie Avenue remain, but when I need a hug, just a few grains in my cup takes me back to that kitchen table.

The English Tea

BY MURIEL HARRIS

Excerpted from The North American Review, *Feb. 1, 1922.*[1]

If the English tea has not always been the foundation of English society, it is simply because Marco Polo began his travels a few centuries
late. The germ of English tea was as much a part of the English con-
stitution as is the Bible, Beethoven, or *Blighty*.[2] And just as the Ger-
mans feel that Shakespeare should have been born in their Fatherland,
so it scarcely occurs to the English mind that China tea really comes
from China and Indian from India. And even if it does, what is China?
What is India? Both are places to which the Englishman takes England
and brings it safely home again. And tea? Tea was being poured in the
panelled drawing-room when he left England, and seven years later he
comes back for his second cup. It is as impossible for the Englishman
to forget English tea as it is for him to forget England.

There are grandmothers today who remember the severity with
which their grandmothers regarded the decadent innovation of afternoon tea. You might have tea, but you might not have it comfortably. It
was brought in under protest, and conversation languished until it was
taken out again. And yet the Great War was run on tea, and the subma-
rine sinkings and the convoy system and the munitions question and
the War Cabinet itself were suspended regularly every afternoon for a
few minutes when the little black teapot made its peremptory appear-

---

1   [Certain British spellings and archaic terms have been amended. Ed.]
2   *Blighty* was a humorous men's magazine printed in London for British servicemen.

ance, flanked with what had once been cake and toast but now was—it is difficult to say what it was in 1918. The apotheosis of tea took place during the Great War. More than this. A certain Georgian virility returned with it. The "dish of tay" which was drunk alike by men and by women after the portentous three and four and five o'clock dinners of more than a century ago, again became masculine as well as feminine. Perhaps it was more the one than the other by the time the war was finished. Certainly the solvent that is tea accommodated a million inter-relationships where friction was possible. If nothing more, it was the weakness to which the truly great succumbed as readily as any one of their minions. Queen Anne is dead—though she was once a real person with a marked liking for playing at the game of "Let's Pretend"—but her tall glass cupboards with their Lowestoft and egg-shell china found real successors in the rude earthenware of the funny, ramshackle, shabby old Whitehall buildings which constitute the heart of the British Empire. If you go to Regent's Park today, if you visit the pleasant town of Cheltenham or of Bath, you will see by the hundred the houses in which the "dish of tay" flaunted it with parrots and black servants and marmosets and coiffures of astounding geography. You will see where the Nabobs lived and you will hear faint echoes of John Company, and perhaps also some of the fantastic old tea-chests will remain and the red lacquer trays and the dragon china, and a memory of the days when the trial of Warren Hastings was the gossip of the day and a few other Anglo-Indians felt uneasy, even though the word "profiteering" had not yet been invented. And so the old Government offices, in which the Pepys and the Norths—also of tea fame—and the Pitts and the Foxes had had their being, positively clamored for the revival of the beverage of which the regalia was still there.

Nor could an institution be neglected which so instantly reflected the genius of the times. It is only necessary to compare the classic Georgian tea service with the redundant curves of the Victorian teapot; the Victorian teapot—prosperous, stout-waistcoated—with the miscellany, the democratic diversity, if you will, of the Great War china—the silver was mostly at the Bank—to realize the part in English society played by tea. And why? Because tea—afternoon tea, nowadays, and not the ten o'clock nightcap of the Victorian era—makes a halfway house between English formality and English expansion. Strangers are often at pains to reconcile the English stiffness and coldness with the expansiveness of the English house and its manner of hospitality. In one sense, the Englishman's house is his castle, strongly barred against intruders, extremely jealous of its privacy, resentful of any attempt to penetrate its fastness. In another, it is an open door, welcoming, free, hospitable. You have to be given the freedom of the castle and it is yours. Without this freedom, you are a mere outsider. The English tea is at once a preliminary to this freedom and a relaxation from the forms of life. There is no set service, no special time within an hour or so. It comes after the day's efforts and provides the little stimulus which overcomes fatigue. The shining silver reflecting the leaping fire, the sound of the kettle, the warm scent of the flowers, the low book-box or stand, full perhaps of brand new books, all these elements which have grown up round the tea function, provide a quiet, expansive atmosphere in which both friend and family can feel themselves most perfectly at home. The secretive Englishman delivers himself most astoundingly at tea. You have a share in his confidences. For once he becomes conversational, easy, even eloquent. There are subjects suited for the dinner-table; the people who breakfast with each other are usually the rulers of our destinies; lunch is an uneasy meal, booted and spurred for the afternoon's avocations. At tea there are no rules—nothing but arm-chairs and relaxation and informal converse, and perhaps the children in clean frocks for an hour or so before dinner. The tea hour represents the English home in its fullest sense in that it conveys a sense of intimacy even to the stranger. He can see the household out of the office, off the stage, when it is content thus to dispense with trappings of ceremony and of form.

Perhaps the penetration of the English tea into the Versailles Conference was one of the most remarkable of its achievements. In a sense, of course, the Conference was itself something of a return to a state of society when society was small and international and not, as today, large and intensely national. Nobody who was unconnected with the Conference had for the moment any particular interest, and a limited and cosmopolitan society was thus the cynosure of every eye. When

Mr. Balfour diverted M. Clémenceau with tea, it was an international incident,[3] in the sense almost that upon the frown of a king's mistress depended the fate of nations. And it was tea made with canned milk, too! Was it a ruse of the wily Lloyd George? Did he realize how tea helped the inarticulate Englishman? How it gave him something to do with his hands, filled in the pauses in his conversation, compensated for his French—or lack of it—and, most of all among the voluble Latins, gave him the feeling of being after all at home?

For the Englishman has to feel at home in order to deliver himself at all. The Frenchman is most truly gracious in public. The *beau geste*, of its nature, implies an audience. The German needs officialdom, almost a book of etiquette, behind him to be most impressive. For the things he cares most about he puts on a uniform; for the things an Englishman cares most about, he takes off his uniform, or never puts it on. And the English tea is for the Englishman the taking off of his uniform and feeling himself at home and therefore free to act and speak. In India he divests himself of officialdom and takes his tea. In China he brings England into the home of tea, just as, after a life-time, he takes China back to England and his porcelain and his jade and his Mandarin robes and his carved ebony for the background of the tea-table. It is the oddest thing to see in Cairo or Quebec English chintzes and perhaps an array of photographs in court trains upon which is the name of a South Kensington photographer; to drink tea among these household gods, just as though the thermometer were not above a hundred or below zero and the Red Sea and the St. Lawrence River were merely the Thames a little geographically displaced. It is the oddest thing to return to South Kensington and Regent's Park and again to drink the self-same blend amid brass bowls and mirrored hangings; amid perhaps Egyptian hieroglyphs and *ushabtis*;[4] or among *assegais*[5] and Zulu shields and elephant tusks and lion skins.

---

3   This refers to Georges Clemenceau (French Prime Minister, 1906–1909 and 1917–1920) and Arthur James Balfour (UK Prime Minister turned British Foreign Minister).
4   "*Ushabtis*" are small statues placed in tombs in Ancient Egypt.
5   An "*assegai*" is a light spear from southern Africa.

For here again the Englishman's home may be his castle, but it is also his point of departure. You might define it as a place to come back to—and to come back to from Asia or Africa or the South Pole, laden—as John Company used to be laden—with shawls and spices, with the insignia of your travels which you laid at the foot of the steaming altar in the drawing-room. There are hundreds of these homes in England, repositories of successive tides of travel spoils, each of which leaves its high water mark. And the teakettle goes steaming on, whether it be surrounded with stuffed birds from Australia or *kakemonos*[6] from Japan or carved chessmen from India, or latest of all, polished shell-cases and shell-noses and German helmets and saw-bayonets, trophies of the last tide in the English adventure.

Perhaps the oddest contrast of all was tea in the Tower of London itself, in the building where Sir Walter Raleigh languished and wrote his *History of the World*, himself the typical Englishman who loved England to go away from her. And the tea kettle hissed and bubbled as though the twelve-foot walls were upon no Roman site, as though no countless tragedies of Kings and Queens and courtiers had filled the very atmosphere. Perhaps the Englishman is lacking in the sense of time or place. Perhaps he has so complete a sense of continuity that time and place do not matter. Perhaps again, his one-idea-ed mind sees only that one thing is right and that thing must be done. It would account for his stolid bringing to America of eighteenth-century bricks for his house in the cockle shells of the period, although boundless forests were at his disposal. It would account equally for his perfect naturalness in applying his own customs amid the most incongruous surroundings. Of course he has his tea, whether he is in London or in Timbuktu; whether empires are falling or rising. It is the same instinct which makes him apply quite gravely the English form of government to the Kaffir[7] or the Yoruba[8] peoples. *Civis Romanus sum;*[9] and tea is part of it all, part of a great freemasonry.

---

6 A "*kakemono*" is a wall hanging, either a scroll or calligraphy, that can be rolled up for storage.

7 "*Kaffir*" is an old term, now considered derogatory, used by white South Africans to refer to black South Africans people.

8 "*Yoruba*" are people from West Africa.

9 "*Civis Romanus sum*" means "I am a Roman citizen" and implies certain rights.

In the life of every country there are certain illuminating moments in the day. The Frenchman dines with mellowness and joy in living. The American thrills by doing something differently. The German expands under the influence of opera with ham sandwiches. The English love of formalism makes tea a regular institution and then proceeds to remove any suggestion of regularity about it, except its every day existence. Nor does this apply to any particular class. The cottage tea with its big loaf and its thick black liquor is just as much of an institution as is the Cathedral tea with a delicate blend from China and thin bread and butter. There is the same warm, generous feeling about it as in the crispness of the falling leaf and the pungent smell of its burning and the glow of the flames against the blue mist of the darkening autumn afternoon. The English drawing-room is nearly always formless. It has just come about; it is rarely conscious. And the English tea party is formless too, apart from its being an institution; apart from the sense of its always having been. Now, it is a gathering in an old London house, on the gates of which places for the linkman's torches still survive. And the guests come in at any time, and there is no guest of honor, though affairs of state may be settled or a plea put through for somebody's appointment, or a traveler may have returned from a big game expedition, or a writer may have uttered a *mot* which penetrates to all the groups in the various corners of the room, who are as publicly private as it is possible to be. Now, it is definitely a tea party in an old provincial or cathedral town. And old ladies wear their seed-pearls, and, proud of their ancient family, look quite incredibly shabby, and the room is uncommonly full of furniture of every period, and there are glass cases with miniatures and perhaps a wax relief portrait or two, of which, if you are favored, you may be told that it was my great-uncle, who served under Lord X—during his first ministry. "Yes, I do value them a good deal." And there is nothing of the antique shop about it, because the things have always been there, have accumulated there. And here sometimes a lion may be found, though it is not openly confessed. And if he can be persuaded to roar, why then, there is all the more to talk of [*it*] afterwards and it is very pleasant, of course, to hear of something from the great world and perhaps to learn that Dr. *Y*—is to have the next bishopric.[10] And the atmosphere is warm and friendly and quite incredibly dignified, and the young people whisper together, and in a few days it all begins again, only the exquisite luster and the Queen Anne silver and the Chippendale tray are in a different house, and the glass table contains a tray of orders, and my great-uncle is this time my great-grandfather or a cousin who fought under Wellington.[11] And once again, it is perhaps tea in the University town. And the rusty dons make jokes at each other's expense, and Greek and Latin tags fly round, and sometimes the fresh-faced undergraduate looks in and his breezy slang can be heard penetrating the attenuated accents of the Oxford manner. And nobody is very rich and many are very poor and this is an exclusive society, and town—meaning the inhabitants—and gown—meaning the University—are separated by a great gulf, and there is the same study and the same reference books and the same dust upon the writing-table, and there is the same tea kettle, the fountainhead of all the converse, indeed of all the gathering.

Withal, perhaps the English tea is best alone; when it comes in of its own accord and is set down silently by your great armchair near the fire. And you reach out to it vaguely from the engrossing book upon your knee, and you read and dream and sip your tea and relax beatifically, and the day seems smoothed out and you walk on air and a spell is over you, pointed only by the rhythm of a falling coal, and you are conscious of a great release.

---

10 A "bishopric" is a district that is overseen by a bishop.
11 The Duke of Wellington led the Anglo-Allied Army against Napoleon's Imperial French army at the Battle of Waterloo in 1815.

FOURTH STEEP

TEA CAREERS

Life Immersed in Tea

by Katrina Ávila Munichiello

As children we dream of being firefighters or ballerinas...or both. We are fixated on the idea of a job that is full of wonder and excitement and, often, costumes.

As we grow older, the priorities begin to shift. We realize that being a superhero will not pay a mortgage. We become unsettlingly practical. We keep our hobbies, but "get a day job."

There are some people, however, who find the temerity to make their hobby their career. They take a leap of faith and create their own opportunities. Sometimes they are successful. Sometimes they are not. In either case, they tried.

It does not take long in the world of tea to discover that there are many ways to make a life of it. There are, of course, tea shops with the varied roles that make them run. There are those, like me, whose tea career involves putting pen to paper...or fingers to keyboard. There are growers, processors, importers, marketers, and academics. The field needs historians, business minds, culinary experts, and scientists.

For some, sipping tea is the ultimate goal. For others, true happiness will not be found unless their lives are immersed in tea.

The Tea Effect

BY GEORGE CONSTANCE

A couple of weeks after Hurricane Katrina ripped through New Orleans, I sat alone in our café, staring through propped open doors at the burned remains of a row of buildings across the street, a victim of post-Katrina mayhem that gripped the city.

It was a difficult day indeed. Small business owners with proper identification were allowed past heavily-armed checkpoints to enter the city and salvage what they could. My wife Daya and I took full advantage to tour what we could of the city before heading to the shop. It was a devastating trip. Streets clogged with debris, fallen trees, swamp grass, mud—many feet thick in places, cars, boats, and pieces of buildings that were formerly homes, made many routes impassable. Those roads that were open were eerily quiet; no traffic, no people, not even a bird could be heard. Both Daya and I experienced severe headaches, possibly from the smell of raw sewerage, mold, and swamp gas or simply from the unexpected intensity of so much devastation. This scene stretched far beyond what we could see that day, covering an area nearly the size of the state of Connecticut.

Our café was situated on the small strip of high ground along the Mississippi River that was spared heavy flooding and is now affectionately known as the "Sliver on the River." The main route along the sliver is Magazine Street, six miles of small businesses like my own, that contributed to the city's unique flavor and international appeal. Our shop was located about two miles from the checkpoint. Again, we saw no pedestrians and no cars, save for the occasional emergency vehicle or military transport. A helicopter was landing in front of the Audubon zoo. Surreal.

We arrived at mid-morning, just as the dress shop owner across the street was pulling up to her shop. We talked for a few minutes standing in the middle of what was once one of the busiest streets in New Orleans. Not a soul passed by. Two blocks to the south was the levee and two blocks to the north was flooding. It's tough enough in the best of times to operate a small business. We knew this was the end of what we had. Plan B was already in our minds, until, hopefully, the city could allow a return to plan A. We parted to our respective shops and took inventory. The shops smelled much like the city: of raw sewerage and of cinders from the fire across the street. The roof had been damaged and the large stores of tea we had stocked up on for the fall were moldy and smoke damaged. The awnings were in tatters and signs were missing. We later discovered some of the equipment had been fried by electrical surges.

Ironically, I sat in the only tea café in the city of New Orleans desperately wanting a cup of tea. My daily ritual was a cup of chai or black tea in the morning and then I worked my way through the day with lighter teas, *oolong* in the afternoons, green tea for evenings and redbush at closing twelve hours later. I know that even if I did have a stash of tea, the water was either completely unavailable or hazardous.

As I stared at the door my mind raced back to my first cup in the shop. The café was in a small front addition made to an old Victorian residence that had previously held an optometrist office, an antique shop before that with the owner living in the attached residence, and a pharmacy before that. It was a mess when we found it, but had potential and a good location, near three universities and in one of the busiest and coolest neighborhoods in the city. I had scraped away years of neglect and carpet glue from the entire cement floor with a 4-inch scraper, then painted it with Indo-Victorian designs. I repaired and painted walls, built all the furniture by hand. It was my shop.

I vividly remember that first cup. The shelving was finished and tea in place, the electrical service had been upgraded and fixtures plugged in. All that was necessary was an inspection and we were in business.

It was a gorgeous day and I propped open the old heavy wooden doors to let the fresh air in. The hot water dispenser hissed and, after an eternity, clicked loudly announcing it was time for tea. I immediately steeped a Darjeeling Makaibari Estate black tea and sat to admire my work. After my second sip of one of the best cups of tea I'd ever had, and without a sign or any indication of what was to come, our first customer walked in.

She was tall or gave the illusion of tall with six-inch black heels. The extremely short black shorts and fishnet stockings, likewise, lengthened her legs. The rest of her ensemble consisted of a tight leather vest and a Betty Page-like hairdo and makeup. I was really enjoying that Darjeeling! I quickly learned that she was a Bourbon Street dancer and that she loved the mango tea; I was quick to provide it at no charge, as we were still not officially open. She and her boyfriend, whom I barely noticed, were extremely friendly and welcomed us to their neighborhood, where, we learned, we were very anxiously anticipated. The rest of the afternoon was quiet, with our second customer, a Catholic priest, arriving just before we shut down for the day.

That first day was indicative of what we had started in New Orleans and a reflection of what New Orleans was and may become again. I'm a fan of history and loved the concept of a tea shop because of its historical attachment. I especially enjoyed reading about the first seventeenth-century tea shops, called coffee houses as coffee began to make its appearance in England, and their posted rules of behavior. In these first truly democratic businesses, no man was compelled to surrender his seat to a nobleman. Freedom of speech was the rule of the day, so much so that the newly restored monarch King Charles II attempted to outlaw them as houses of sedition. And so, the tradition lived on in my own Indonique Tea & Chai Café.

It bears repeating that our first customer was a Bourbon Street stripper and our second a Catholic priest. Our customers were from every walk of life, and represented every race and mindset. So many events highlighted this free egalitarian draw that only a cup of tea could have. The vast diversity of tea available, the range of flavors, and its ancient roots attracted the most diverse group of people that

I've ever encountered. My customers included Jude Law, Congressman William Jefferson, local jazz and funk musicians, and even an authentic British Knight, Sir Eldon Griffith. It also included the folks at the tattoo parlor down the block, a beautiful young girl who wore fairy wings everywhere she went, and university students. I once witnessed a woman exit a chauffeur-driven limo and take a table opposite a young man who had just received his tenth tattoo from the parlor on our block. She asked to see the latest and they talked and laughed for half an hour before parting. The priest, my second customer, came regularly to counsel parishioners in dire need, as the café offered a relaxed and comfortable environment. Yoga groups poured into our shop after classes; sitar players offered intimate concerts. One group, including an Emergency Room surgeon, a realtor, and others, met informally to discuss Eastern philosophy. Small business venture capitalists met on other occasions. There was a sense of freedom and camaraderie that existed nowhere else, and tea—by its nature—was the draw and the binding particle.

It's funny how things work out. I had originally attempted to sell tea wholesale, but couldn't sell a bag of tea to save my life. The café was in fact a desperation move. If I couldn't sell tea to existing cafés, then I was determined to go directly to the customer. It was an expensive proposition, but it worked. We made ends meet and posted a profit within 16 months.

What surprised us was how infectious our desperation move was. Infectious not only because it spread from customer to new customer, but because it spread through those customers to other cafés. Reminiscent of those early tea shops, our tea appealed to a very diverse group of business owners who asked us to sell them our tea as their customers demanded it. The first was an edgy café on trendy Oak Street. The owners, one with a bone through his nose—as can only happen in New Orleans, ran a very successful coffee shop. They told us their customers wanted our chai and they wanted to support a local business. They didn't see us as competition. If they were buying chai, why not from us? In turn, I sent coffee lovers to them. Another trendy coffee shop in the Faubourg area—next to the jazz club Snug Harbor, where

Charmaine Neville sings—likewise asked to buy our tea for their customers, again seeking quality products from a local business. A third business owner asked us to open a kiosk in his newly renovated retail complex that housed a nationwide kitchen store franchise.

We hadn't seen this coming, what we termed the "Tea Effect" in the community. I expressed surprise to one of the owners who freely offered his primary reason for buying: Indonique had tapped into a very broad market with tea. He wanted to broaden his market share in his neighborhood by association. Offering his customers our tea made his shop part of the new tea community. We all benefited from the highly infectious Tea Effect.

My thoughts were jolted back to the present in the wreckage of the shop when a well-armed National Guardsman peered through the same door my first customer entered to ask if everything was all right, if we needed water, or had injuries. A group of five more soldiers waited outside. It was a stark contrast to that first day, a very different emotion. I thanked them for coming down to help and apologized for not having tea to offer them. They laughed a bit and continued their rounds. We salvaged what we could over the next few days, sold what equipment we could, and concentrated on repairing our home. Daya took our children to Connecticut while I attempted to rebuild in New Orleans. In the end, rebuilding the café was hopeless. I joined my family in Connecticut.

Post-Katrina, we consider ourselves fortunate—fortunate that we live in a wealthy nation that offered a place to which we could evacuate, and the help of friends and family to rebuild our lives. So many around the world don't have these resources. Tea-producing regions in particular are vulnerable. The tea industry does little to alleviate this. Indonique was rebuilt with this in mind. We pledged to return 10% of every sale we make to the communities that pick our tea through Non-Governmental Organizations like Mercy Corps that can most effectively make change and provide oversight. Our accounting records are open and our website is dedicating percentages to organizations that fight the trafficking of children. We believe that if all industries did the same, we could alleviate poverty, disenfranchisement, extremism and the need for large military expenditures. We're rebuilding Indo-nique as a cause. The trick for us is to recreate that Tea Effect, so easily obtained in our shop, and duplicate it in cafés and retailers around the nation, to make the cause as infectious as the Tea Effect. We're in discussions now with brokers and venture capitalists to do just this. Perhaps the storm that caused so much misery will lead to something that will alleviate misery everywhere.

Fingers crossed.

Unfurled

BY DHEEPA MATURI

Have you watched—really watched—your tea leaves steeping in your cup? At one time in my life, I would not have stopped long enough to do such a thing. During that time, I was a lawyer and a mother and a wife, and I barely paused to eat, much less contemplate the goings-on in a tea cup.

And yet, one day, that's what I did.

One evening, I sat down to tea with a good friend. I remember that I snatched that time out of my schedule, because she was soon relocating to another state. During our conversation, I reached into a tin of silken sachets and felt the lovely little bags slide and slip over my fingers. I placed one in a tea cup, poured boiling water over it, and then inhaled the scent of green leaves harvested from rich, fertile soil. And I watched those leaves, watched them swell with hot water and then twist and unfurl.

As I watched, I suddenly felt alone in the room. In that strange silence, I recognized that so much was swelling and twisting within my own head and heart that something inside me was ready to unfurl. I still recall that moment of stillness and clarity as the birth of my tea company and my own rebirth as an entrepreneur.

I was a lifelong tea drinker, but tea drinking certainly hadn't prepared me for tea entrepreneurship. After that evening, a great deal of research, learning, and work lay ahead of me. Those challenges, however, did not compare to the difficulty of foregoing my professional identity as a lawyer. In return for those hours of legal paperwork and drudgery, I had received instant respect and regard from my peers and my family. There was a feeling of belonging, of knowing my role in life. There was a feeling of security, of knowing where the long (although dull) hours were leading.

I had stepped off a sturdy platform that was reinforced with certainty and credibility. Without the knowledge base and experience to which I was accustomed, I felt alone and disoriented. Slowly—very slowly—I began to learn the ropes, immerse myself in a new industry, and lay the groundwork for a new company. I learned a great deal, very rapidly. And I found out quickly that counseling a business is entirely different from building an enterprise from the ground up.

Each step produced many new issues to handle. And each new issue required time and research and effort. I struggled to ignore the naysayers, the people who expressed astonishment about my choices and pessimism about my prospects. I grappled with recurring feelings of uncertainty and self-doubt. I experienced frustration, concern, and worry....

And exhilaration.

After years of dragging myself out of bed in the morning, I was now leaping to start my days. After years of counseling caution and conservative steps, I was pushing through my own intense risk aversion. After years of limiting my professional interactions to the minimum necessary to complete the tasks at hand, I was expanding my networks assertively and finding people of varied voices, backgrounds, and visions. I was spending my days joyfully talking tea, business, and life. I was *living*.

Moreover, I was doing something I felt to be worthwhile. As the head of a tea company, I was teaching the benefits of tea drinking. I was explaining tea's wonderful wholesomeness and its utter compatibility with the body. Most importantly, I was helping others to understand that each cup is much more than a beverage, but rather, an invitation to pause; to savor sight, smell, touch, and taste; and to be mindful. Why should we schedule later times and faraway places for such moments? We can—and should—have them throughout our day, quiet moments to recharge and reset.

Only a few years have passed since that evening of tea and contemplation. At times, when remembering my pre-tea existence, I barely recognize my current life and self. The landscape around me has become dense with life, color, and sound. It has become full of people, and rich with support and encouragement. And I myself feel as though I am blooming, just as the flowers in my tea blends do. I have discovered in myself a woman who enjoys challenges, meeting new people, and striking up conversations. I've found a person who loves her work. Though the pace of life has not decreased (as any entrepreneur will tell you), in the mirror I see ease and happiness.

Certainly tea has given me a new identity, a new routine to my days, and a new relationship with the world. More importantly, tea has also taught me that all of our moments, no matter how small, carry the potential for our own transformation. Within each cup I drink, I remember an evening when a new path and dream unfolded before me. I remember that my own life, once rolled tight, suddenly unfurled, bloomed, and became full of possibilities.

Comedy at the Customs with a Barrel of Water and Other Stories

by Thomas J. Lipton

Excerpted from Leaves from the Lipton Logs, *1931.*[1]

An early discovery which I made concerning tea was that it varied in taste and "body" according to the water in which it was brewed. Thus, a blend which excellently suited one town became flat and insipid as a beverage when brewed in another town perhaps forty miles away. The explanation, of course, lies in the varying chemical properties of the different water supplies. Accordingly I issued instructions to each of my branch managers to forward, periodically, samples of the water drunk by the inhabitants of his town or city to my tea tasters in London, and the latter, in their turn, were instructed to prepare the most suitable blends for the different districts. The result was that I was able to advertise "the perfect tea to suit the water of your own town," an idea that had never been hit upon before and which scored heavily for Lipton's teas. I know that this may sound rather far-fetched but it is nevertheless true. The tea I was selling in Edinburgh was quite a different blend from that retailed in Glasgow, while the London tea, specially blended to suit the water, was a different article altogether to the hard-water tea sent from my headquarters to Manchester, for instance.

Even when I had started my continental branches the practice of testing the water was still adhered to. I remember a shop manager returning

---

1   [Certain British spellings and archaic terms have been amended. Ed.]

from Hamburg with a fairly large cask of water and finding great difficulty in getting his "luggage" past the Customs. The first official who fell foul of him simply stared when he was told that the cask contained nothing but water. Then he went and called the Chief Examiner.

"Come along, now, what have you got in that cask?" demanded the chief with some asperity.

"Drinking water!" explained my manager.

It was now the chief's turn to stare. This was a new experience in a long life spent in the customs service!

"Plain drinking water?" he demanded, non-plussed. "Do you mean to tell us that you have traveled from Hamburg with a cask of water? What do you think we are—children? Open the cask an' let's taste this precious water of yours!"

Water, of course, it was, but only after every officer at Dover had carefully tasted and sniffed it did they allow our man to pass. And from the glances they bestowed upon his retreating figure they plainly took him for a harmless lunatic!...

...I had been in the tea trade barely a year when an opportunity presented itself for me to go out to Sri Lanka. This was after the coffee crop failure in the Island.[2] Certain London bankers, representing a group of Sri Lanka estates, had approached me with the object of prevailing upon me to purchase these and go in for tea planting on a large scale. I was already buying tea in stupendous quantities; why not grow a lot of the commodity myself?—they urged. The idea did not displease me in the least. It coincided entirely with the rule I had laid down for the abolishing, wherever possible, the middle-man or intermediary profiteer between the producer and the consumer. But I did not intend to buy a "pig in a poke." So instead of coming to a decision with the bankers I secretly booked a passage to Australia on the first available liner, but got off at Colombo, Sri Lanka.

On arriving at Colombo I at once went up-country to the Kandy and Matele tea districts where I inspected the estates for sale. Although

---

2   In the mid-1800s, the coffee growing industry in Sri Lanka was devastated by a leaf disease. The hope was that replacing the coffee plantations with tea farms could save their agricultural industry.

I knew as much about tea planting as Euclid knew about motoring, I liked the look of the estates. They seemed good to me. Without further consideration of the matter I cabled off a very low offer to the London bankers and when they replied "Can't you do better?" I knew the plantations were mine! Within a few hours, and at the small additional cost of one or two more cables, I became their sole proprietor. That I was not likely to repent of my hurried bargain was made fairly clear to me no later than next morning when another would-be buyer, one with some experience, too, of the planting business came along and offered me ten thousand pounds profit on my deal....

...I would not like you to imagine that in these early Sri Lanka transactions, and in the subsequent important developments of my eastern interests, everything "came off" for me as easily as if I had been shelling peas. Far from it. A lot of hard thinking had to be done and much more hard work. Many problems had to be faced, human and economic. I had to apply myself diligently to a completely new set of facts and circumstances. "East is East and West is West!" and I speedily found it out. But, East or West, common sense generally comes out on top and my chief aim, after becoming a tea planter on a large scale, was to improve my properties and the conditions of my native employees, banish waste, introduce up-to-date methods and install modern machinery. Without doing all these things I could see that my investments were not going to be so profitable as at first seemed likely....

..."Direct from Tea Garden to the Teapot!" This was the slogan I came home with from my trip to Sri Lanka and I made the utmost of it in all my advertising for several years thereafter. It must have made a very strong appeal, too, for my sales of tea went up by leaps and bounds. Often, in spite of my Sri Lanka supplies and the great parcels I continued to purchase in Mincing Lane and subsequently at the Colombo Tea Sales I was actually hard put to it to let all my branches have all that they required so that my millions of customers could be satisfied....

In Mincing Lane, opposition against me became rife. It was but to be expected that the man who was running his own plantations and selling "direct from the tea garden to the teapot" would not be joyfully received in the Lane devoted to brokers and middlemen, but all the same I got as much tea as I wanted there because they knew that my money was good and always forthcoming on the spot. Several attempts were made to belittle "cheap tea" by running up prices for specially-selected and extra fine packets of tea to as much as five and ten guineas per pound. However, I proved more than a match for tactics of this kind. To prove to the Lane and to the public that my estates in Sri Lanka were capable of producing the best tea in the universe, I cabled my manager in the island to send me home a parcel of the very finest, gold-tipped tea grown on our own ground. In due course it arrived and was sold by public auction in Mincing Lane at the amazing price of thirty-six guineas per pound! After this there was no further attempt to decry Lipton's tea; it had set up a record difficult, almost impossible, to beat.

There's Nothing Like the First Time
BY CYNTHIA GOLD

I have been fortunate to have the opportunity to visit a wide variety of tea farms, tea gardens, and tea estates throughout the world. Each time is a pleasure and an honor, as well as a tremendous learning experience. Still, nothing will ever match the impact on me of my first experience.

It was in Hangzhou, China—a beautiful family-owned tea farm producing Lung Ching tea, also known as Dragonwell. It was a cool and misty day. Throughout the morning I was able to participate in the harvest. After teaching me the right flicking motion to harvest the leaves without bruising them or getting farther down the stem than was desired, I set to work filling my basket. By midday—several baskets later—I was soaked but very happy. We brought the leaves in and laid them out for a brief wither. While waiting, the farmer lit a fire outside and we huddled around it to warm up and possibly dry off a touch. In the glow of that fire I watched those around me, and although nobody seemed in any way unhappy, part of me wondered why they didn't have the same wide grin on their faces that I did! Wet or not, I couldn't think of a single place on earth that I'd rather be.

It was time to fire the leaves. After several demos, I sat down at my wok and began to wok fire the leaves. The gentleman who had loaned me his wok was careful to watch and correct my hand movements and guide me through knowing when each batch was adequately fired. Batch after small batch, the repetitive movements where hypnotic. I was in a happy blur scooping out my leaves in batches to cool. When I got up from my wok at the end of the day it suddenly hit me as to what I had just been so fortunate and privileged to experience: to take those leaves from the field to the finished product. What an incredible feeling. I "lost it" then. I literally started to cry. The farmer was quite worried, thinking perhaps that I had burnt myself on the wok, but as a chef, I had long ago deadened my nerve endings, so that was no real risk for me. And even if I had, so what? What a small price that would have been to enjoy this incredible day. Our translator explained to him that I was simply overwhelmed by the beauty of the experience.

It was a life-changing experience for me. As clichéd as it sounds, at that moment, tea literally became a part of my soul. It was no longer a commodity that I respected and loved, but something much more. It is difficult to articulate, but I have never looked at tea the same way since.

Tea Journey

BY AHMED RAHIM

I have been an artist for the past twenty plus years, and I assure you that running a business in the United States is not a Bohemian adventure. Business works more from the conscious mind, with lots of financial capital need, intricacies with human resources, and the legalities of operating a company. The creation of art for me is living more in the unconscious and tapping into the spiritual powers of one's emotions, thoughts, and the intangible world of dreams and fantasies to create what "feels right." I spent fifteen years living in various cities across Europe and the United States developing skill in photography, film making, painting, and playing musical instruments, while also getting my hands busy with many types of building projects: from mosaic making and stone work, to building houses and planting gardens. Now that I am focused on creating a business, I remind myself every day that I can use what I have learned. We too can create something different—an experience and lifestyle that can have an effect similar to an art piece. The dream in this adventure is born every moment and lives strong in our company—Numi—because of our core values of creativity, sustainability, and a commitment to saving the planet and the people that make our products exist. It gives us a profound purpose that business can have meaning when you do it with more intention than just selling a product. We want to celebrate the mystery of art and innovation as well as the feeling that you are making a difference with the decisions made each day, from our supply chain to the types of products we market. This is the beauty and inspiration that keeps me going every day, fueling me to continue to open boundaries and either create new experiences that have never existed before or revisit ones that have lived in deep tradition. Through Numi we try to have these traditions be shared and cared for by the greater public.

It is hard to find words to describe being part of a vision that incorporates creativity, strong values for nature and people, and love, and has been turned into a product enjoyed by thousands of people across the world. It is incredible to watch teas and herbs travel across the globe, starting in small and remote villages that are so far removed from what most of us take for granted in our lives. These villagers who have very little in their lives are dedicated to cultivating and producing the best quality organic teas and herbs possible. The journey the tea takes to leave these villages and get across the world feels like a miracle. Each time it happens, it is like we have been blessed by the powers of nature and by the people who love what they do every day. Our commitment to organic and Fair Trade products provides us another and even greater reward, the chance to act as stewards to Mother Earth and the farmers and villagers. Being a part of this global "communitea" is a rare feeling, one that I believe we are in need of more and more, as the world gets smaller through ease of travel, access to communication, and the use of Internet technology.

Traveling across the world to remote villages in China, India, Africa, South America and other countries to source our organic herbs and teas always reminds me to become even more intimate and further solidifies my commitment to the core values of organic farming and Fair Trade. When I witness the way people live in these developing countries, I feel that I must take ownership and responsibility to care for them, especially as we strive to grow our partnerships and find more ways to create stronger Fair Trade programs. I learn so much during my travels about the local farming, the villages, their needs to live simple lives, and how we can bring the ceremonial attributes of these teas and herbs to the United States.

One particular experience I recall took place in the Yunnan Mountains of China. I met a man who, at the age of 31, was called a hero! The Chinese Government had leased him hundreds of acres of land in the high mountains to grow tea, but there was no road access to these mountainous regions. He recruited a very poor community from Northern China where he grew up to pave the road. In doing so, they were all given housing and paid well beyond a fair wage. With his help they experienced many things in their lives that they may have never seen if they lived their entire lives in their poor village.

I really wish everyone could see and experience the journey these herbs and teas take to get from one place to another and meet the farmers responsible. It is an experience and education that is life long, and reminds me that I can make a difference each and every day by making decisions that help our "communitea." The people we can touch and help every day—if we really care—is so inspiring and gives me a purpose to forge ahead with the business at Numi.

These intentions have a ripple effect, and I personally hope that Numi's business model has an impact on our customers, our farmers, the earth and other businesses. I hope that we can all learn and experience a life full of abundance and commit to the care of nature around us. It is what feeds us and keeps us strong every day. Sometimes, we miss the obvious and look through the forest without ever seeing the trees. If we stop more often to smell the roses and watch the beauty right in front of us, we have more love and create so many magical wonders that make all our moments matter so much more.

Tea: Its Stirring Story

BY WILLIAM GORDON STABLES

Excerpted from Tea: The Drink of Pleasure and Health, *1883.[1]*

A cup of tea at early morn. Do you indulge in such a luxury, reader? I do. And my servant knows how to make it; knows the exact amount of the herb to put into the tiny teapot (the herb itself is India's most fragrant and best), the exact amount of sugar, and the exact proportion of sweetest cream. I give the signal for infusion ere I get into my cold bath, and by the time I have done and enrobed myself in loosely flowing toga, the salver stands on the mat. Just the tiniest milk biscuit is all that is needed as fitting accompaniment, and no better beginning could possibly be made to a day. After this slight but efficient refection, I shave; but while I shave I think, and arrange the work and business of the day that is before me; for my intellect feels as sharp as my razor after that morning cup of tea. I often sing while dressing, and if there be anyone in the room I (Scot though I am!) even fire off jokes and perpetrate puns. These jokes come spontaneously. Fact! I haven't got to go feeling around for them, so to speak. If my wit didn't dry up with the heat of the day, if it only could be kept wet till dinner time, I feel sure I should pass for a fellow of infinite jest and humor. However, I am convinced of one thing, that is, there is a deal of virtue in a cup of tea at early morn....

...The following is a true and succinct account of a little adventure that befell me in 1862. I was then a student in the university of

---

1   [Certain British spellings have been amended. Ed.]

Aberdeen, and one day while walking along on the sunny side of Union Street, I came upon a man standing beside a sack evidently well filled with something. He wasn't a prepossessing man by any means, nor was he very well dressed. He was perspiring freely, holding a dirty Glengarry in one hand, while with the other he wiped a bald *at frontalis*[2] with an objectionable looking cotton handkerchief. The man, as I have said, was perspiring, and what is more, the sack seemed perspiring too; both man and sack were damp.

"I'm saying, sir," said this fellow to me.

"Well," I replied, "what are you saying?"

"Would you mind givin' me a lift on to ma shouther wi' this bit baggie?"

Now I am naturally one of the most obliging men in the world, so I did not hesitate a moment to do what the man requested.

"It *is* heavy!" said I, hoisting up the sack. "And how very wet it is! Whatever does it contain, my good fellow?"

"Seaweed," was the curt reply.

"Now listen," I answered sharply, "it doesn't smell like seaweed, and it isn't seaweed; so as you have told me a lie, and if you don't divulge, I'll pull you down by the run, sack and all."

"What do you want to now for?" said he.

"Only curiosity perhaps," I replied; "but this may be some poor wretch you've drowned, and you may be carrying his cold slimy body to the dissecting room. You remember the lines:

'Burke and Hare
Cam' doon the stair,
With a body in a box,
A ghastly corpse, for Dr. Knox.'

This, my dear friend, may be a body in a bag."

"There's precious little body in it," said the fellow with a good laugh; "it's tea leaves, and deil haet else."

"Tea leaves?"

"Tea leaves, nothing else; I've been round hotels and inns and places collecting them."

---

2   "*At frontalis*" refers to the forehead.

"But what," I continued, really moved by curiosity this time, "what the mystery do you collect tea leaves for? Look here" (seeing that the fellow hesitated to answer), "are you thirsty?"

"Man!" he replied, "I could drink a glass o' whiskey at any hoor o' the day or nicht."

After such a candid confession of course we adjourned. The sack was placed at the door of an inn in Adelphi Lane, and I treated him to two consecutive "glaisses," which he swallowed after the manner of men eating oysters (or Scotchmen drinking whiskey).

"Weel, sir," he said, "I'll tell you the truth. I buy tea leaves and sell them over again to wivies to spread over their carpets, when sweepin' them, to keep doon the dust. That's the truth."

"It isn't the truth, my man; Aberdeen wivies, of all wivies in the world, are not so averse to dust as all that."

"Weel, sir, I'll tell you the *real* truth this time, I sell the tea leaves to laddies to feed their rabbits wi'. That's the *real* truth this time."

I referred the man to my eye after that, and requested to know if he saw anything the color of cabbage in it. Then I threatened to kick over the bag and call the constable; and finally I called for another "glaiss of whiskey."

Glug! One gulp, down went the liquor, and then having had "the truth," and "the real truth," he told me what he termed "the honest truth," which I was bound to believe. This *honest* fellow it seems bought the tea leaves from *honest* landladies of inns and hotels, and sold them to an *honest* "firm" who dried and doctored them, mixed them with a modicum of full flavored tea, and sold them to *honest* shopkeepers to retail to the public as pure tea.

So much honesty is somewhat confusing; but far be it from me to impute *dis*honesty to anyone, and least of all to an Aberdeen.

When this honest bagman had glugged down the fifth "glaiss" his eyes watered, as well they might, and he winked and smiled with unutterable satisfaction.

"Man!" he said, "the fun o' the thing is this: the wivies, I mean the innkeeper wivies that I buy these tea leaves from, have a good guess what I do wi' them. They ken the leaves will be made ower again, as

Morrison made his mither; but they little ken what I ken, for as sure as I hold this empty glass between me and the licht, they often *buy their ain tea leaves back again*, and no' a bit the wiser."

After reading the above no Englishman need be told that the Scotch are far more fond of tea than they are of—of anything else to drink. They are really, I'm not joking.

Growing Tea in Paradise

BY ROB NUNALLY

I'm not sure what prompted the idea of growing tea in Hawaii. Before the change in century (remember Y2K?), my partner and I had started looking for a place to live in Hawaii. Initially we thought we were looking for a daylily farm. Mike had done some daylily hybridization in Hawaii in the early 1990s, which led to the development of an online auction site. Our search focused on Hawaii Island, north of Hilo near Onomea Bay, a beautiful area bordering a scenic drive and botanical gardens. We really didn't want vacant land which would require home construction; however, once we saw what was being offered we couldn't resist. This area was formerly sugar cane land and zoned for agriculture. It has soil, which is of limited quantity where active lava flows down the slopes of steaming volcanic vents. However, the land along this part of the island has lots of rich, red and quickly draining soil that can handle upwards of 180 inches of rainfall a year. It's an incredible location with temperatures that are rarely under 60 or over 85 degrees and it has scenic views of a rocky coast with textured green hills and gulches. It lies at the foot of a 14,000 foot mountain called Mauna Kea. Referring to this area as paradise is not often argued. It is one of the most beautiful spots I had ever seen. In consideration of all these factors, a decision to buy this incredible land was made.

Buying agricultural land meant we instantly became farmers looking for a crop. I recall musing about different plants when tea came to mind. I've always been a tea drinker, starting each day with a cup of

Earl Grey and a glass or two of iced tea during warm tropical afternoons. My partner was a tea drinker too. But growing tea? With a bit of research we discovered that tea is made from the *Camellia* plant and that tea plants grow well in subtropical environments. Investigating more we found that our local U.S. Department of Agriculture (USDA) office was encouraging people to try to grow tea.

Hawaii has been looking for a replacement crop for sugar cane since cane production left the island in the 1970s. Many things have been considered: tea, cocoa, vanilla, coffee, tropical fruits, bio fuels, and a host of other crops. I was most interested in tea, so we obtained about twenty tea seeds from the USDA and germinated them. They all sprouted in about 90 days. We transplanted them to the ground and they grew quite well.

We have since added 2,000 more plants. I'm starting to feel like a farmer, paying close attention to weather, always appreciating the rain and becoming concerned when we face more than a few days of cloudless skies. The tea rewards us with rich lovely green leaves. Since our island is subtropical, our tea plants always think it is spring. We get harvests all year round.

We are really excited about the prospects for tea in Hawaii. Despite being a well-established commodity in other parts of the world, we think it's time the United States had more tea farms. Most tea is imported into this country under less than desirable import regulations. We're thrilled with the idea of being one of a handful of tea growers in the U.S. We decided to grow organically and offer clean, pesticide-free tea.

Today we have enough tea in the ground to begin research on our plants. Plants grown from seeds have the genes of the mother and father plants. They can be slightly different from each other. We're looking for plants that offer the best in flavor and growing habit. Our long term project is to taste different plants and propagate plants that produce a taste we desire. Then we'll propagate that plant to expand the farm with a few more acres of tea that offers unique Hawaii grown tea characteristics.

Propagating tea is not as easy as we'd like and we continue to experiment with taking and rooting the cuttings to obtain a genetic duplicate or clone of particular plants. Growing by seed is much easier, but then we have genetic differences in each plant with little control in growing and flavor characteristics. While this can be interesting, and we do want to keep some variety in our crop, we'd also like to establish some unique plants which are cloned so that we have plants that taste and grow in a very consistent manner.

Processing tea is fun and challenging. We've met many people traveling the island that enjoyed drinking tea, but didn't know much about how tea is processed. One of the most frequent questions I am asked is, "What kind of tea do you grow?" The reply is that there really is only one tea plant and it is *Camellia sinensis*. We grow *Camellia sinensis* and it is the processing of the leaves of this plant that make white, green, *oolong*, or black tea.

White tea is the least processed, made by simply picking the newest leaf and drying it. Green tea is tea leaf that is usually heated, rolled and dried before it oxidizes, keeping the leaf green. *Oolong* tea production allows some oxidation of the leaf; the leaf is allowed to start to turn brown. This contributes to distinctive floral and complex flavors. When creating our *oolong*s, we chase that floral quality of the leaf, typically producing a nice sweet fragrance and a smooth taste with good mouth feel. Black tea is fully oxidized tea. After picking, the leaf is rolled and allowed to fully turn brown/black before it's dried. Our black tea has a wonderful malty tone without a bite, even when brewed for extended periods of time. We have processes in place that allow us to make green, *oolong* and black teas with reliability. We've also played a bit with white tea and flavored tea.

One of our biggest challenges is facing the economics of farming. Farming tea is a lot of work. There are so many variables that make it difficult and it hasn't proven to be a profitable venture on a small scale. At the same time, I feel addicted to it. I love looking out over the tea field, with the plants all being pruned to a pluckable height. The new flush creates a yellow-green layer over dark green older leaves. The smell of tea leaf is glorious, a sweet floral fragrance, like honeysuckle or our a locally grown vine called *maile*. The growing of tea has spawned a new reason to visit Hawaii and this could help with the profitability of growing tea. We have started offering tours of our place so people can learn about and taste some of our teas.

We think it is important to honor the whole ceremonial side of drinking tea: brewing in artful ways and drinking from ceramic vessels. Tea is an art and can be elegant or simple and spiritual. Drinking tea is a reflective time to share and be with friends. The act of sharing tea is one of awareness and consciousness. It is to be enjoyed and used to stimulate discussion and exploration of the wonders of occupying this place in time.

Ballad of the Tea Picker

BY LE YIH

Translation from The Middle Kingdom *by Samuel Wells Williams, 1897.*[1]

Where thousand hills the vale enclose, our little hut is there,
And on the sloping sides around the tea grows everywhere;
And I must rise at early dawn, as busy as can be,
To get my daily labor done, and pluck the leafy tea.

At early dawn I seize my crate, and sighing, Oh, for rest!
Thro' the thick mist I pass the door, with sloven hair half dressed;
The dames and maidens call to me, as hand in hand they go,
"What steep do you, miss, climb today—what steep of high Sunglo?"

Dark is the sky, the twilight dim still on the hills is set;
The dewy leaves and cloudy buds may not be gathered yet:
Oh, who are they, the thirsty ones, for whom this work we do,
For whom we spend our daily toil in bands of two and two?...

...My face is dirty; out of trim my hair is, and awry;
Oh, tell me, where's the little girl so ugly now as I?
'Tis all because whole weary hours I'm forced to pick the tea,
And driving winds and soaking showers have made me what you see!

---

1   [Certain British spellings have been amended. Ed.]

With morn again come wind and rain, and though so fierce and strong,
    With basket big, and little hat, I wend my way along;
      At home again, when all is picked, and everybody sees
How muddy all our dresses are, and drabbled to the knees....

    ...Oh, weary is our picking, yet do I my toil withhold?
      My maiden locks are all askew, my pearly fingers cold;
        I only wish our tea to be superior over all,
O'er this one's "sparrow-tongue," and o'er the other's "dragon-ball."...

    Oh, for a month I weary strive to find a leisure day;
      I go to pick at early dawn, and until dusk I stay.
    Till midnight at the firing pan I hold my irksome place;
      But will not labor hard as this impair my pretty face?...

    ...But though my bosom rise and fall, like buckets in a well,
      Patient and toiling as I am, 'gainst work I'll ne'er rebel.
    My care shall be to have my tea fired to a tender brown,
And let the *flag* and *awl*[2] well rolled display the whitish down.

    Ho for my toil! Ho! for my steps! Aweary though I be,
In our poor house, for working folk, there's lots of work, I see;
    When the firing and the drying's done, off at the call I go,
And once again this very morn, I'll climb the high Sunglo.

My wicker basket slung on arm, and hair entwined with flowers,
    To the slopes I go of high Sunglo, and pick the tea for hours;
How laugh we, sisters, on the road; what a merry turn we've got;
I giggle and say, as I point down the way, There, look, there lies our cot!...

    ...Today the tint of the western hills is looking bright and fair,
And I bear my crate to the stile, and wait my fellow toiler there;

---

2   The "flag" and "awl" are developmental stages of young tea leaves when they are just beginning to open.

A little lass is she—she leans upon the rail
And sleeps, and though I hail her she answers not my hail.

And when at length to my loudest call she murmurs a reply,
'Tis as if had to conquer sleep, and with half-opened eye;
Up starts she, and with straggling steps along the path she's gone;
She brings her basket, but forgets to put the cover on!...

...Our time is up, and yet not full our baskets to the mouth—
The twigs anorth are fully searched, let's seek them in the south;
Just then by chance I snapped a twig whose leaves were all apair;
See, with my taper fingers now I fix it in my hair.

Of all the various kinds of tea, the bitter beats the sweet,
But for whomever either seeks, for him I'll find a treat;
Though who it is shall drink them, as bitter or sweet they be,
I know not, my friend—but the pearly end of my finger only see!

Ye tittering swallows, rise and fall, in your flight around the hill;
But when next I go to high Sunglo, I'll change my gown, I will.
I'll roll up the cuff to show arm enough, for my arm is fair to see:
Oh, if ever there were a fair round arm, that arm belongs to me.

This ballad was intended to be sung by girls and women as they picked tea leaves. It was written by Le Yih in the early Ch'ing dynasty (mid-1600s).

Starting In Pursuit of Tea

BY SEBASTIAN BECKWITH

"Tea is said to be a way. This is because it is something one learns to appreciate through feeling, not through verbal instruction. If a person maintains a state of quietness, only then will one appreciate the quietness inherent in tea."

—Lu Yu

Taoist philosophy teaches a path, or a way, to life. Weaving work together with life makes one more centered and balanced—combining skills to make a living while allowing one to enjoy life and nature. Being aware of and living in rhythm with the natural world leads to a richer sense of fulfillment.

In Pursuit of Tea was founded at a time of personal change, it was the pursuit of a new path. It grew out of my former livelihood, which involved leading treks and spending time in Bhutan—a small, mountainous country in the Himalayas. The journeys from there to visit friends in the Kingdom of Sikkim took me through the incredible scenery of West Bengal and the hills of Darjeeling on a regular basis. My interest in tea and immersion in the region helped to solidify the direction of that change.

I'm a proponent of one inventing one's own job—combining the skills you have with work that's fulfilling. It's often not easy, as creativity and hard work are required. I began the company based on my values which I hoped would lead to such fulfillment.

For example, diversity has always been important for me, I've often held several part time jobs instead of one full time job. The interaction with different people in different environments is more stimulating than just plugging away at the same thing day after day. I was able to find the diversity I craved by putting all these interests together.

It was also important for me to choose a livelihood that contributed to the health of the planet and the people living on it, and wasn't just a means to make money. Education would be a large part of what I wanted to do, teaching people about cultural issues, culinary traditions, and how to expand their enjoyment of tea.

Today, I'm fortunate to be able to spend time in tea fields with farmers and producers; though the travel is arduous, it balances the time that I spend at home in New York City. The farmers are folks who make tea using techniques learned from their families and communities through generations, as well as through the important and continual process of trial and error. Dialog with producers is always interesting, as we're both trying to learn and grow through our exchanges. For example, they would want to know what people in the United States think of the tea and how they drink it. They're curious about what kind of water is used to brew the tea and what the trends of tea drinking are. Learning the nuances these farmers look for when making as well as drinking the tea helps me understand more about the tea plant itself on a first-hand basis. This knowledge is invaluable to tastemakers and connoisseurs in the culinary world, as many of the most amazing teas never leave Asia. Being a bridge from people of ancient cultures living close to the earth to culinary experts in modern cities is quite an interesting and challenging process and one that I find particularly rewarding.

It's equally inspiring to share with people who simply became interested in tea through tastings and discussions. Just spending time, drinking tea with people who enjoy it most, can be the best reward of all. Through In Pursuit of Tea, I've created an occupation that satisfies many aspects of my core values, as well as supporting the infinite pathways of learning, teaching, and sharing something healthy and spiritually uplifting.

Around the World with a Cup of Tea

BY JANE PETTIGREW

When I decided, one weekend in April 1983, to give up my job as a language and communications trainer and open a tea shop with friends in London, I had absolutely no inkling of how that one decision would totally change my life. My life up to that date had been quite ordered, quite typically middle class English, teaching by profession, traveling on holiday once or twice a year to nearby European locations, and in my spare time, baking and cooking to entertain friends at home and going out to concerts, movies and theater.

Later that year, once Tea-Time—our little shop in Clapham Common—was ready for the first rush of eager local tea drinkers, my days (starting at 4:00 A.M.) became a whirlwind routine of rolling out scone mix, whisking bowlfuls of lemon drizzle and carrot cake, ironing table cloths, drawing up staff rotas,[1] cleaning carpets and vacuuming up crumbs, chatting with customers, organizing the cake counter, and working out costs. For the first ten months of our new venture, I slept four hours a night, lost weight, learned all sorts of new skills, and had the most enormous (if exhausting) fun! Famous faces started to appear regularly at the door, and actors, rock singers, TV personalities, musicians, writers and film stars mingled happily with our local regulars—moms with toddlers, elegant elderly ladies, chefs and waiters on split

---

1 A "rota" is a roster or staffing schedule.

shifts, and our friends. Shared tables helped forge new friendships and the atmosphere was one of relaxed and chatty enjoyment.

Then, one afternoon, a group of American ladies called me over to their table—where they were digging into smoked salmon sandwiches, scones with Dorset clotted cream and our special sherry trifle—and asked me if I would go and speak to their group about the history of tea drinking in Britain. Of course I said, "Yes, I'd love to!" realizing as I spoke that I knew absolutely nothing about the history of tea drinking in Britain. We agreed on a date and I took a couple of hours off the next day to dash down to the local reference library to see what I could find out. To my utter surprise (and relief), I found a wealth of books that told me of London's first coffee houses where tea was offered both wet and dry, how tea had first been sold at great expense to the upper classes as a medicinal tonic, how various grades of both green and black tea had been shipped in from China, and how we eventually started growing our own tea in India in the nineteenth century to meet a growing demand.

At school I had loathed history with its boring lists of battles and faceless kings and queens, but those two hours in the Brixton Tate Library were a turning point. What I read forced open a great fortified, nail-studded door and shone a floodlight on our past, showing me that history can be exciting, illuminating, and very, very real. I simply had to find out more. I knew that if I found this fascinating, then so too would the American ladies. So, I joined the British Library (in those days hidden in the gloomiest depths of the British Museum in Bloomsbury) and spent any spare moment away from the mixing bowls and chopping boards to discover more details of the tea story. I scribbled, I photocopied, I found images that added color and helped explain the facts. I had some of those turned into little slides ready for projection during presentations, and I bought the first of many box files that would keep these new treasures safe.

The talks and presentations became a regular part of my tea routine and, as I read and researched, I found that there were more strands to the story than I could ever have known when I started out. I discovered Chinese teapots and bowls, tea gowns and tea dances, the reason for locks on tea caddies, the fascinating facts behind the social history of familiar parts of London, the link between opium and tea, and the part that tea played in the design of tables, trays, trolleys and Gothic temples in the grounds of stately homes. I kept adding new elements to my talks and people, it seemed, were as amazed as I was.

As well as giving these talks to groups of Japanese, Americans, Canadians and Europeans, I started to write and found I could draw on the same material to add background and interest to my first recipe book, then to my little *Book of Days*, and a few years later I found that I had gathered enough facts, figures, images and stories to suggest to the National Trust that we should create a book called *A Social History of Tea*. My tea travels took me all over Britain, to libraries, record offices, museums, tea company archives, and private homes. I pored over old invoices and inventories, packaging designs, entries in diaries, extracts from novels, pages in books of etiquette, and company records. I still thrill at the memory, in a record office in Kent, of coming across a rolled parchment document that listed all the porcelain tea wares owned by Frances Cranfield, Dowager Duchess of Dorset, in 1682. The fragile paper revealed that she had purchased "two tea potts," "twelve Blew tee dishes," "eighteene white tee dishes," and that the word "china" (which had previously only referred to the country and now also meant all these fine tablewares) was spelled "cheyny" or "cheyney" in the seventeenth century. It took my breath away! The hours during which I found nothing of interest, the endless piles of yellowing documents and dusty old books that yielded nothing were so totally worthwhile when I came across gems like this.

By now I had been invited to Paris to speak to the French tea club, *Le Club des Buveurs de Thé*, to Japan to take part in the annual British fair in Hankyu's Osaka store and to give lectures in different parts of the country, to Brazil to give a series of lectures to students and teachers of the Cultura Inglesa, a teaching organization that had been set up by the British Council 60 or so years earlier, and to the U.S. to participate in Harney & Sons' first Tea Conference in Connecticut. My life was beginning to change beyond all recognition! I was accommodated in five-star hotels and treated like visiting royalty, flowers and champagne were set ready in my room, cars and drivers were provided to take me wherever I had to go, and I was invited to important cocktail parties to meet ambassadors and local dignitaries. I was overawed! I found that I loved hot climates! I learned that the British way is not the only way. I discovered how people in warm countries smile so much more than we do in the northern hemisphere. I danced samba in clubs in Copacabana and I felt more relaxed and happy with my life than ever before.

Pulled in too many different directions, I sold my share in the shop in 1989 to write, lecture, research, and eventually to edit *Tea International* (published by The UK Tea Council). And there was so much more to come, more doors to push open, more tea trails to follow. I knew now that I should not wait to be invited to some of the world's most important tea countries but that I should go and see for myself how tea is produced in India, Sri Lanka, China, and Taiwan. My list of contacts was beginning to grow, and I had written about or been involved in public relations work for various Indian companies, so it was not difficult to organize a first visit to Darjeeling. How I loved the misty peaks and valleys at Goomtee, Okayti, and Ambootia. How satisfying and relaxing to take breakfast on the lawn in a garden surrounded by soaring pine trees and clambering morning glory with its intensely blue trumpet flowers. What fun we had delving inside little antique shops in Darjeeling town to buy Buddhist prayer bowls and beautiful rings and pendants. How we smiled as we rode the little steam train down from Kurseong, past the waving schoolchildren in their blue and white uniforms and the chattering monkeys that skittered about on rocks and scampered up nearby trees. In Sri Lanka, while gathering material for my biography of Merrill Fernando's very successful tea company—Dilmah, the family took me from noisy bustling Colombo up through rubber plantations and spice groves to the higher tea country where we stayed in the stunningly beautiful Tea Trail bungalows that once were estate homes for managers and their assistants but have now been refurbished as luxury holiday homes. We dined like princes, slept in four-poster beds and sipped cocktails on terraces that overlooked carefully tended rose gardens, huge bamboo stands, and, in the background, a vast lake with its curving shore and a scattering of small islands.

For my first visit to China's tea regions, I joined a group led by Dan Robertson of Chicago's Tea House and adventured to Tibet, Sichuan, Zheijiang, and Fujian provinces, and via Hong Kong to Taiwan. Less luxurious and cosseted but a real adventure, we found the old tea lands, watched smoky *lapsangs* and rich, woody *oolongs* being made in the small factories of the Wuyi Mountain. We sipped tea in traditional tea houses while watching Beijing opera, we rode chair lifts over ancient tea gardens to reach Buddhist temples at the top of craggy mountains. We rode a bus, a steam boat and a rickety tractor to see how the famous green tea is made in the small family manufacturing units of Taiping Village where the locals were surprised to find a bunch of pale-faced "big noses" watching their every move.

Today, my passport bears the stamp of many of the most important tea-growing and consuming countries of the world—India, Sri Lanka, China, Taiwan, Japan, Russia, the US, and Canada. But there too are the marks of less well-known tea lands—Malaysia, Guatemala, Georgia, South Korea, Brazil, Thailand, Tibet, and Italy. And there are more still to collect. Soon I shall be drinking several cups of tea in South Africa and Hawaii and then, who knows, perhaps also in Bolivia, Vietnam, Cambodia, Laos, and Eastern Europe. I have been so lucky! How could I have known 27 years ago in an ordinary suburb of southwest London that my working life would one day take me all over the world, or that I would sip tea served in so many different ways in so many countries? And the wonder for me is that it's not just about the tea—it's about all the wonderful people I have met along the way who have shared their passion and their knowledge with me and helped me to pass it on.

TEA TRAVELS

Wanderlust

BY KATRINA ÁVILA MUNICHIELLO

When you have crossed the line from casual tea drinker to enthusiast, it is inevitable that you begin to dream of the tea world.

As a child, I imagined my future travels would be filled with names I'd read in family histories—Miraflores, Mexico; County Cork, Ireland; Ávila, Spain; and Mainz, Germany. As tea began to take hold of my life in a more significant way, my travel horizons grew. I started dreaming of walking through fields, sipping tea as I embraced the beauty of the mountains. I imagined visiting the immaculately cultivated fields of Japan, the tropical climates of Sri Lanka and India, and the ancient tea trees of China. I must admit that my parents have been a little baffled by these interests, but fortunately, I share my life with a partner who is also game for these adventures.

Until the day my traveling no longer involves packing diapers and playpens, my grand tea travels are dreams in my head. In the meantime I live vicariously through those who are taking the leap. From filmmakers who bring stories to the screen, to those who write them, to those who make it possible for others to travel, we all owe a debt of gratitude to the people making the tea world feel a bit smaller.

Tales from *All In This Tea*: Part One
BY LES BLANK, AS TOLD TO KATRINA ÁVILA MUNICHIELLO

Les Blank was the Co-Producer, Co-Director, and Cameraman for the 2007 documentary All In This Tea. *This film chronicled one of tea expert David Lee Hoffman's trips through remote China in search of the finest teas. Les was asked to share some of his unique experiences and memories of creating this critically acclaimed film. The stories are shared here, as told to author Katrina Ávila Munichiello.*

Tea Beginnings

I got started on tea when I was having horrible allergic reactions (to foods). I went to a specialist who put me on an elimination diet. For one week they removed everything from my diet except vegetables, brown rice, turkey, and tea. Then each week I could add one more food until I reached the food causing the reaction. I never discovered the food causing the reaction, but I did find that drinking tea instead of coffee put a different slant on the start of my day. It was a slow infusion of consciousness...or caffeine...or both.

First Meetings

The Himalayan Fair happens once a year in Berkeley, not far from my house. There is food, dancing, singing, and various performances all day long. David Lee Hoffman had a tent set up there for his company, Silk Road Teas. He was giving away free tea, and I always take free samples. This tea did something to my mind that I had never experienced. I listened to David speak and then I talked to him myself. He knew about my films and invited me to his property in West Marin County for tea and beer or wine and food cooked outside over his fire pit.

Initially, I was just interested in David Lee Hoffman and the world of tea. I visited David's place and was interested in what he was doing on his acre and a half of property. He spent 20 years building a tea house with special tile from China or Japan and he has a worm bin that looks like a Buddhist temple.[1] I was very interested in his stories of wandering around monasteries in Asia. It all seemed intriguing.

The Film

Filming began in 1997 and Mr. Blank worked on the film until its release in 2007. Filming took them through China's Guangdong, Fujian, and Zhejiang provinces.

I was interested in an adventure. David was planning a trip with a friend. He had seen my film about Werner Herzog (*Burden of Dreams*, 1982), so the idea came together for me to go. I bought a $5,000 digital camera and a plane ticket.

We had such wonderful meals on that trip—banquets and feasts. I never had a bad meal or even a mediocre meal. It didn't matter how poor the hovel or how rich the restaurants. It was mind blowing.

A Favorite Tea Site…That Wasn't a Favorite

We visited the ancient tea trees. The old trees were fascinating. There are trees that are 600 years old. The tea is harvested from these same trees and it's one of David's favorite places. The roots go down so deep that they pick up things you wouldn't get from the cultivated tea trees.

As a filmmaker, though, this was a terrible place. It is so far up in the mountains that the humidity is always too high. It never dries out up there. There's lots of clay in the ground so it's hard to walk while shooting. My feet kept slipping out from under me—190 pounds of weight tossed around with my camera flying.

---

1 Hoffman is an ardent organic farmer and environmentalist.

David dragged me back up there on our second trip over and I complained bitterly. On that trip, the fog was so dense that I couldn't see a foot in front of me.

Priceless Tea Memory

It's not what you would think of as ideal tea, especially when compared with the aesthetics of something like a Japanese tea ceremony where everything is done in very deliberate, beautiful ways.

We took a long hike up a steep cliff to see a tea farmer. You can get in and out only by animal and you have to go down these slippery slopes. This farmer took out tea-stained cups and got spring water from a nearby spring—beautiful pure water. He heated it up in a grimy old pot, dingy and grim. The tray was rusted and funky. He picked those cups up so lovingly and carefully served us ready-to-drink tea. People there always offer you tea, as soon as you cross the threshold. It is humble in quality and very moving. The care, the warmth of extending his hospitality, even though the cups were a "different standard of cleanliness," was powerful.

And Now...

I'm not the best example of a tea person. David (Hoffman) makes fun of my tea-making methods. He does it properly, in small amounts, re-steeping and pouring out the tea for each cup. I like to read the "New York Times" and I don't want to be bothered so I make one big pot. I have a stainless steel kettle (which David said is horrible.) I steep for 6 minutes and then strain it into a teapot. I throw a cozy on it and it lasts me 1½ to 2 hours.

Tales from *All In This Tea*: Part Two

BY GINA LEIBRECHT

When I began work with Les Blank on *All In This Tea* in 1998, I immediately realized I was a natural fit for the job. Luxuriating in the sensu-
ous footage of tea gardens, farmers roasting tea in their woks, and the
ongoing scenes of pouring, sniffing and sipping allowed me to delve
deeply into a subject I had always wanted to know more about.

My parents are European, and unlike the average American kid, I
drank a lot of tea. I would drink it with meals, or my mother would
fix me a strong cup of black tea if I wasn't feeling well—and it always
worked! At the age of fourteen, I spent a snowy and blustery holiday in
my mother's hometown of Hamburg, Germany. One afternoon I was
carousing around the city with a friend when we stumbled upon a tea
shop nestled in a hidden alley. Entering the shop was like traveling back
in time, to the days when camels carried chests of tea to distant lands
along the Silk Road. The aroma was intoxicating. There were stenciled
wooden crates piled on top of one another. Some had been pried open to
reveal mounds of dried leaves. I was transported. I had a few Deutsch-
mark in my pocket, so I bought a small bag of tea and brought it back
to the states with me, where I kept it in a small canister on a bookshelf
in my bedroom. I never actually drank the tea, but every now and then
I would sit on the edge of my bed, close my eyes, and take a good long
sniff, which invariably transported me to distant, exotic, and mysterious
lands in far away times. Years later, when I was in college, I remember
sitting in my father's dining room having long conversations over tea.
He always had a special discovery that he was eager for me to try.

When I first saw the footage that Les Blank had shot in China, I knew I had never seen anything like it before: scenes of farmers on the lush and mist covered mountains of rural China, picking and firing their teas—traditions they had learned from their parents, who learned from their parents, and so on, and so on. I knew these images would be new to Westerners, who view tea as a quick beverage that you don't put much thought into. Throw a tea bag into a cup, pour hot water, and that's it. The images I saw in the China footage revealed a totally new context for tea—a far cry from the bland, brown dust found in tea bags. Each leaf is carefully picked by hand at a certain time of day, and dried, rolled, and fired, depending on the type of tea. The tea makers use all of their senses to make the tea just the way they want it.

Although China is the homeland of tea, it is a mysterious country that has historically not been open to foreigners. The images of China that we in the West are most familiar with have been politicized by the news media. *All In This Tea* shows us a country with a history and culture that goes back thousands of years, with a breadth and depth of knowledge and tradition that makes Western countries look like teenagers. It's the human side of China, which reveals the universal desire to honor and uphold tradition, as well as a type of culinary artistry and connoisseurship that makes us civilized. I have to ask myself: What would the world be like if we didn't promote citizen-to-citizen relationships? I think *All In This Tea* underscores the necessity to create cultural bridges with countries even if we don't agree with their politics or their business practices.

The biggest irony in *All In This Tea*, however, is that a Californian is opening the eyes of these seemingly oblivious Chinese businessmen to the value of one of their own country's oldest and most prized tradition—not to mention an organic method of fertilization that's been around for millions of years. By buying tea directly from the farmer, small family farms are able to maintain their livelihood, which in turn preserves the ancient art of making tea. This art cannot be learned from a book, and in most cases, it upholds the environmentally sustainable practices of growing the tea with a special appreciation for the concept of "*terroir*." As the West gains increasing access to these finer teas, we can begin to develop our own tea-drinking traditions. In short, it's good for everyone!

For a filmmaker, having this kind of dimension in a story is a dream, and it all sprang from my partner, Les Blank, doggedly following David Lee Hoffman around China with a small, handheld digital camera. Hoffman's passion and invincibility sparked a lot of conversation, and viewers asked themselves a lot of questions—usually nothing having to do with tea, but more about how we Americans relate to other countries, whether we are living according to our ideals, and what is out there that we feel passionately enough about that we would take a stand for it?

I believe American tea drinkers have always felt like a minority, and now they are having their day. Next to water, tea is the second most popular beverage in the world. The tea renaissance that began in the early 1980s seems to be coming to a culmination with tea sales increasing, even during recessions, and tea houses popping up everywhere. Now, when I have a really great tea on the shelf of my kitchen, I drink it!

Visit to the Ningpo Green Tea District[1]

BY ROBERT FORTUNE

Excerpted from Three Years' Wanderings in the
Northern Provinces of China, *1847.*[2]

Having despatched my collections to England by three different
vessels from Hong Kong, I sailed again, at the end of March 1844,
for the northern provinces. During the summer of this year, and in
that of 1845, I was able to visit several parts of the country, which
were formerly sealed to Europeans, and which contained subjects of
much interest.

About the beginning of May I set out upon an excursion with Mr.
Thom, the British consul, and two other gentlemen, to visit the green
tea district near Ningpo. We were informed that there was a large and
celebrated temple, named *Tein-tung,* in the center of the tea district,
and above twenty miles distant, where we could lodge during our stay
in this part of the country. Twelve or fourteen miles of our journey
was performed by water, but the canal ending at the foot of the hills
we were obliged to walk, or take chairs for the remainder of the way.
The mountain traveling chair of China is a very simple contrivance.
It consists merely of two long bamboo poles, with a board placed between them for a seat, and two other cross pieces, one for the back and

---

the other for the feet; a large Chinese umbrella is held over the head to afford protection from the sun and rain.

The Chinese are quite philosophers after their own fashion. On our way to the temple, when tired with sitting so long in our boat, we several times got out and walked along the path on the sides of the canal. A great number of passage-boats going in the same direction with ourselves, and crowded with passengers, kept very near us for a considerable portion of the way, in order to satisfy their curiosity. A Chinese man never walks when he can possibly find any other mode of conveyance, and these persons were consequently much surprised to see us apparently enjoying our walk.

"Is it not strange," said one, "that these people prefer walking when they have a boat as well as ourselves?" A discussion now took place amongst them as to the reason of this apparently strange propensity, when one, more wise than his companions, settled the matter by the pithy observation, "It is *their nature* to do so;" which was apparently satisfactory to all parties.

It was nearly dark when we reached the temple, and as the rain had fallen in torrents during the greater part of the day, we were drenched to the skin, and in rather a pitiable condition. The priests seemed much surprised at our appearance, but at once evinced the greatest hospitality and kindness, and we soon found ourselves quite at home amongst them. They brought us fire to dry our clothes, got ready our dinner, and set apart a certain number of their best rooms for us to sleep in. We were evidently subjects of great curiosity to most of them who had never seen an Englishman before. Our clothes, features, mode of eating, and manners were all subjects of wonder to these simple people, who passed off many a good-humored joke at our expense.

Glad to get off our clothes, which were still damp, we retired early to rest. When we arose in the morning, the view which met our eyes far surpassed in beauty any scenery which I had ever witnessed before in China. The temple stands at the head of a fertile valley in the bosom of the hills. This valley is well watered by clear streams, which flow from the mountains, and produces most excellent crops of rice. The tea shrubs, with their dark green leaves, are seen dotted on the lower sides of all the more fertile hills. The temple itself is approached by a long avenue of Chinese pine trees. This avenue is at first straight, but near the temple it winds in a most picturesque manner round the edges of two artificial lakes, and then ends in a flight of stone steps, which lead up to the principal entrance. Behind, and on each side, the mountains rise, in irregular ridges, from one to two thousand feet above the level of the sea. These are not like the barren southern mountains, but are clothed nearly to their summits with a dense tropical looking mass of brushwood, shrubs, and trees. Some of the finest bamboos of China are grown in the ravines, and the somber-colored pine attains to a large size on the sides of the hills. Here, too, I observed some very beautiful specimens of the new fir *(Cryptomeria japonica)*, and obtained some plants and seeds of it, which may now be seen growing in the Horticultural Gardens at Chiswick.

After we had breakfasted, one of the head priests came and gave us a very pressing invitation to dine with him about mid-day; and in the meantime he accompanied us over the monastery, of which he gave the following history: "Many hundred years ago a pious old man retired from the world, and came to dwell in these mountains, giving himself up entirely to the performance of religious duties. So earnest was he in his devotions that he neglected everything relating to his temporal wants, even to his daily food. Providence, however, would not suffer so good a man to starve. Some boys were sent in a miraculous manner, who daily supplied him with food. In the course of time the fame of the sage extended all over the adjacent country, and disciples flocked to him from all quarters. A small range of temples was built, and thus commenced the extensive buildings which now bear the name of "Tein-tung," or the "Temple of the Heavenly Boys;" *Tein* signifying heaven, and *tung* a boy. At last the old man died, but his disciples supplied his place. The fame of the temple spread far and wide, and votaries came from the most distant parts of the empire—one of the Chinese kings being amongst the number—to worship and leave their offerings at its altars. Larger temples were built in front of the original ones, and these again in their turn gave way to those spacious buildings which form the principal part of the structure of the present day.

All the temples are crowded with idols, or images of their favorite gods, such as the "three precious Buddhas," "the Queen of Heaven"— represented as sitting on the celebrated lotus or nelumbium—"the God of War," and many other deified kings and great men of former days. Many of these images are from thirty to forty feet in height, and have a very striking appearance when seen arranged in these spacious and lofty halls. The priests themselves reside in a range of low buildings, erected at right angles with the different temples and courts which divide them. Each has a little temple in his own house—a family altar crowded with small images, where he is often engaged in private devotion.

After inspecting the various temples and the belfry, which contains a noble bronze bell of large dimensions, our host conducted us back to his house, where the dinner was already on the table. The priests of the Buddhist religion are not allowed to eat animal food at any of their meals. Our dinner therefore consisted entirely of vegetables, served up in the usual Chinese style, in a number of small round basins, the contents of each—soups excepted—being cut up into small square bits, to be eaten with chopsticks. The Buddhist priests contrive to procure a number of vegetables of different kinds, which, by a peculiar mode of preparation, are rendered very palatable. In fact, so nearly do they resemble animal food in taste and in appearance, that at first we were deceived, imagining that the little bits we were able to get hold of with our chopsticks were really pieces of fowl or beef. Such, however, was not the case, as our good host was consistent on this day at least, and had nothing but vegetable productions at his table. Several other priests sat with us at table, and a large number of others of inferior rank with servants, crowded around the doors and windows outside. The whole assemblage must have been much surprised at the awkward way in which some of us handled our chopsticks, and, with all their politeness, I observed they could not refrain from laughing when, after repeated attempts, some little dainty morsel would still slip back again into the dish. I know few things more annoying, and yet laughable too, than attempting to eat with the Chinese chopsticks for the first time, more particularly if the operator has been wandering on the hills all the morning, and is ravenously hungry. The instruments should first of all be balanced between the thumb and forefinger of the right hand; the points are next to be brought carefully together, just leaving as much room as will allow the coveted morsel to go in between them; the little bit is then to be neatly seized; but alas! in the act of lifting the hand, one point of the chopstick too often slips past the other, and the object of all our hopes drops back again into the dish, or perhaps even into another dish on the table. Again and again the same operation is tried, until the poor novice loses all patience, throws down the chopsticks in despair, and seizes a porcelain spoon, with which he is more successful. In cases like these the Chinese themselves are very obliging, although scarcely in a way agreeable to an Englishman's taste. Your Chinese friend, out of kindness and politeness, when he sees the dilemma in which you are, reaches across the table and seizes, with his own chopsticks, which have just come out of his mouth, the wished-for morsel, and with them lays it on the plate before you. In common politeness you must express your gratitude and swallow the offering.

During dinner our host informed us that there were about a hundred priests connected with the monastery, but that many were always absent on missions to various parts of the country. On questioning him as to the mode by which the establishment was supported, he informed us that a considerable portion of land in the vicinity belonged to the temple, and that large sums were yearly raised from the sale of bamboos, which are here very excellent, and of the branches of trees and brushwood, which are made up in bundles for firewood. A number of tea and rice farms also belong to the priests, which they themselves cultivate. Besides the sums raised by the sale of these productions, a considerable revenue must be derived from the contributions of the devotees who resort to the temple for religious purposes, as well as from the sums collected by those of the order who are out on begging excursions at stated seasons of the year. The priests are of course of all grades, some of them being merely the servants of the others, both in the house and in the fields. They seem a harmless and simple race, but are dreadfully ignorant and superstitious. The typhoon of the previous year, or rather the rain which had accompanied it, had occasioned a large slip of earth on one of the hillsides near the temple, and completely buried ten or twelve acres of excellent paddy land. On our remarking this, the priests told us with great earnestness that every one said it was a bad omen for the temple; but one of them with true Chinese politeness remarked that he had no doubt any evil influence would now be counteracted, since the temple had been honored with a visit from us.

After inspecting the tea farms and the mode of manufacturing it, Mr. Thom, Mr. Morrison, a son of the late Dr. Morrison, and Mr. Sinclair, returned to Ningpo, leaving me to prosecute my research in natural history in this part of the country. I was generally absent from the temple the whole day, returning at dark with the collections of plants and birds which I had been lucky enough to meet with in my peregrinations. The friends of the priests came from all quarters of the adjacent country to see the foreigner; and, as in the case of a wild animal, my feeding time seemed to be the most interesting moment to them. My dinner was placed on a round table in the center of the room, and although rather curiously concocted, being half Chinese and half English, the exercise and fresh air of the mountains gave me a keen appetite. The difficulties of the chopsticks were soon got over, and I was able to manage them nearly as well as the Chinese themselves. The priests and their friends filled the chairs, which are always placed down the sides of a Chinese hall, each man with his pipe in his mouth, and his cup of tea by his side. With all deference to my host and his friends, I was obliged to request the smoking to be stopped, as it was disagreeable to me while at dinner; in other respects, I believe I was "polite" enough. I shall never forget how inexpressibly lonely I felt the first night after the departure of my friends. The Chinese one by one dropped off to their homes or to bed, and at last my host himself gave several unequivocal yawns, which reminded me that it was time to retire for the night. My bedroom was upstairs, and to get to it I had to pass through a small temple, such as I have already noticed, dedicated to *Tein-how,* or the "Queen of Heaven," and crowded with other idols. Incense was burning on the altar in front of the idols; a solitary lamp shed a dim light over the objects in the room, and a kind of solemn stillness seemed to pervade the whole place. In the room below, and also in one in an adjoining house, I could hear the priests engaged in their devotional exercises, in that singing tone which is peculiar to them. Then the sounds of the gong fell upon my ears; and, at intervals, a single solemn toll of the large bronze bell in the belfry; all which showed that the priests were engaged in public as well as private devotion. Amidst scenes of this kind, in a strange country, far from friends and home, impressions are apt to be made upon the mind, which remain vivid through life; and I feel convinced I shall never forget the strange mixture of feelings which filled my mind during the first night of my stay with the priests in the temple of Tein-tung. I have visited the place often since, passed through the same little temple, slept in the same bed, and heard the same solemn sounds throughout the silent watches of the night, and yet the first impressions remain in my mind distinct and single.

The Tokaido

BY ELIZA RUHAMAH SCIDMORE

Excerpted from Jinrikisha Days in Japan, *1891.*[1]

Great once was Shidzuoka, which now is only a busy commercial town of an agricultural province. The old castle has been razed, its martial quadrangle is a wheat field; and the massive walls, the creeping and overhanging pine-trees and deep moats are the only feudal relics. Keiki, the last of the Tokugawa Shoguns, lived in a black-walled enclosure beyond the outer moat, but the modern spirit paid no heed to his existence, and his death, in 1883, was hardly an incident in the routine of its commercial progress.

The great Shinto temple at the edge of the town is famous for the dragons in its ceiling. The old priest welcomed us with smiles, led us in, shoeless, over the mats, and bade us look up, first at the Dragon of the Four Quarters, and then at the Dragon of the Eight Quarters, the eyes of the monster strangely meeting ours, as we changed our various points of view.

At the archery range behind the temple our *danna san*[2] proved himself a new William Tell with the bow and arrows. The attendant idlers cheered his shots, and a wrinkled old woman brought us dragon candies on a dark-red lacquer tray, under whose transparent surface lay darker shadows of cherry blossoms. The eye of the connoisseur was quick to descry the tray, and when the woman said it had been

---

1 [Certain British spellings and archaic terms have been amended. Ed.]
2 "*Danna san*" can refer to a boss, manager, or husband.

bought in the town, we took *jinrikishas* and hurried to the address she gave. The guide explained minutely, the shopkeeper brought out a hundred other kinds and colors of lacquer, and children ran in from home workshops with hardly dried specimens to show us. All the afternoon we searched through lacquer and curio shops, and finally despatched a coolie to the temple to buy the old woman's property. Hours afterwards he returned with a brand-new, bright red horror, and the message that "the mistress could not send the honorable foreigner such a poor old tray as that."

The fine Shidzuoka baskets, which are so famed elsewhere, were not to be found in Shidzuoka; our teahouse was uninteresting, and so we set forth in the rain, unfurling big flat umbrellas of oil-paper, and whirling away through a dripping landscape. Rice and wheat alternated with dark-green tea bushes, and cart-loads of tea-chests were bearing the first season's crop to market. The rain did not obscure the lovely landscape, as the plain we followed turned to a valley, the valley narrowed to a ravine, and we began climbing upward, while a mountain-torrent raced down beside us. One picturesque little village in a shady hollow gave us glimpses of silk-worm trays in the houses as we went whirling through it. The road, winding by zigzags up Utsonomiya pass, suddenly entered a tunnel six hundred feet in length, where the *jinrikisha* wheels rumbled noisily. On cloudy days the place is lighted by lamps, but on sunny days by the sun's reflection from two black lacquer boards at the entrances. The device is an old one in Japan, but an American patent has recently been issued for the same thing, as a cheap means of lighting ships' holds while handling cargo.

On the other side of Utsonomiya Pass the road winds down by steep zigzags to the village of Okabe, noted for its trays and boxes made of the polished brown stem of a coarse fern. We bought our specimens from an oracular woman, who delivered her remarks like the lines of a part, her husband meekly echoing what she said in the same dramatic tones, and the whole scene being as stagey as if it had been well rehearsed beforehand.

From the mountains the road drops to a rich tea country, where every hill-side is green with the thick-set little bushes. At harvest-time cart-loads of basket-fired, or country-dried, tea fill the road to the ports, to be toasted finally in iron pans, and coated with indigo and gypsum to satisfy the taste of American tea drinkers. In every town farmers may be seen dickering with the merchants over the tough paper sacks of tea that they bring in, and within the houses groups sitting at low tables sort the leaves into grades with swift fingers.

At Fujiyeda, where we took refuge from the increasing rain, the splashing in the large bathroom of the teahouse was kept up from afternoon to midnight by the guests, and continued by the family and teahouse maids until four o'clock, when the early risers began their ablutions. A coughing priest on the other side of our thin paper walls had a talkative massagist about midnight and refreshments later, and we were glad to resume the ride between tea fields at the earliest possible hour.

At Kanaya, at the foot of Kanaya Mountain, the teahouse adjoined a school-house. The school-room had desks and benches but no walls, the screens being all removed. The teacher called the pupils in by clapping two sticks together, as in a French theater. Spying the foreigners, the children stared, oblivious of teacher and blackboard, and the teacher, after one good look at the itinerants, bowed a courteous goodmorning, and let the offenders go unpunished.

Up over Kanaya Pass we toiled slowly, reaching at last a little eyrie of a teahouse, where the landlord pointed with equal pride to the view and to several pairs of muddy shoes belonging, he said, to the honorable gentlemen who were about piercing the mountain under us with a railway tunnel. Under a shady arbor is a huge, round boulder, fenced in carefully and regarded reverently by humble travelers. According to the legend it used to cry at night like a child until Kobo Daishi, the inventor of the Japanese syllabary, wrote an inscription on it and quieted it forever. No less famous than Kobo Daishi's rock is the *midzu ame*[3] of this Kanaya teahouse, and the dark brown sweet is put in dainty little boxes that are the souvenirs each pilgrim carries away with him.

---

3   "*Midzu ame*" is malt glucose or, literally, "water candy."

Farther along the main road, with its arching shade-trees, the glossy dark tea bushes gave way to square miles of rice and wheat fields. Here and there a patch of intense green verdure showed the young blades of rice almost ready to be transplanted to the fields, whence the wheat had just been garnered, the rice giving way in turn to some other cereal, all farming land in this fertile region bearing three annual crops.

A few villages showed the projecting roofs peculiar to the province of Totomi, and then the pretty teahouse at Hamamatsu quite enchanted us after our experiences with the poor accommodations of some of the provincial towns. A rough curbed well in the court-yard, with an odd parasol of a roof high over the sweep, a pretty garden all cool, green shade, a stair-way, steep and high, and at the top a long, dim corridor, with a floor of shining, dark *keyaki* wood. This was the place that made us welcome; even stocking-footed we half feared to tread on those brilliantly-polished boards. Our balcony overlooked a third charming garden, and each little room had a distinctive beauty of wooden ceilings, recesses, screens, and fanciful windows.

The most enviable possession of Hamamatsu, however, was O'Tatsu, and on our arrival O'Tatsu helped to carry our traps upstairs, falling into raptures over our rings, pins, hair-pins, watches, and beaded trimmings. She clapped her hands in ecstasy, her bright eyes sparkled, and her smile displayed the most dazzling teeth. When we ate supper, sitting on the floor around an eight-inch high table, with little O'Tatsu presiding and waiting on us, not only her beauty but her charming frankness, simplicity, quickness, and grace made further conquest of us all. The maiden enjoyed our admiration immensely, arrayed herself in her freshest blue-and-white cotton kimono, and submitted her head to the best hair-dresser in town, returning with gorgeous bits of crape and gold cord tied in with the butterfly loops of her blue-black tresses. At her suggestion we sent for a small dancing-girl to entertain us, who, with a wand and masks, represented Suzume and other famous characters in legend and melodramas. When we left Hamamatsu, affectionate little O'Tatsu begged me to send her my photograph, and lest I should not have understood her excited flow of Japanese sentences, illuminated, however, by her great pleading eyes, she ran off, and, coming back, slipped up to me and held out a cheap, colored picture of some foreign beauty in the costume of 1865. When at last we rode away from the teahouse, O'Tatsu followed my *jinrikisha* for a long way, holding my hand, with tears in her lovely eyes, and her last *sayonara* broke in a sob.

A hard shell-road winds down to the shores of Hamana Lake and across its long viaduct. The *jinrikisha*s run, as if on rubber tires, for nearly three miles over an embankment crossing the middle of the great lake, which at one side admits the curling breakers of the great Pacific. Until a few years ago this mountain-walled pool was protected from the ocean by a broad sand ridge, which an earthquake shook down, letting in the salt waters. The Tokaido railroad crosses the lake on a high embankment, which was sodded and covered with a lattice-work of straw bundles, while seed was sown in the crevices more than a year before the road could be used. The whole railroad, as we saw in passing its completed sections, is solidly built with stone foundations and stone ballast, and intended to last for centuries. The Japanese seldom hurry the making of public works, and even a railroad does not inspire them with any feverish activity. Not until the last detail and station-house was finished was the line opened for travel, and following so nearly the route of the old Tokaido, through the most fertile and picturesque part of Central Japan, it keeps always in sight Fujiyama or the ocean.

In the course of the afternoon plantations of mulberry-trees came in sight. Loads of mulberry branches and twigs were being hauled into the villages and sold by weight, the rearers of silk-worms buying the leaves and paper-makers the stems for the sake of the inside bark. Climbing to one high plateau, we rested at a little rustic shed of a teahouse, commanding a superb view down a great ragged ravine to the line of foam breaking at its boulder-strewn entrance, and so on to the limitless ocean. One of the *jinrikisha* coolies preceded us to the benches on the overhanging balcony, and, kindly pointing out the special beauties of the scene, took off his garments and spread them out on the rail in the matter-of-fact, unconscious way of true Japanese innocence and simplicity of mind.

The guidebook calls the stretch of country beyond that high-perched teahouse "a waste region," but nothing could be more beautiful than the long ride through pine forest and belts of scrub-pine on that uncultivated plateau, always overlooking the ocean. At one point a temple to the goddess Kwannon[4] is niched among towering rocks at the base of a narrow cliff, on whose summit a colossal statue of the deity stands high against the sky. For more than a century this bronze goddess of Mercy has been the object of pious pilgrimages, the pilgrims clapping their hands and bowing in prayer to all the thirty-three Kwannons cut in the face of the solid rock-base on which our lady of pity stands.

We reached the long, dull town of Toyohashi at dusk, to find the large teahouse crowded with travelers. Two rooms looking out upon a sultry high-walled garden were given us, and for dining room a tiny alcove of a place on one of the middle courts. This room was so small and close that we had to leave the screens open, though the corridor led to the large bathroom, where half a dozen people splashed and chattered noisily and gentlemen with their clothes on their arms went back and forth before our door as if before the life class of an art school. The noise of the bathers was kept up cheerfully, until long after midnight, and no one in the teahouse seemed to be sleeping. By four o'clock in the morning such a coughing, blowing, and sputtering began in the court beside my room that I finally slid the screens and looked out. At least a dozen lodgers were brushing their teeth in the picturesque little quadrangle of rocks, bamboos, and palms, and bathing face and hands in the large stone and bronze urns that we had supposed to be ornamental only. Later, the gravel was covered with scores of the wooden sticks of tooth-brushes, beaten out into a tassel of fibers at one end, and with many boxes emptied of the coarse, gritty tooth-powder which the Japanese use so freely.

The last day of our long *jinrikisha* ride was warm, the sun glared on a white, dusty road, and the country was flat and uninteresting. Each little town and village seemed duller than the other. Wheat and rape

---

4   "Kwannon" is sometimes referred to as the *bodhisattva* Kuan Yin or Guan Yin.

were being harvested and spread to dry, and in the farm-yards men and women were combing, beating out the grain with flails, and winnowing it in the primitive way by pouring it down from a flat scoop-basket held high overhead. Nobody wore any clothes to speak of, and the whole population turned out to watch the amazing spectacle of foreigners standing spell-bound until our *jinrikisha*s had gone by.

At Arimatsu village we passed through a street of shops where the curiously-dyed cotton goods peculiar to the place are sold. For several hundred years all Arimatsu has been tying knots down the lengths of cotton, twisting it in skeins, and wrapping it regularly with a double-dyed indigo thread, and then, by immersion in boiling water, dyeing the fabric in curious lines and star-spotted patterns. A more clumsy and primitive way of dyeing could not be imagined in this day of steam-looms and roller-printing, but Arimatsu keeps it up and prospers.

At sunset we saw the towers of Nagoya castle in the distance, and after crossing the broad plain of ripening rape and wheat, the coolies sped through the town at a fearful pace and deposited us, dazed, dusted, and weary, at the door of the Shiurokindo, to enjoy the beautiful rooms just kindly vacated by Prince Bernard, of Saxe-Weimar.

The Shiurokindo is one of the handsomest and largest of the teahouses a foreigner finds, its interior a labyrinth of rooms and suites of rooms, each with a balcony and private outlook on some pretty court. The walls, the screens, recesses, ceilings, and balcony rails afford studies and models of the best Japanese interior decorations. The *samisen*'s[5] wail and a clapping chorus announced that a great dinner was going on, and in the broader corridors there was a passing and repassing of people arrayed in hotel kimonos.

As the wise traveler carries little baggage, the teahouses furnish their customers with *ukatas*, or plain cotton kimonos, to put on after the bath and wear at night. These gowns are marked with the crest or name of the house, painted in some ingenious or artistic design; and guests may wander round the town, even, clad in these garments, that so ingeniously advertise the Maple-leaf, the Chrysanthemum, or

---

5 A "*samisen*" is a musical instrument with three strings, a square body, and a long neck.

Dragon teahouse. All guides, and servants particularly, enjoy wearing these hotel robes, and travelers who dislike to splash their own clothing march to the bath ungarmented, assuming the house gowns in the corridor after their dip. These *ukatas* at the Shiurokindo were the most startling fabrics of Arimatsu, and we looked in them as if we had been throwing ink-bottles at each other.

Until the long *jinrikisha* ride was over we had not felt weary, as each day beguiled us with some new interest and excitement; but when we stepped from those baby-carriages at the door of the Shiurokindo we were dazed with fatigue, although the coolies who ran all the way did not appear to be tired in the least. Their headman, who marshaled the team of ten, was a powerful young fellow, a very Hercules for muscle, and for speed and endurance hardly to be matched by that ancient deity. At the end of each day he seemed fresher and stronger than at the start, and he has often run sixty and sixty-five miles a day, for three and four days together. He led the procession and set the pace, shouting back warning of ruts, stones, or bad places in the road, and giving the signals for slowing, stopping, and changing the order of the teams. On level ground the coolies trotted tandem—one in the shafts, and one running ahead with a line from the shafts held over his shoulder. Going downhill, the leader fell back and helped to hold the shafts; going uphill, he pushed the *jinrikisha* from the back.

The *jinrikisha* coolies make better wages than farm laborers or most mechanics. Our men were paid by the distance, and for days of detention each man received twenty-five cents to cover the expense of his board and lodging. They earned at an average one dollar and ten cents for each day, but out of this paid the rent of the *jinrikisha* and the government tax, Where two men and a *jinrikisha* cover one hundred and eighty miles in four days they receive thirteen dollars in all, which is more than a farm laborer receives in a year. As a rule, these coolies are great gamblers and spendthrifts, with a fondness for saké. Our headman was a model coolie, saving his money, avoiding the saké bottle, and regarding his splendid muscle as invested capital. When he walked in to collect his bill, he was clean and shining in a rustling silk kimono, such as a well-to-do merchant might wear. In this well-dressed, distinguished-looking person, who slid the screens of our sitting-room and bowed to us so gracefully, we hardly recognized our trotter of the blue-cotton coat, bare knees, and mushroom hat. He explained that the other men could not come to thank us for our gratuities because they had not proper clothes. In making his final and lowest bows his substantial American watch fell out of his silk belt with a thump; but he replaced it in its chamois case with the assurance that nothing hurt it, and that it was with the noon gun of Nagoya castle whenever he came to town.

Tea Pilgrimage

BY JAMES NORWOOD PRATT

Whoever said "the past is not dead; it's not even past" could have been speaking of tea history, for the history of tea lives on in the cups we drink every day. A taste that's been known sometimes for centuries comes back to life. There is not a tea you can ask for which does not bear witness to strange and wonderful stories, if only one cares to discover them. Every tea contains history. It is a history which begins thousands of years before we Westerners first began drinking tea only 400 years ago and stretches right back to ancient-most China.

Everyone who takes much of an interest in tea runs considerable risk of falling into a love affair, sooner or later, with the homeland of tea. After long infatuation, last September I boarded a flight from San Francisco to Shanghai as part of a special tour in pursuit of romance. The next morning I headed south of Shanghai on the road to Yixing, home of China's famous purple sand clay earthenware teapots. Teapots have been made since about the time of Christopher Columbus, which makes the teapot a fairly recent development in the history of China tea, if anything in China may be considered recent. To watch these master potters was to witness antiquity alive and vibrant in the present moment.

From Yixing we continued south through the hills around Lake Taihu where Lu Yu lived while he wrote the world's first book about tea over twelve hundred years ago. The rows of tea hugging the contours of the hills produce the famous *Biluochun* and *Guzhu* or "Purple Bamboo Shoot" just as they did when Lu Yu lived there and enjoyed them, though under different names. By nightfall I entered Hangzhou, one of the most beautiful cities in China (or anywhere else) and the ancient capital of the Song dynasty. *Longjing*—the incomparable green tea we call Dragon Well—grows nearby on the surrounding hillsides.

Plucking tender shoots off the Dragon Well tea plants with my own fingers and pressing the mass of leaf against the bottom of a hot wok with my own hand gave the product of these labors a fresher, sweeter taste. We drank the tea we'd made while cruising Hangzhou's West Lake aboard a "dragon boat" and listening to classical Chinese music played on traditional instruments. To be at its best, ancient authorities always agreed, Dragon Well should be made with water from Tiger Run Spring, a source miraculously discovered in the hills above West Lake when Lingyin Temple was founded there by *Chan* (Zen) Buddhists well over a thousand years ago. Ancient Authority is spot on. This spring water will float a Chinese penny, and makes Dragon Well elegance itself, exactly as claimed. Following a short flight south to Fuzhou, directly across the straits from Taiwan, we are welcomed with a jasmine *oolong* Buddhist banquet at Drum Mountain monastery, after sunset chants as old as stone. Gongs' unforgettable peace. Vegetarian delicacies to go with our Drum Mountain tea after dark.

Six hours by train up river, deep in the interior of Fujian Province, grows "Bohea" meaning *oolong* tea, from the obsolete English word for Wuyi, the Chinese name for a spectacular mountain range and the *oolong*s produced there. Wuyi-shan looks like China the way Disney would do its dizzy cliffs to climb and clefts mysterious to enter. Entranced, I float down Nine Bend Creek on a bamboo raft, or is it the peaks and precipices which are floating past as if in a dream? When you enter the canyon where the ancient plants grow and drink the greatest *Wuyi yancha* or "cliff tea" in situ, you see it's no wonder they worshipped Da Hong Pao.

Awesome Beijing, like Buddhism, is inseparable from the culture that tea came from, and, of course, we had to visit. Its splendors included unforgettable teas at a pavilion in Prince Gong's garden-mansion, and dinners prepared in the Imperial kitchens at Fangshan Restaurant. For fourteen days all told, the spirit of ancient China always inhabited whatever tea we drank. Then back to San Francisco. Never to be the same again, of course, returning transformed, as if from pilgrimage to a holy land....

This piece originally appeared in Fresh Cup's Tea Almanac 2001. *Reprinted with permission.*

Sipping and Tripping through Asia

BY LAURA CHILDS

Just before I began writing my *Tea Shop Mystery* series, I spent a fair amount of time traveling through Asia. I think this is where my true passion for tea was finally realized. Not just through sipping tea and broadening my tea-tasting horizons, but experiencing a number of serendipitous tea moments.

One of my most special memories involves traveling on the bullet train from Tokyo to Kyoto on Christmas Day. I was deep into a book and hypnotized by the motion of the train, when my husband suddenly told me to look up. I lifted my head and there, directly out the window, was a spectacular, terraced tea garden with Mt. Fuji in the background. The bright, verdant green of the tea shone like neon against the white snows of Fuji, like a color photo pushed to the max. Later, I learned there are dozens of tea gardens outside the city of Fujinomiya and that several of the local bath houses even offer tea baths. It must be heavenly to steep in a warm, bubbling brew of fresh-picked tea leaves. No agony of the leaves here, just tired muscles unkinking, while tea leaves tickle pink skin and release their sweet, earthy aroma.

Later, while wandering the ancient, narrow streets of Kyoto, marveling at the temples, gardens, and tori gates, we got hopelessly lost. A woman from a small tea shop noticed our wandering and beckoned us in to take a seat. We sat down, a little dazed and travel-worn, and were delighted when she produced cups of bright green tea and fresh-baked yams.

Another trip took us to the oldest tea house in Shanghai: lovely Huxinting Tea House, located in a pagoda-like pavilion in the middle of a lake in Yuyuan Garden. There is nothing like sipping tea while lounging on silk cushions and admiring three hundred year-old Chinese bonsai, also known as *Pen-jing*.

In Hong Kong, we visited the Flagstaff House Museum of Tea Ware. My husband, who teaches Chinese and Japanese art history, was head over heels for the collection. Of course, he already had well over two hundred different Yixing teapots!

On a trip to Bali, a small bowl of hot tea was my comfort after thirty-five hours of air travel. Standing on my hotel balcony, gazing out at a live, steaming volcano with the South China Sea stretching endlessly toward the equator, I sipped Java's own Agung black tea and counted my blessings.

Imagine my surprise when I returned from Bali and found out that Berkley Prime Crime had offered me a three-book contract to actually write my *Tea Shop Mysteries*! Twisting tea lore into tales of history and mystery seemed daunting at first, but after ten books I'm more than up to the challenge. And readers constantly tell me there's something very satisfying about reading a *Tea Shop Mystery* while sipping a cup of Golden Monkey Yunnan or Blue Mountain Nilgiri or classic, aged *pu-erh*. Come to think of it, I wouldn't mind a cup of tea right now myself!

The Tea Gardens of Shanghai

Anonymous Special Correspondent

Excerpted from Hunt's Merchant Magazine, *1858.[1]*

A special correspondent of the London Times, *writing from Shanghai, 23rd October, 1857, describing the manners and customs of the Chinese, writes of the tea gardens of Shanghai thus:*

We bustle our way through the narrow streets. We pass the temples and the *yamuns,*[2] unentered, for we have seen a hundred such before, and we reach the tea gardens of Shanghai city. These are worth a visit, for they are the best I have seen in China. A Chinese garden is usually about 20 yards square, but these cover an area of ten acres. It is an irregular figure flanked by rows of shops, rudely analogous to those of the Palais Royal. The area is traversed in all directions by broad canals of stagnant water, all grown over with green, and crossed by zig-zag wooden bridges, of the willow pattern plate model, sadly out of repair, and destitute of paint. Where the water is not, there are lumps of artificial rock-work, and large pavilion-shaped tearooms, perhaps twenty in number. Here self-heating kettles of gigantic proportions are always hissing and bubbling; and at the little tables the Chinese population are drinking tea, smoking, eating almond hard-cake or pomegranates, playing dominoes, or arranging bargains. There are interstices also of vacant land, and these are occupied by jugglers and peep-show-men.

---

1   [Certain British spellings and archaic terms have been amended. Ed.]
2   A "*yamun*" is a residence that is given to officials of the Chinese government.

From the upper room of one of these teahouses, we shall have a view of the whole scene, and A'lin will order us a cup of tea and some cakes for lunch. The jugglers and gymnasts below are doing much the same kind of tricks which their brethren of England and France perform. M. Houdin and Mr. Anderson would find their equals among these less-pretending wizards. I am told that these peep-shows which old men are looking into and laughing, and which young boys are not prevented from seeing, contain representations of the grossest obscenity.

Here is a ventriloquist, who, attracted by our European costumes at the casement, has come up to perform. "Give him a dollar, A'lin, and tell him to begin." That dirty, half-clad wanderer would make another fortune for Barnum. He unfolds his pack, and constructs out of some curtains a small closed room. Into this he retires, and immediately a little vaudeville is heard in progress inside. Half-a-dozen voices in rapid dialog, sounds, and movements, and cries of animals, and the clatter of falling articles, tell the action of the plot. The company from the tea-tables, who had gathered round, wag their tails, with laughter, especially at the broadest sallies of humor, and at the most indecorous *denouements.* In truth, there is no difficulty, even to us, in comprehending what is supposed to be going on in that little room. The incidents are, indeed, somewhat of the broadest—not so bad as the scenes in our orthodox old English comedies, such as "The Custom of the Country," for instance, or "The Conscious Lovers;" but still they are very minutely descriptive of facts not proper to be described. The man's talent, however, would gain him full audience in Europe without the aid of grossness.

"Ho lai"—"fire there." Shall we light a cheroot and stroll about? Don't make too sure, Mr. Bull, that the gentleman in the mandarin cap, who is holding you by the button and grinning in your face, is saying anything complimentary about you. In a journey up the country a fat Frenchman, who had equipped himself in an old mandarin coat, a huge pair of China boots, and a black wide-awake,[3] was leaning upon a bamboo spear, while his boat was being drawn over one of those

---

3   A "wide-awake" is a type of soft felt hat.

mud embankments, which serve the purpose of our locks. He also was very much flattered at the politeness of an old man who prostrated himself three times before him, and chin-chin-ed him. Unluckily an interpreter was present, who explained that this old man took our French friend for the devil, and was worshipping him in that capacity according to Chinese rites. In fact, the Frenchman in his antique disguise rather resembled a Chinese idol. But ask the French consul at Shanghai about this; he can tell the story better than I can.

Originally published in the London Times *on October 23, 1857 and reprinted in the* Hunt's Merchant Magazine *in April 1858.*

In The Footsteps Of Choŭi

BY BROTHER ANTHONY OF TAIZÉ

A Korean Tea Pilgrimage

I love drinking Korean tea and I love visiting the places where it is produced: the Hwaŏm-sa and Ssangye-sa temples in Chiri Mountain in the southern regions where tea was first planted in the ninth century, and the modern tea fields of Hwagye Valley and Hadong, as well as Posŏng and Cheju Island. There is nothing more beautiful than Korean tea fields in springtime. But the Korean Way of Tea is not simply a matter of drinking tea. There is a rich tradition of tea literature inherited from the past that my friends who "do tea" in Korea insist must be studied. There are tea poems, treatises about tea, even a tea rhapsody! These classics of tea are regularly read in Korea at the same time as the Chinese *Classic of Tea* by Lu Yü.

The main problem for me is that all these texts are written in Classical Chinese, while I can only read modern Korean. Still, I have recently been preparing English translations of the three main Korean tea classics, based on Korean translations by a tea friend. The two most famous, the *Chronicle of the Spirit of Tea* and the *Hymn in Praise of Korean Tea*, are from the brush of the Venerable Choŭi, who in the nineteenth century shared tea with some remarkable scholars at a time when the Way of Tea had been largely forgotten. I persuaded the publisher of the translations that we had to include in our book photographs of the places associated with the writers, and last autumn we set out to visit the places where Choŭi lived—the publisher, a photographer, my tea friend, and myself. The story of Choŭi's life kept us company on our travels round the far southwestern region of Korea; it was an unexpected autumnal tea pilgrimage.

Choŭi was born on the fifth day of the fourth lunar month, 1786, in Singi Village, Samhyang District, Muan County, in the southwestern region of South Chŏlla Province, just outside Mokp'o city. His family name was Chang; his given name was Ŭi-sun. Today the site of his original home is being developed as a memorial park, with grandiose plans for a series of halls and museums devoted to every aspect of Korean tea history and practice. The little house in which he spent his first years has been restored near the entrance but it is dwarfed by the new buildings rising on the hill above it.

We arrived rather late in the afternoon. It was getting dark and we were fortunate to be welcomed by the Venerable Yongun, who is the inspiration for this project. He is probably the greatest scholar of Korean tea history now alive. His room is lined with books, from floor to ceiling, and he has edited many of Korea's most important tea-related texts. Sharing tea with him and talking quietly was probably far more enriching than visiting all the displays in glass cases in the surrounding buildings.

In his sixteenth year, Choŭi first became a monk at Unhŭng-sa temple on the slopes of Tŏkyong-san in Tado District, Naju County, South Chŏlla Province, under the guidance of the Venerable Pyŏkbong Minsŏng. At that time, the temple must have been an impressive sight, with a series of ancient halls rising up the hillside. Alas, time and the Korean War (1950–1953) have demolished everything and we arrived to discover that at present, just one monk is living there, in a very simple house at the end of a rural lane. A single new temple hall has recently been built on the site of the original main hall. Nothing else remains.

Along the slopes of the valley beyond the hall, however, we were amazed to find large plantations of tea growing completely wild and very little tended. The Venerable Hyewŏn, the monk living there, explained that the bushes are growing from roots that are centuries old, that almost certainly already existed when Choŭi became a monk there. He gave us tea he had made using their leaves and it was touching to imagine the young Chŏui arriving in this very isolated spot to begin his quest for enlightenment surrounded by tea! We ate soft persimmons from a tree that might be descended from one he knew, and one huge ginkgo loaded with nuts was almost certainly there then. I enjoy finding such continuities.

In his nineteenth year, after an enlightenment experience in Yŏng'am hermitage on the nearby Wŏlch'ul-san Mountain, Chŏui received ordination from the Sŏn (Zen) master Wanho Yunu at the temple of Taedun-sa (now known as Taehŭng-sa). The rocky heights of Wŏlch'ul-san (the name means "moonrise") once sheltered dozens of hermitages. A few temples remain, and scattered pagodas indicate where others stood. Just below one ancient temple there is a large, newly created tea plantation belonging to the Amore-Pacific group's Sulloc tea company, the largest producers of tea in Korea.

In 1806 Chŏui first met the great scholar and thinker Tasan Chŏng Yak-Yong (1763–1836), who was living in political exile in his mother's native town of Kangjin, only seven or eight miles away from Taedun-sa. Soon after his arrival in Kangjin, Tasan had met one of Korea's last surviving tea masters, the Venerable A'am Hyejang, the head monk of the nearby Paegnyŏn-sa temple. It was from him that Tasan learned tea. The simple house in which Tasan spent much of his exile still exists on the far side of the hill from Paegnyŏn-sa temple. In the temple, too, there remain a couple of buildings that Tasan and Chŏui must have seen.

Wild tea grows in the hillsides all around, a sign of the long history of tea cultivation in this area. Indeed, the name "Tasan," meaning "tea mountain," was originally the name of the hill on which his house stands. From the temple, there would have been a fine view out across the bay, but now much land has been reclaimed from the sea. We did not linger long here, but it was interesting to learn that the head monk of Paegnyŏn-sa is attempting a modern revival of what Koreans call *ttok-ch'a*, caked tea, the form of tea familiar from the classics of China and Korea, and which Tasan and Chŏui drank, whereas modern Korean tea is almost entirely leaf tea. There are similarities with Chinese *pu-erh* tea.

In 1809, two hundred years ago, Choŭi spent several months in Kangjin, learning the *Book of Changes* and classical Chinese poetry from Tasan, who seems to have learned more about tea from him in return. They became close friends, although Tasan was socially superior and a Confucian scholar who had been deeply influenced by the Sŏhak (Western learning) that included Catholicism. Usually such men had little or no sympathy with Buddhism. In addition to scholarly learning, Choŭi was a skilled painter in both scholarly and Buddhist styles, and a noted performer of Buddhist ritual song (*pŏmp'ae*) and dance.

In 1815, Choŭi first visited Seoul and established strong relationships with a number of highly educated scholar-officials, several of whom had been to China, who became his friends and followers. These included the son-in-law of King Chŏngjo, Haegŏ Doin Hong Hyŏn-ju and his brother Yŏnch'ŏn Hong Sŏk-ju, the son of Tasan, Unp'o Chŏng Hak-yu; as well as the famous calligrapher Ch'usa Kim Chŏng-hŭi (1786–1856) with his brothers. It was most unusual for a Buddhist monk, who was assigned the lowest rank in society, together with shamans and *kisaengs* (female entertainers), to be recognized as a poet and thinker in this way by members of the Confucian establishment. Since he was a monk, Choŭi was not even allowed to enter the walls of Seoul and instead received visits from these scholars while living in Chŏngnyang-sa temple outside the eastern gate or in a hermitage in the hills to the north.

Once he was in his 40s, Choŭi withdrew to the mountain above Taehŭng-sa temple, outside the township of Haenam, in the far southwest of Korea, built a hermitage known as Ilch'i-am in 1824, and lived there alone for the next 40 years, practicing meditation in a manner he developed and wrote about. After his death the hermitage ceased to exist. In the late 1970s, scholars involved in the twentieth-century tea revival discovered where it had been. They built a couple of small halls on the site, and monks with an interest in tea began to live there, cultivating a tea field. I had been there once before, ten years ago, and retained the image of a tiny thatched tea room and a small wooden hermitage lost on a wild mountainside.

It is a steep climb from the main temple, I was gasping a bit by the time we reached the hermitage, but not as much as some of the younger members of our group! Recently several additional halls and buildings have been added and we were welcomed for tea by the Venerable Muin, who is currently living there. The views from the hermitage across the late-autumn colors of the mountainside were wonderful and we soon recovered. The Venerable Muin is also in charge of the 'temple-stay' program at the main temple, and organizes tea-making sessions for groups of international visitors in the spring months of April and May. We drank tea with him and were touched by his ready welcome. He certainly sees many more people in a year than Choŭi did, and from many different countries!

In 1828, during a visit to Ch'ilbul Sŏn (Zen) Hall in Chiri Mountain, several miles to the north, Choŭi copied out from a Ming Chinese encyclopedia dating from the late sixteenth-century the *Ch'asinjŏn* *(Chronicle of the Spirit of Tea)*, a simple guide to the basic principles involved in making and drinking tea. In 1830, back at Ilch'i-am, he prepared a clean copy of his rapidly written text. Ch'ilbul-sa (temple), as it is now called, lies high up in peaceful isolation at the very end of the road that climbs through Hwagye Valley, the site of many recently planted tea fields. Its old buildings were burned during the Korean War and it is now much larger than when Choŭi was there. A modern monument in one corner of the lower car-park commemorates his visit. It always reminds me that we are not being very authentic, zooming up in a car along a smooth modern road while Choŭi had to climb several miles up a rough mountain path.

I visit the Hwagye valley every year. In it is the home of the woman who produces my favorite tea; its name is *Kwan Hyang*—vision of fragrance! She makes my favorite Korean meals, too, from fresh mountain herbs. When we visit her house, we almost always drive on up to Ch'ilbul Temple and I have slept there several times, too. The sound of night birds singing among the trees in the intense silence that follows the morning chanting at around 4:00 A.M. on spring mornings is quite wonderful. And well hidden from visitors on a slope above the temple is a modern meditation hall, where monks continue the meditation practiced by Choŭi.

In 1831 Choŭi once again visited his friends in Seoul, reading and writing poems with them. He then returned to his hermitage and in 1837 he wrote his *TongCh'aSong* (*Hymn in Praise of Korean Tea*), at the request of Hong Hyŏn-ju. This is an impressive poem in classical Chinese, designed to affirm that Korean tea is equal in quality to Chinese tea. Its main text is broken into short sections by many prose annotations and explanations added by Choŭi while he was writing. In 1838 we find him climbing to Piro Peak, the topmost peak of the Diamond Mountains (now in North Korea), before visiting the hills around Seoul. In his fifty-fifth year, he received the honor of being recognized as a Great Monk by King Hŏnjong. In his fifty-eighth year he visited his childhood home and saw his parents' graves covered with weeds, an event he marked in a poem.

From 1840 until 1848, the scholar and calligrapher Ch'usa Kim Chŏng-hŭi was exiled to the southern island of Cheju and during those years, Choŭi visited him no less than five times, once staying for six months, bringing him tea and teaching him about Buddhism. When Ch'usa was freed, he visited Choŭi at Ilch'i-am as soon as he arrived on the mainland on his way back to Seoul. Ch'usa died in the tenth month of 1856 and a little later, when he was already 71, Choŭi visited his grave near Asan, to the southwest of Seoul. Ch'usa's family home still stands close to his grave and can be visited. The house on Cheju Island where Ch'usa lived also survived until the mid-twentieth century, when it was burned in the troubles that heralded the approach of the Korean War. It has now been rebuilt and I love to go there in February when the special Cheju narcissus is in flower in the garden, with its extraordinary jasmine-like perfume.

In the nineteenth century, there was probably no tea growing on the island. Today, the Amore-Pacific group's vast Sulloc tea fields with their tea museum and research institute have made Cheju Island the main center of Korean tea production. Choŭi and Ch'usa would have been amazed. It is surely fitting that the same company has established a museum just outside Seoul which houses some of Korea's most precious tea relics, including the oldest copies of Choŭi's texts, his formal memorial portrait, and some relics of his tea drinking.

Choŭi remained vigorous and healthy to the end, all the time practicing meditation at Ilch'i-am hermitage. Early in the morning of the second day of the seventh month of 1866 he called his attendant to help him get up, sat in the lotus position and entered Nirvana. At the entrance to Taehŭng-sa temple, among a large group of stone urns and memorial stones, tea pilgrims can pay their respects to the urn containing the ashes of Choŭi, the greatest master of Korean tea.

It was moving to stand there, recalling his life story, with crowds of Korean families visiting the temple for an autumn outing rushing past. Few of them will have heard of Choŭi. Few of them ever drink tea. Very few stopped to think even for a moment of the many monks whose remains rest there. But perhaps Choŭi would have been surprised to think that after so many years he would still be remembered, admired and celebrated by people who still drink tea in a world so different to his own. He would have been even more surprised at the idea that the texts he wrote more than 150 years ago might be translated into English (a language he probably never heard of) and read across the world. His life story offers a vivid illustration of two main dimensions of the Way of Tea. It nourishes meditative inwardness, that is the Zen of Tea; and it nourishes quiet friendship, that is the Heart of Tea. Our pilgrimage constantly reminded me that our life itself is a pilgrimage, full of moments in which we experience what a Korean poet called "the Mystery of Meeting." That is the Joy of Tea.

The Tea Lands of Sri Lanka and India

BY DANIELLE BEAUDETTE

It's no surprise that they call Sri Lanka the "Island of Delight," with its tropical island weather and warm, friendly greetings. We heard "*ayubowan*" (hello and long life) everywhere we went. Our stay here was during their New Year holiday, giving us the opportunity to see many of their holiday celebrations. In traveling through the tropical landscape to the different tea estates, we stopped at roadside fresh fruit stands, an old British-built Anglican Church, and a batik workshop where we saw the beautiful batik artwork being created by hand.

At the New Vithanakende Tea Estate, owner Navaratna Pilapitiya showed us how their tea is manufactured under the most hygienic and modern conditions. This tea estate is situated next to a tropical rain forest in the beautiful mountains of Ratnapura. Their teas were exquisite; my favorite being the extra special grade.

My most tranquil experience in Sri Lanka was when we stayed at the Strathdon Tea Estate Bungalow. We awoke early to catch the magnificent sunrise on the veranda. The bungalow was beautiful, surrounded by rolling hills of tea and a plethora of flowers. When the sun peaked from behind the hills, time stood still for a moment and all the elements of nature created a peace you could feel deeply within you.

After leaving Strathdon, we traveled to the Kirkoswald Tea Estate where Mr. Venmathirajah provided us with an in-depth tour of his factory and a unique visit to the nursery. Here, we learned the process of producing different varietals of tea, as well as how to grow new bushes from seed or a grafted mature plant. This was followed by a visit with Anil Cooke, President and CEO of the Asia Siyaka Commodities. It was enlightening as he explained the "ins and outs" of how the brokerage firm works.

All of our accommodations in Sri Lanka were fabulous, including our one-night stay in the glorious Mahaweli Reach Hotel in Kandy. We were surrounded by endless amounts of brightly colored tropical flowers and trees, had a choice of multiple pools to lounge by off the veranda, and were treated to buffets of exquisite food!

We then traveled to India, where our stay was equally spectacular. Our gracious hosts, Mr. Udayakumar, Owner of the Glendale Tea Estate, and Mr. Vinod Shenai, Group Manager, made sure that our trip was exceptional from the moment we landed. We stayed the entire time in the Adderley Tea Estate Bungalow, situated high in the Nilgiri Mountains, surrounded by tea fields wherever you looked. The grounds were impeccably kept with hundreds of varieties of plants and flowers, each labeled with their Latin and English name, and the staff was outstanding.

Our first stop was at the Glendale Tea Estate in the spectacular Nilgiri Mountains. The Glendale Estate is a leader in the industry for their ethical trade practices and their high standards earned certification from the Rainforest Alliance and from ISO. They provide schooling for the children on their estates as well as education for the workers through their Tea Research Institute. And now, Mr. Udayakumar's commitment to education will continue internationally. I'm incredibly grateful to him for the opportunity to share writings from our fifth grade class in Brookline, NH with the fifth grade class on the Glendale Tea Estate, and to begin international communications between the two schools. While visiting with Mr. Udayakumar, we enjoyed an SFTGOP white tea which was exceptionally smooth, along with fried tea leaves that were *Naladiku*—very good! It was interesting to learn that they've broadened their agricultural production not only with tea, but with a variety of tree farms: cloves, nutmeg and cinnamon to name a few. From there, we enjoyed a tour of one of the only green tea producing tea estates in the Nilgiris, the Glenmorgan Tea Estate with owner Rasik Vadera. Here, they produce a shiny gunpowder tea, along with other types of primary grade green tea.

After visiting the auction house where we watched the tea buyers purchasing at raging speed, we met with Mr. Indrajit Chatterjee of Container Tea Commodities, who refers to his organization as the "voice for the planters." He explained to us the flow process of the tea from estate to the broker house and how important it is to them that the workers on the estates are well cared for.

Throughout our stay in India, we had the opportunity to have lunch with the owners of the tea estates in their homes. Their wives were incredibly gracious, preparing elaborate eight to ten-course meals, and sharing with us stories of their work in India. In addition to a stop in Coonoor to have spectacular hand-sewn saris made for us, we had the opportunity to ride in the old-fashioned steam train. We started in Coonoor and exited the train with a special stop in the middle of the Glendale Tea Estate. The cramped ride and the fever of excitement on the train conjures up a memory I will long remember!

The last estate we visited in India was the Warwick Tea Estate, now part of the Havukal Tea Estate. We met with the manager, Mr. Surrendra Mohan. This Tea Estate looks like a scene from an Irish countryside—impeccably built rock walls that outline the crossroads of the tea fields with built-in staircases for the tea pickers to climb to get to the bushes. At this estate, they produce a very unusual tea, called Frost Tea. It was absolutely magnificent—slightly dry with hints of honey and a lightly scented aroma of sweet flowers—almost like a very lightly oxidized *oolong*. As we drove through the estate, we were surprised to find that we had to share the thin, winding road with an enormous water buffalo grazing on the grass on the side of the road! Also grown on this estate are coffee and cardamom plants, where we witnessed a "monkey watchman" chasing the monkeys away with his sling shot. I was very pleased to hear that the Havukal Estate sponsored a school for the mentally-challenged students, which the Havukal owner's wife set up. It was indeed a pleasure to learn that the estates in this region are all well aware of sustainability, the importance of fair trade, and helping those less fortunate in the community.

In closing, take a moment…picture yourself with a steaming cup of freshly brewed tea from yesterday's harvest—seven-thousand feet high in the mountains, surrounded by hundreds of rows of tea bushes glistening in the warmth of the hot sun, and the soft song of Buddhist prayer heard off in the distance. This connectedness with nature, and the beautiful people who labor in the fields each day, reminds me to thank them with each perfect cup of tea I sip.

Drinking Tea in a Back Room in China

BY JOHN MILLSTEAD

There are many perks to being a foreigner teaching in China. The tasty food with its exotic aromas, artistically displayed on round tables with cups of steamy tea on the side ranks high on the list. Another perk is enjoying the magnificent scenery and varied terrain across the ancient lands. I've always enjoyed going on long walks and hiking mountain trails, so it wasn't long before I paid a visit to one of the local outfitters to purchase new gear. I desperately wanted to get back on the trail and start exploring the Hulan Mountains not far from my new home in Ningxia Hui Autonomous Zone in northwest China.

One day, Emily, a Chinese English Teacher and fellow hiker, took me to a living room-sized hiking store. Although it was small, it was packed with all the clothing, gear, gadgets, and equipment needed for a Himalayan-sized expedition. I was amazed at what was available in this part of the world. I soon found myself walking down a short hall-way and heard voices coming from an adjacent room. Not wanting to miss out on the latest widget, I stepped into the smoke filled room; I quickly looked around and almost stepped out just as fast.

The dimly lit room had a large table in the middle, old tents and backpacks leaning against the walls, pictures of past escapades tacked here and there, and the skull of a bull nailed in the middle of the mustard colored back wall. Surrounding the table were four Chinese men smoking, chatting, and drinking tea.

Emily quickly grabbed my arm, encouraging me to leave. The men around the table looked up at the strange sight and quickly encouraged me to stay. I was intrigued and talked my way into the room. I quickly found myself sitting next to an elderly gentleman with long gray hair and an even longer matching beard—not typical in this part of China. I didn't (and still don't) speak Chinese very well so I had to depend on Emily to translate. She told me that the man with the beard was a famous explorer and author in China. She said he had hiked the entire length of the Great Wall several times, and scaled many mountains. She also explained that the men were drinking a special kind of tea called *pu-erh*.

I was mesmerized by the way the men sat around the little tea table, sipping the dark tea out of dainty little cups. Although the tea pouring seemed very complicated, the shopkeeper appeared nonchalant as he carefully poured the hot water into the pot, over the tea, into the sharing pitcher and then into the cups. I also took pleasure in watching the shopkeeper as he pried small pieces of the compressed tea from the disk that was wrapped in delicate rice paper.

Four hours later I was dizzy from all the tea, the smoke filled room, and the chatter I didn't comprehend, but I was also hooked on this new discovery. My bladder was begging me to leave, Emily needed to get home, my eyes were burning from all the smoke, and yet my palette was alive and I wanted more. As I stood up to bid farewell to my new friends, I was elated when they invited me to return the next day.

The man with the beard asked me to write down how I became a Christian. He said he wanted to include it in his next book. He also said I could bring a friend. And this I did. I typed up my testimony and used software to translate it. I called an American friend who was fluent in Chinese. He and I returned to the small room in the small shop. We quickly found our seats around the table and started drinking tea—but not for four hours. No, that wasn't enough. This time we stayed for five hours, interrupted with a short break for Chinese noodle soup with steamy chunks of vegetables and fatty mutton.

When we returned from lunch, the man with the beard laid out a long piece of rice paper, picked up a calligraphy brush and dabbed it in a bottle of ink. He then gracefully penned a special word for the shop-keeper to hang in the tea drinking room, near the bull's skull on the mustard-colored wall. A very satisfying day and a nice complement to the *pu-erh* tea, new friendship, and a cool spring day in a foreign land.

A Thousand Cups of Tea

BY STEFANI HITE

One cup of tea led to another...and another...and before we knew it, our lives would always be different.

I grew up in places all over the world and have always loved traveling. But becoming a teacher and having a kid ties you down a bit. So when my husband suggested we think about running a student exchange program, I was both intrigued and horrified. It would be great to travel again, even to countries I had visited as a child. But with middle school students? I mean...really?

Nevertheless, we established an e-mail relationship with a School Head in Winchester, England. With some back and forth, we managed to settle on some dates and advertised for students. Twenty-five hearty 7th and 8th graders took the plunge. We booked tickets, organized trips, exchanged e-mail addresses, and were off and running.

The British visit to the U.S. went extremely well. There were a few bumps and bruised egos, but we organized visits to New York City, Philadelphia, and Washington, D.C. Kids had parties and parents arranged sleepovers. Before we knew it, they were leaving for the airport to fly home. Kids were crying all over our yard while we frantically loaded suitcases onto the bus and wondered how it was going to turn around on our street.

Phew. We collapsed after a job well done—but that was just the half of it. Our turn to visit England was only a few months away. This would not be luxury travel or tourist sightseeing; we were going to live with families and experience the "every day" of their lives.

Our trip was exciting, nerve-wracking, and exhausting. (We lost a record of five passports between security and the gate, leading me to insist on travel wallets thereafter.) We arrived at the school, greeted by balloons and cries of delight as the students were reunited with their partners. One by one they drove off and we finally left for the tiny cottage that would be home for two weeks.

"You must be shattered!" Julia greeted us as we cautiously entered the kitchen. "Sit down and I'll make you a cup of tea."

And so we drank the first of many....

First we had to learn the difference between the teas offered. "I like English Breakfast," Joseph declared. "I can't abide that wussy, flowery Earl Grey my wife drinks." Then there was the issue of milk and/or sugar. "You really want to drink it black?" Julia marveled at my request. Turns out, my little family would require three different preparations: black for me, black with (a large amount of) sugar for my husband Gary, and our seven-year-old daughter, Cory, requested milk and sugar—with a smidgen of tea.

We grabbed the variety of chipped, flowered mugs and sat down in the garden, relaxing in the warm English sunshine, sipping our cups of tea. Thus began an outstanding experience we felt compelled to repeat over and over.

The student exchange program couldn't have been any more spectacular. We visited historic sites, sat in on lessons in our host school, and were invited to dinners by the students' families. Whether we were chatting in the teachers' lounge at school, or enjoying a high cream tea at the local manor, we requested our personal preferences and drank a cuppa with gusto. We downed dreadful British Rail tea traveling on the trains. We drank delicious tea in a bakery on the Winchester High Street. We huddled over Styrofoam cups of tea in the driving rain in Portsmouth. We slurped exotic tea while giggling at our "busking" students in Bath. We took high tea at Fortnum and Mason in London (with scones and clotted cream, of course.) And we enjoyed a cup at the end of a long day, visiting with our new friends.

During our exchanges over the past several years, we've matched up hundreds of students. Our first "alumni" group is now attending college and the students report that the opportunity to become immersed in a non-American culture had a profound effect on their lives. Families have continued to maintain contact and some visit each other each year.

Was it all perfect? Of course not. During one visit to England, I insisted on dragging our group to see "Richard III" performed at the Globe Theatre. This was not everyone's cup of tea, especially a 13-year-old American teenager. During the third act, I noticed Dustin looking particularly agonized. I moved next to him and said, "I know you're not really appreciating this now, but just think...one day, you'll be in college, and you'll be talking to a pretty girl who's majoring in English Lit. When you tell her that you saw 'Richard III' at the Globe, you will definitely get a date with her!" Dustin simply rolled his eyes and asked if he could wait in the lobby.

Fast forward six years later. Gary and I were sitting in a Starbucks drinking tea (of course). Dustin walked in—now a college sophomore. He greeted us enthusiastically and filled us in on his life in college, his plans, and that he's still in contact with his English partner from the first exchange. As we stood up to leave, Dustin turned to me and casually asked, "Do you remember what you said to me about 'Richard III' and how I'd get a date because of seeing that play?"

"Yes!" I replied, anxiously awaiting the punch line, sure he was going to announce that he now has a fabulous English Lit-majoring girlfriend.

"Yeah...It hasn't happened." Dustin grinned, and we all laughed.

Our lives now are too busy, our daughter off and running in too many directions. Running another exchange seems out of the question. But I think back to all the cups of tea we drank on our exchanges...each one representing a connection with kids and families far away. Perhaps there are more cups of tea in our future....

Miyanoshita

BY SIR EDWIN ARNOLD

Excerpted from Japan as Seen and Described by Famous Authors, *1909.*[1]

About fifty miles away from Yokohama, along the seashore, and then by a sharp turn into the highlands which are grouped around Fuji-San, lies embosomed the lovely and salubrious Japanese health resort, whence I am writing this. Fifteen hundred feet above the Pacific and the hot plains, we have escaped hither, for a time, shunning the now somewhat sultry weather of the capital and its ubiquitous mosquitoes, which are more bloodthirsty and importunate in Tokyo than anywhere. The *ka,* bred in the rice-fields and ditches of Nippon, is truly a most relentless and insatiable little pest, against which natives and foreigners equally defend themselves with *kaya* or nets of green muslin, made either large enough to cover a European four-poster, or small enough to place over a sleeping baby. At this season of the year you may indeed see hundreds of tiny brown Japanese infants sleeping, stark naked, beneath what looks like a green meat-safe, where the flies and mosquitoes cannot get at them. Not only the babies, moreover, but their fathers, mothers, "sisters, cousins, and aunts," and the Japanese world in general, largely discard clothing as the July heats come on; and, in the country especially, one sees at this time more of the people—in a very literal sense—than during the cooler weather. One result is to disclose the really splendid illustrations with which

---

1   [Certain British spellings and archaic terms have been amended. Ed.]

a great many of the men are adorned by the tattooer. The *jinriki-sha* pullers in particular are oft-times gorgeously pictorial from nape to heel, and you may study for an hour the volutes, arabesques, flowers, gods, dragons, and poetical inscriptions on the back of your coolie as you bowl along, without exhausting the wealth of design and coloring upon the saffron surface of his skin.

The journey hither from Yokohama leads by railway through interminable rice fields lying between the hills and the sea, all the spare patches now "green as grass" with the sprouting roots of the *ine*.[2] Last year Inaré, the deity of the rice plant gave Japan a bad harvest, and the poor are greatly suffering in consequence. But this year all looks well for a bumper crop, and the purple and silver of the iris and lily-clumps—everywhere at present blossoming—fringe verdant squares of exuberant promised plenty, where the great dragon-flies buzz, and the frogs croak all day long. A run of two hours brings you past Kamakura, the region of the old glories of the warlike house—which ruled Japan from A.D. 1192, to the middle of the fifteenth century—past Enoshima, the ever beautiful "Isle of Dragons," to Kodzu, where you take a tramcar, and bump through the town of Odawara to Yumoto village, whence the ascent to Miyanoshita commences. The ladies and the luggage ride up the three miles of hilly road in *kuruma* drawn by *no-nim-biki*.[3] The gentlemen, glad of a little rural walk after the hot streets of Tokyo, contend with the ascent on foot. We reach Miyanoshita just as the lights begin to twinkle in the windows of the two hotels which receive the innumerable visitors to this green and pleasant glen. A hot spring, slightly mineral, has created Miyanoshita, affording perpetual and pleasant bathing; and the air, whether it breathes from the sea below or from the thickly-wooded hills above, is always fresh and pleasant.

To inhale that air, and to bathe in the soft waters heated for you in the subterranean furnaces, are the main business of life in this hill village. The only industry of the place, apart from guides, teahouses, and waiting *musumës,* is the manufacture of all kinds of small articles from the wood of the various timber trees growing on the hills around.

---

2   "*Ine*" is a rice plant.
3   A "*kuruma*" is a carriage or chariot. "*No-nim-biki*" suggests that it was drawn by two men.

Some of these are of incredible ingenuity in construction and neatness of finish, making the most elaborate work of Tunbridge Wells[4] utterly commonplace. Many of the woods employed, such as the camphor, the ivy, the *kaki, kari* and *sendan*,[5] are of great beauty, and there seems to be almost nothing that a Japan turner cannot produce from them. He sells you, for a few *sen,* a box of ivy-wood delicately grained and polished, containing a dozen lovely little saucers of the same material; or a lunch-box which folds into next to nothing until you want it, and then expands into a complete and handsome table service. Sellers of photographs are also numerous, and softly importunate, for the Japanese have become very skillful with the camera. When you have purchased all the photographs and wooden knickknacks which you desire, the next thing is to organize excursions into the wild and beautiful wilderness of mountains everywhere surrounding you. These must be performed either on foot or on chairs lashed on bamboo poles, and carried upon the shoulders of four of the sturdy hill men of the district. The paths are very steep and narrow, and the foothold very often merely the loose stones of a mountain stream. Yet the sturdy *ninsoku*[6] trudge along, up hill and down dale, in their sandals of rope, apparently insensible to fatigue, or sufficiently refreshed from time to time by a cup of pale tea and a sugar biscuit, and willingly accepting fifty *sen,* or about eighteen pence, for a tremendous day's work. With a thin blue calico coat, a blue handkerchief tied around the close-cropped head, and their small brass tobacco pipes stuck in their girdles, they chatter gaily as they trot along under the bamboo poles, shifting these every now and then from shoulder to shoulder with a little harmonious murmur of "*go-issho*," which means "at the same honorable time," i.e., "all together, boys." Arrived at the teahouse, they patiently pick from their legs the leeches which have fastened there in the wet and narrow forest paths, wipe the profuse perspiration from their brown

---

4   Royal Tunbridge Wells is a borough in west Kent, England that was considered a destination for the upper class.

5   "*Kaki*" is a Japanese persimmon tree. "*Kari*" is another wood that is carved; it is often used for chess sets. "*Sendan*" or "*Melia azedarach*" is also known as white cedar and is part of the Mahogany family.

6   "*Ninsoku*" are laborers.

necks, smoke a pipe or two, and slowly sip a cup of the "honorable hot tea," and are then ready to trudge on again for another *ri*[7] under their heavy burdens.

Charming and instructive beyond description are some of the expeditions which may thus be undertaken from Miyanoshita as a center, the hills containing all sorts of natural wonders, as well as being of wonderful beauty in regard of scenery. We made two out of many favorite explorations yesterday and the day before; on the first occasion to the mountain lake of Hakoné, on the second to no less formidably-named a spot than "the Great Hell"—O Jigoku. The general character of the country being the same, I will make one description serve for the impressions of the two journeys.

The Hakoné Mountains are for the most part intensely green in aspect, "darkly, deeply, beautifully green"—of a green to make an artist despair, it is so magnificently monotonous, and beyond imitation by the palette. This results principally from the long bamboo grass everywhere growing over the highland country, which, though it rises to the height of eight or ten feet, presents the appearance of an unbroken verdant mantle of herbage rolling in light waves before the wind. The trees—chiefly beech, fir of various kinds, and oak—grow at one time sparsely, at another in extensive groves, from the jungle of the dwarf bamboo; intermixed with which are a few inconspicuous wild flowers—white andromedas and spiræs, yellow lilies, wild hydrangea, dog roses, and the Canterbury bell. Little or no animal life is to be seen; the cover seems too dense for four-footed creatures, but on the less-wooded mountains the fox and badger exist, and there are deer, wild boar, and monkeys of a single species, to be found not far off. A lark—almost exactly identical with the English species—sings the familiar carol as we pass, and an oriole, which flutes very sweetly, is seen and heard; but the general silence of the mountains is remarkable and almost unbroken, except by the noise of streams everywhere descending. Some of these smoke in the cool hillside air, and discolor the stones with sulphurous or mineral deposits, notably at Ko-ji-go-

---

7   A "*ri*" is a bit less than 2½ miles.

ku, near to Ashino-yu, where some of us enjoyed the luxury of hot sulphur baths, and found them immensely refreshing in the middle of a long walk. The central spot, however, for witnessing this kind of phenomenon is at the "Great Hell" itself, near to the pass of O Tomi Toge, from which a glorious view is obtained of the ever wonderful Fuji-San. There was nothing to indicate that we were approaching a spot to justify the name given to this place, except the sudden appearance of many large dead trees, which had been killed by the fatal breath emanating from the *solfataras*[8] near. The hillside at large spreads on either hand as fair and green as before, with waving bamboo grass and silvery flowers of the *deutzia*,[9] and white bells of the Japan anemone. The earliest intimation was by the nostrils, which become abruptly aware of odors distinctly infernal; and on reaching a solitary farmhouse you come in sight of a torrent, running over black and speckled rocks, on a bed yellow as the rind of an orange. The ladies must now leave their chairs and toil by a steep ascent round a shoulder of the valley, from which issues this Japanese Styx; and by a perilous and broken path, winding now through the thickets, now along the brink of a crumbling precipice, we come suddenly in sight of a gully, destitute of every shred of vegetation, and hideous with all the Cocytian colors associated with flame and smoke, death and desolation, ruin and ravage. It is a corner of the world abandoned to despair—a mountain hearth on fire—which one beholds; a nook of nature whence everything lovely and living has been banished to give vent to the secret forces of the under world. The earth all around is poisoned and parti-colored with livid blotches and gangrenes; the rocks are crusted with a leprous tetter; pimples and ulcers of purple and black and yellow break out from the level spaces. Some of these are alive with an evil activity, and hiss and fume and bubble, emitting jets of fat yellow and green smoke, with now and then a crackling noise when the crust sinks in, to open by and by at another black and yellow gash in the diseased ground. It is not safe even to stand near the melancholy amphitheater where reek

---

8   "Solfataras" are volcanic areas where sulfuric gases are released.
9   "Deutzia" is a genus of shrubs, mostly with white flowers.

these caldrons of Acheron.[10] To pass along the black edge of the stream itself and into this ghastly corry would be rash in the extreme, for no one knows where the surface may not yield, and suddenly plunge the foot or limb into a bath of boiling sulphur. A lady of our acquaintance was severely burned here some time ago, and a Russian officer lost his life in the treacherous morass of flame.

I am requested by an amiable and charming young lady of our party to inscribe upon her bamboo staff the Japanese name of the place—which she will certainly never visit again—together with some suitable record. Sitting out of reach of the winds from Hades, under a great cryptomeria, blasted by its neighborhood, I carve on the Japanese alpenstock a verse which she means to preserve:

"Staff, which to O Jigoku went,
Good news to Sinners tell;
Demons may climb to Paradise,
Now angels walk to Hell."

And yet, just over the ridge, spreads a scene as beautiful as that just quitted is forbidding. On the slopes of the O Tomi Pass box-trees and the milky-blossomed *asemi*,[11] with the pines and bamboos, the azaleas and lilies, make the mountain fair and glad again; and Fuji-San is seen towering up in perfect beauty at the end of a vast valley. The snow is almost gone from the Lady of Mountains. Just here and there are visible, if I might quote my own new poem, the "Light of the World":

"Dark hollows where sad winter hides away
From summer, with the snow still in her lap."

By another path the matchless mount may be seen looking down upon the deep waters of Hakoné—a great lake of unknown depth, and perpetual coldness, lying two thousand feet above the sea. Hakoné Lake has for its Japanese name *Yoshi-no-Midzu-Umi*, or the "water of the reeds," and is a very beautiful highland sea, the abode, it is said, of supernatural beings, till a Buddhist priest penetrated these recesses and gave to the world knowledge and possession of lovely and cool

---

10 The "Acheron Cauldron" is an extinct volcano.
11 "*Asemi*" is another name for *Pieris japonica*, an evergreen ornamental shrub with cascading flowers.

Hakoné. We drink to the pious memory of Mangwan Shónin as we sit in the upper gallery of the teahouse looking over the rolling blue wavelets of the lake. Close by Japanese woodmen are cutting fir-trees into thin boards, to make *ori*, the boxes in which sweetmeats and cakes are presented. We return in drenching rain, but well rewarded for this and for all our exertions by the splendid scenery and the countless objects of interest on the road. Perhaps it would not have rained if we had remembered to put some stones in the lap of the great rock image of Jizo, whom we passed in accomplishing the ascent. He is the god of travelers and the protector of children, and the correct thing is to pay him the little attention alluded to. As we wend homewards through the picturesque village of Kiga, we stop to look again at the wonderful fish in the gardens of a teahouse near at hand. Swimming about in a pool under a little waterfall there are exhibited some hundreds of variegated carp—the Japanese *koi*—which are of every imaginable brilliancy of color—purple, russet, citron, saffron, orange, rose-red, gold and silver. They are tamer than any pigeons, and come voraciously to the bank to be fed, scrambling for slices of bean cake, and putting their gold and brown noses high out of the water in their struggles to secure the morsel. When a piece of cake falls on the dry rock, near the water, they try to throw themselves on shore, and even use their fins for legs in their eagerness to obtain the prize. The fish in the opening story of the *Arabian Nights,* who were colored blue, yellow, white, and red, and who talked in the frying-pan, could not have been more marvelous in hue, and certainly not more intelligent.

Memorandum of an Excursion to the Tea Hills

by G. J. Gordon, Esq. (Communicated by Dr. N. Wallich)

Excerpted from the Journal of the Asiatic Society of Bengal, *1835.*[1]

Having been disappointed in my expectations of being enabled to visit the Bohea hills, I was particularly anxious to have an opportunity of personally inspecting the tea plantations in the black-tea district of the next greatest celebrity, in order to satisfy myself regarding several points relative to the cultivation, on which the information afforded by different individuals was imperfect or discordant.

Mr. Gutzlaff, accordingly, took considerable pains to ascertain, for me, from the persons who visited the ship, the most eligible place for landing with the view of visiting the Ankoy hills; and Hwuy Taou bay was at length fixed upon as the most safe and convenient, both from its being out of the way of observation of any high Chinese function-aries, who might be desirous of thwarting our project, and from its being equally near the tea hills, as any other part of the coast, at which we could land. As laid down in the map of the Jesuits, there is a small river, which falls into the head of this bay, by which we were told we should be able to proceed a good part of our way into the interior. We should, of course, have preferred proceeding by the Ankoy river, which is represented in the same map as having its source to the west

---

1   [Certain British spellings have been amended. Ed.]

of Ngau-ki-hyen and falling into the river which washes Sneu-chee-foia, were it not for the apprehension of being impeded or altogether intercepted by the public functionaries of that city. In order to make ourselves as independent as possible of assistance from the people, we resolved to dispense with every article of equipment which was not necessary for health and safety. The weather had for some days been comparatively cold, the thermometer falling to 55° at sunrise, and not getting higher than 66° during the day, so that warm clothing not only became agreeable, but could not be dispensed with during the nights; arms for our defence against violence from *any* quarter, formed likewise a part of our equipments, and, trusting to money, and Mr. Gutzlaff's intimate knowledge of the language and of the people, for the rest, we left the ship on the morning of Monday, 10th November, proceeding in the ship's long boat towards the head of the bay, where the town of Hwuy Taou is situated.

The party in the boat consisted of Mr. Gutzlaff, Mr. Ryder (second officer of the "Colonel Young"), Mr. Nicholson, late quartermaster of the "Water Witch," whom I had engaged for the projected Woo-re journey, and myself, one native servant and eight *lascar*s.[2] The wind being unfavorable, we made rather slow progress by rowing, but taking for our guidance the masts of some of the junks which we observed lying behind a point of land, we pulled to get under it, in order to avoid the strength of the ebb tide, which was now setting against us. In attempting to round the point, however, we grounded, and soon found that it was impossible to get into the river on that side, on account of sand-banks, which were merely covered at high water, and that it was necessary to make a considerable circuit seaward to be able to enter. This we accomplished, but not till 1:00 A.M. At this time a light breeze fortunately springing up, we got on very well for some time, but were again obliged to anchor, at ¼ past 2, from want of water....

...At daylight we found that there was not six inches of water in any part of the channel, and from the boat we stepped at once upon dry sand. The survey from the bank showed us plainly that it would

---

2   A "*lascar*" was an East Indian sailor who was hired to work on a British ship.

be impossible to proceed any farther by water. We accordingly prepared to march on foot, taking with us three *lascar*s who might relieve each other in carrying our cloak-bag of blankets and great coats, as well as some cold meat. We ordered the people to prepare a meal as fast as possible, intending to make a long stretch at first starting, and Mr. Nicholson was directed to remain in charge of the boat with five *lascar*s, to move her down under the bridge on the return of the flood, and there to wait our return for four or five days. Crowds of people now began to crowd round the boat, moved by mere curiosity. Mr. Gutzlaff induced some of them to get ducks and fowls for the use of the boat's crew, and, strange to say, prevailed on one man to become our guide, and on two others to undertake to carry our baggage, as soon as we should be a little farther off from the town and out of the way of observation....

...It was, however, past 9 o'clock before Mr. Ryder had completed his arrangements for the boat's crew, and the sun was already powerful. We were soon joined by our guide and the coolies, and our cavalcade winding along the footpaths, which are the only roads to be met with, made an imposing appearance. Mr. Gutzlaff and the guide led the way, followed by a *lascar* with a boarding pike; next came the baggage, attended by a *lascar* similarly armed. I followed, with pistols and attended by a *lascar* armed with a cutlass. Mr. Ryder, carrying a fowling piece and pistols, brought up the rear.

Skirting the town of Hwuy Taou, we proceeded in a N. N. E. direction at a moderate pace for an hour and a half, when we stopped at a temple and refreshed ourselves with tea. Nothing could be more kind or more civil than the manners of the people towards us hitherto, and if we could have procured conveyance here, so as to have escaped walking in the heat of the day, loaded as we were with heavy woollen clothes, we should have had nothing farther to desire; as it was, my feet began already to feel uncomfortable from swelling, and after another hour's marching, I was obliged to propose a halt till the cool of the evening. Fortunately, we found, however, that chairs were procurable at the place, and we accordingly engaged them at half-dollar each. These were formed in the slightest manner, and carried on bamboo poles, having a cross bar at the extremities, which rested on the back of the bearer's neck, apparently a most insecure as well as inconvenient position; but, as the poles were at the same time grasped by the hands, the danger of a false step was lessened. We had not advanced above a mile and a half before the bearers declared they must eat, and to enable them to do so, they must get more money. With this impudent demand we thought it best to comply, giving them an additional real each. After an hour's further progress, we were set down at a town near the foot of the first pass which we had to cross. There the bearers clamorously insisted on an additional payment before they would carry us any further. This we resisted, and by Mr. Gutzlaff's eloquence gained the whole of the villagers, who crowded round us, to join in exclaiming against the attempted extortion. Seeing this, the rogues submitted and again took us up. Mr. G. mentioned that, while we were passing through another village, the people of which begged the bearers to set us down that they might have a look at us, they demanded 100 cash as the condition of compliance. The country through which we passed swarmed with inhabitants, and exhibited the highest degree of cultivation, though it was only in a few spots that we saw any soil which would be deemed in Bengal tolerably good; rice, the sweet potatoes, and sugarcane were the principal articles of culture. We had now to ascend a barren and rugged mountain, which seemed destined by nature to set the hand of man at defiance....

...At half past four, we arrived at a rather romantic valley, which was to be our halting place for the day. We proposed to the bearers to carry us on another stage next day, but for this they had the impudence to ask five dollars per chair. This, of course, we would not listen to for a moment, and were afterwards happy that we got rid of such rascals, as good bearers and on moderate terms were procurable at the place. The name of this village is Lung-tze-kio. It seems once to have been a place of greater importance than now, exhibiting marks of dilapidation and decay....

...*Nov.* 12th—Got into our chairs at a quarter past 6:00 A.M., and proceeded along a narrow rugged dell to a town called Koe-Bo. Several nice looking hamlets were seen on the way. The people were engaged in reaping the rice, which seemed heavy and well-filled in the ear. In several places, I observed that they had taken the pains to tie clumps of rice stalk together for mutual support. Sugarcane is bound in the same way, and, for additional security, the outside canes are mutually supported by diagonal leaves, which serve at the same time to form them into a kind of fence. The leaves are not tied up round the stalks as in Bengal; the cane is slender, white, hard, and by no means juicy or rich; yet, bating the black fungus powder, which is very prevalent, their surface is healthy, and close growing in a remarkable degree. We arrived at Koe-Bo at eight o'clock, and finding we could get water conveyance for part of the way on which we were proceeding, we engaged a boat for that purpose. After a hearty breakfast we embarked at 10:00 A.M., amidst crowds of people who covered the banks of the river at the *ghát*....[3]

...We had been in vain all yesterday and today looking out for a glimpse of tea plantations on some of the rugged and black looking hills close in view, though at almost every place where we halted, we were assured that such were to be found hard by. At 3:00 P.M. we reached a town near the foot of the pass by which we were to reach Taou-ee, the place of our destination. There we proposed selling our gold, which for the sake of lightness, I had brought with me in preference to silver, not doubting that I should find little difficulty in exchanging it at its proper relative value whenever required. In this, however, we had been disappointed at our last abode, and we were therefore much vexed at learning from our conductors that the inhabitants of Aou-ee were of such a character that the less we had to do with them and the shorter our stay amongst them, the better....

...The hill we had now to ascend was more rugged, and in some places more abrupt, than that over which we were first carried; and though we had set out at three o'clock, the sun had set long before we came to the end of our journey. The moon was unfortunately obscured by clouds, so that nothing could be more unpleasant than the unfortunate *hits* our toes were constantly making against stones, and

---

3   A "*ghát*" is a broad set of steps or a passage that leads down to a pond or river.

the equally unfortunate *misses*, where an unexpected step downwards made us with a sudden jerk throw our weight on one leg. At length we reached a village at the further end of the pass, the inhabitants of which were so kind as to light us on the remainder of our way, by burning bundles of grass, to the eminent danger of setting fire to their rice fields, now ripe for the sickle. Arrived at Taou-ee, we were hospitably received by the family of our guide, and soon surrounded by wondering visitors.

Mr. Gutzlaff speedily selected one or two of the most intelligent of them, and obtained from them ready answers to a variety of questions regarding the cultivation of the plant. They informed him that the seed now used for propagating the plant was all produced on the spot, though the original stock of this part of the country was brought from *Wae-eshan*; that it ripened in the tenth or eleventh month, and was immediately put into the ground where it was intended to grow, several being put together into one hole, as the greater part was always abortive, that the sprouts appeared in the third month after the seeds were put into the ground; that the hole into which the seeds were thrown are from three to four inches deep, and that, as the plants grow, the earth is gathered up a little round their root; that leaves are taken from the plants when they are three years old, and that there are from most plants four pluckings in the year. No manure is used, nor is goodness of soil considered of consequence, neither are the plants *irrigated*. Each shrub may yield about a *tael* of dry tea annually (about a twelfth of a pound). A *mow*[4] of ground may contain three or four hundred plants. The land tax is 300 cash (720 to a dollar) per *mow*. The cultivation and gathering of the leaves being performed by families without the assistance of hired laborers, no rate of wages can be specified; but as the curing of the leaf is an art that requires some skill, persons are employed for that particular purpose, who are paid at the rate of one dollar per *pecul*[5] of fresh leaf, equal to five dollars per *pecul* of dry tea. The fire-place used is only temporary, and all the utensils as well as fuel are furnished by the owner of the tea. They stated that the

4 A "*mow*" is equal to 240 square paces.
5 A "*pecul*" or *picul* is a weight of about 133 ¹/₃ lbs. (approximately 60 kg).

leaves are heated and rolled seven or eight times. The green leaf yields one-fifth of its weight of dry tea. The best tea fetches, on the spot, 23 dollars per *pecul*, (133⅓ lbs.) and the principal part of the produce is consumed within the province, or exported in baskets to Taiwan. That the prevailing winds are north-westerly. The easterly winds are the only winds injurious to the plants. Hoar frost is common during the winter months, and snow falls occasionally, but does not lie long, nor to a greater depth than three or four inches. The plant is never injured by excessive cold, and thrives from 10 to 20 years. It is some-times destroyed by a worm that eats up the pith and converts both stem and branches into tubes, and by a gray lichen which principally attacks very old plants. The period of growth is limited to six or seven years, when the plant has attained its greatest size. The spots where the tea is planted are scattered over great part of the country, but there are no hills appropriated entirely to its culture. No ground, in fact, is formed into a tea plantation that is fit for any other species of cultiva-tion, except, perhaps, that of the dwarf pine already alluded to, or the *Camellia Obeifora*. Mr. Gutzlaff understood them to say that the plant blossoms twice a year, in the eighth moon, or September, and again in winter; but that the latter flowering is abortive. In this I apprehend there was some misapprehension, as seed of full size, though not ripe, were proffered to me in considerable quantities early in September, and none were found on the plants which we saw. I suspect that the people meant to say that the seeds take eight months to ripen, which accords with other accounts. We wished much to have spent the fol-lowing day (the 13ᵗʰ) in prosecuting our inquiries and observations at Tawand and its neighborhood, but this was rendered impracticable by the state of our finances. We had plenty of gold, but no one could be found who would purchase it with silver at any price. We, therefore, resolved on making the most of our time by an early excursion in the morning previous to setting out on our return.

We accordingly got up at day-break, and proceeded to visit the spot were the plants were cultivated. We were much struck with the variety of the appearance of the plants; some of the shrubs scarcely rose to the height of a cubit above the ground, and those were so very bushy that a hand could not be thrust between the branches. They were also very thickly covered with leaves, but these were very small, scarcely above ¾ inch in length. In the same bed were other plants with stems four feet in height, far less branchy and with leaves 1½ to 2 inches in length. The produce of great and small was said to be equal. The distance from center to center of the plants was about 4½ feet, and the plants seemed to average about two feet in diameter. Though the ground was not terraced, it was formed into beds that were partly leveled. These were perfectly well dressed as in garden cultivation, and each little plantation was surrounded by a low stone fence, and a trench. There was no shade, but the places selected for the cultivation were generally in the bottoms of hills, where there was a good deal of shelter on two sides, and the slope comparatively easy. I should reckon the site of the highest plantations we visited to be about 700 feet above the plain; but those we saw at that height, and even less, appeared more thriving, probably from having somewhat better soil, though the best is little more than mere sand. I have taken specimens from three or four gardens. Contrary to what we had been told the preceding night, I found that each garden had its little nursery, where the plants were growing to the height of four or five inches, as closely set as they could stand; from which I conceive that the tea plant requires absolutely a *free* soil, *not wet* and *not clayey,* but of a texture that will retain moisture; and the best site is one not so low as that at which water is apt to spring from the sides of a hill, nor so high as to be exposed to the violence of stormy weather. There is no use in attempting to cultivate the plant on an easterly exposure, though it is sufficiently hardy to bear almost any degree of dry cold.

By half-past 10:00 A.M. we set out on our return, in chairs which we were fortunate enough to procure at this village, and reached the banks of the river at Aou-ee a little before one o'clock. In the first part of our way, we passed by some more tea plantations on very sterile ground. One in a very bleak situation, with nothing but coarse red sand by way of soil, seemed to be abandoned. Our reception at Aou-ee was much more civil than it had been the preceding day; the people suggested that we should remain there till a boat could be procured. The day, however, being tolerably cool, we crossed the river, and proceeded on foot along its banks to Kre-bo, where we arrived about 4:00 P.M....

...We found that one of the seed contractors had despatched a quantity of Bohea seeds, arrived during our absence, with a letter stating expectation of being able to send a further supply and to procure cultivators, who would join the ship in the eleventh or twelfth month. On the same evening I embarked on the Fairy, and reached Lintin on Monday the 17th November, with my tea seeds, just one week after our landing at Hwuy Taou to explore the Hwuy tea hills.

I have been more minute in my details of this little expedition, than may at first sight appear needful, with the view of showing the precise degree and kind of danger and difficulty attending such attempts. Our expectation was, at leaving the ship, that we should reach the head of the bay by nine or 10 o'clock A.M., and attain a considerable distance from Hwuy Taou the same day, and thus have a chance of passing without attracting the notice of any of the *wanfoo*, or government officers. Had we waited to ask their permission, it would of course have been refused, and we should have been directed in the most authoritative manner to return to the ship. We were not a little alarmed when aground in the morning, lest the old gentleman who measured our boat should have deemed it his duty to intercept our progress; but we took care to go on with preparations for our march, as if nothing of the kind was apprehended. It is this sort of conduct alone that will succeed in China. Any sign of hesitation is fatal. Had we shown any marks of alarm, every one would have kept aloof for fear of being implicated in the danger which we seemed to dread; on the other hand, a confident bearing, and the testimony borne by the manner in which we were armed, that we would not passively allow ourselves to be plundered by authority, inspired the like confidence in all those with whom we had to do; for the rest of the narrative shows that from the people left to themselves we experienced nothing but marks of the utmost kindness and good nature, except indeed, where money was to be got....

The Invisible Companionship of Tea

BY WINNIE W. YU

A decade ago, my buddies and I climbed Hua Shan, known as the most treacherous mountain range in China. Expert rock climbers challenge themselves on this mountain, and the week before we embarked, apparently, ten climbers died in one week. It is little wonder then that throughout history, only Taoist hermits lived up there in those shrouded peaks, invisible and seeming to float in and out of the clouds. But you'd never see many temples or structures. The hermits lived in caves, carved out of the bare, vertical faces of the boulders. At 1,600 meters or so, Hua Shan was not really impossibly tall. Instead, it was the scary verticalness that many were challenged by. The bare rock surfaces were carved with slivers of shallow footholds, and we would ascend with the help of metal chains.

The first day of climbing and hiking was a straight eleven hours, a test of endurance, nerves, and the resistance to look down. By the second day, we were in some pretty far reaches and no birds or even ants were seen anywhere. Pine trees jut out of the crevices of the rocks. A sea of clouds were under foot. Many cave dwellings of the hermits were visible but impossible to get to. On the second day, we came upon the most intriguing cave of all: an inset on a sheer boulder the size of a closet, just tall enough for someone to sit cross-legged, and also just wide enough. Straw bedding formed a comfortable cushion for the meditator. A thatched screen of some kind served to shield the cave opening from the elements. No one was home, so I sat down on the straw mat, and noticed that the cave interior was just deep enough to hold one person. Looking out into the sea of white clouds, a sheer vertical drop of 5,000 feet below churned my stomach. Momentarily, I noticed something to my side, and it was a small stove powered by some sticks of charcoal. On top of the stove, a teapot. I sniffed briefly, and the tea inside must have been of a fermented tea like a *pu-erh*.

I sat waiting in the cave for some time, but the hermit did not return. Was this his entire home? Possibly. We had passed by many caves belonging to other Taoist hermits. They practice immortality by living on the dew drops on the morning plants, and flower petals mashed into wine. They can scale Hua Shan with the lightning speed of monkeys, and indeed, watching some of them fly up and down the mountain, you can barely see their straw shoes touch the rocky steps. They practice circulating their *chi*, and various esoteric breathing and internal exercises completely unknown to the modern city dweller. But the one I did not meet apparently practiced drinking tea as part of his meditation. Did he subsist on tea alone? Or was tea his one and final worldly attachment? Did he travel to share his tea with another hermit that day we chanced upon his cave, or was tea his only friend? Seeing his teapot and imagining who this hermit was made an indelible connection for me.

Hua Shan was a mystical place. No tea bushes can grow on it; the rocks are too smooth and steep for any soil to settle on them. But the spirit of tea was abundant, the idea of transformation, of possibilities, of cultivation and exploration of self—the invisible experience of tea on Hua Shan. Tea has always been connected with society, of culture and sharing. But the people who dared to live on Hua Shan, took with them the one worldly attachment: tea. An old Chinese proverb came to mind: One can live without food for weeks, but not without tea for even one day! For some of us, tea was our constant companion, if not sometimes, the only companion.

If one can point to a seminal point where the idea of Teance[1] was created, this experience was certainly one such defining moment. Tea is unlike other beverages. It connects invisibly through time and space, to the past and to others who find solace in tea. The companionship that is in that cup extends beyond the drinker's immediate surroundings. With my tea, I am connected to the Taoists who live alone inside a cave, thousands of feet up a cliff, wondering when they will find their next batch of tea. When I am drinking tea at Hua Shan, I am connected to my friends in Berkeley, struggling with their last bit of High Mountain *Oolong*, wondering when I will bring back another batch. Thus, Teance was created to connect the world of tea lovers everywhere, by importing tea directly from these remote mountain regions where they grow. The city-dweller can then share that universe of tea together in spirit with their Taoist counterpart from thousands of miles away, or with tea drinkers from thousands of years ago. Tea transcends time and space.

---

1   The Teance Fine Teas store in Berkeley, CA.

Tea in Tibet

BY ELIZABETH KNIGHT

"Tea can remove worry as well as thirst." —Tibetan saying

One sweltering hot summer, bored to tears with my eighth-grade life, I escaped Dayton, Ohio by reading James Hilton's *Lost Horizon*. I was enchanted by the tale of stranded travelers who found sanctuary at a hidden Himalayan monastery, called Shangri-La. Years later, I discovered that the first novel published in paperback had been made into a movie directed by Frank Capra. Munching popcorn in a darkened theater on Manhattan's Upper West Side, captivated by a revival of the classic, I never dreamed that I'd ever visit Tibet.

But last spring, a friendly Boston-based importer, whom I'd met on a tea tour of Darjeeling and Assam, told me about a China tea tour hosted by Dan Robertson, owner of The Tea House in Naperville, Illinois. Delighted to discover that the tour included a side trip to the legendary "Land of the Snows," as well as an opportunity to sip butter tea with a local family, I signed up.

Tibet shares a border with Sichuan and Yunnan, two Chinese provinces that cultivated tea as early as the Qin Dynasty (221–206 B.C.). Although Tibetan troops had captured tea, and other luxury goods, in numerous border wars, legend tells that tea from Sichuan was introduced—along with medicine, vegetable seeds, textiles, and the calendar when Princess Wencheng married Tibetan king, Songtsen Gampo (A.D. 617–650). The dainty Chinese bride supposedly drank tea to dilute the powerful taste of yak milk. Later, she mixed tea and milk, adding pine nuts, and *ghee* (clarified butter) to make a nutritious drink.

Tibetans traditionally ate meat and dairy products because the cold climate and thin air of the "roof of the world" made it difficult to grow fruits and vegetables. Princess Wencheng's new beverage acted as a stimulant and fortified nomadic mountain dwellers against the fierce cold. Tea also aided digestion adding much-needed vitamins and minerals to their spartan diet.

Getting tea to Tibet proved to be a problem, however. Under pain of death, the Chinese Royal Court ordered that no tea plants, seeds, or even processed leaves mixed with seeds could be exported to other countries. Eventually, a network of trails was laid out over the treacherous, icy mountains. Caravans of Tibetan horses, medicinal herbs, wool, fur, feathers, and turquoise were traded for highly taxed "border tea."

The processed tea leaves, especially those that came from Yunnan, were pressed into bricks to make them easy to transport. People broke the bricks, soaking crumbled, dried leaves overnight in water. The next day, the infused tea was churned in a wooden cylinder with salt, yak butter, and sometimes goat milk. The salt helped prevent dehydration; yak butter, with twice the fat of cow's milk, provided energy. This buttery broth-like brew, called *bocha*, was poured into a copper or silver teapot kept on a low fire until ready to serve. After the tea was drunk, the butter residue, left behind in the cup, was spread on chapped skin.

The Tang Dynasty, and all the Chinese governments thereafter, used tea to control the border countries until 1949 when the policy came to an end. In 1951, The People's Liberation Army invaded Tibet forcing the ruling Dalai Lama to flee to India. Once the region was firmly under Chinese control, tea seeds and plants were shipped to the territory and technicians helped develop tea cultivation. Today, Tibetans grow their own organic green tea and also drink black Nepalese tea or *pu-erh*.

Long before ships shuttled tea from Asia to Europe, the Tang-Tibet Road and The Tea-Horse Road were the main trunks of the tea trail which wound through Nepal, India and Russia into Europe. Modern highways, and the world's highest railway (16,000 feet above sea level in some places) shadow the tracks of these ancient roads, but our tour group flew cross-country from Beijing to Lhasa, the spiritual and cultural capital of Tibet.

My adventure began on the plane when the director of Heifer International's China-Tibet program happened to be my seat mate. Delighted to use his English, Dr. Huosheng, who has a degree in animal genetics, was thrilled to discover that my husband and I support Heifer's global programs to end hunger and care for the earth.

Flipping open his laptop computer, Dr. Huosheng shared photos of various projects. Many poor Tibetans still live a nomadic life following their herds of sheep, yak and *dzo* (a hybrid yak-cow) to steep mountain pastures. The Tibetan Autonomous Regional Heifer Programs focus on improving animal breeds, disease prevention and raising animals in ways compatible with the environment.

Participating families are given animals and taught how to keep them healthy. The gift is passed on to others in the community when the animal reproduces. Boys as young as ten are expected to care for goats, but the government is trying to enroll children in boarding schools to learn woodworking, sewing, reading, writing and math. As a weekend beekeeper, I was especially interested to learn that bee hives have been introduced to replace the income lost when chicken and ducks were eliminated to prevent the spread of bird flu.

Every single photo showed rugged mountains sharp against an impossibly bright, blue sky. "The sky in Tibet is horrible," Dr. Huosheng exclaimed. "It is so big and we are so small." When I replied that I was looking forward to sunny skies after a week in dusty Beijing, he warned me that in spring, the amount of oxygen in the thin mountain air is one third less than usual. To combat altitude sickness he advised moving slowly, eating several small, high-calorie meals, resting often, and drinking lots of liquids. Chinese Red Flower and Tibetan tea would be readily available, he said.

Spring winds made for a bumpy landing, so the doctor stowed his laptop, but I was enthralled by glimpses of snow-covered peaks poking through the clouds. On the ground, our tour group was met by Tibetan guides who draped silk prayer scarves around our necks and helped haul our mountain of luggage onto a bus.

Dr. Huosheng was right, the effort of climbing just a few steps left many of us struggling for breath, but the view was even more breathtaking. Turquoise rivers snaked through stony ground staked with wind-blasted trees. Turnip-shaped, white-washed stone *chortens*, containing the ashes of spiritual leaders, were crowned with flapping prayer flags. An old woman patted yak dung on a stone wall to dry it for cooking fuel. A man crisscrossed a plowed field, dipping his hand in and out of a shoulder bag, sowing barley seeds. Black and white yaks, tufts of red wool tied to their horns, watched me watch them as the bus poked along behind a huge caravan of Chinese army trucks.

At last, we reached Lhasa. The name means "the habitation of supernatural beings" and it has been Tibet's capital since the seventh century. The city, spread out over a stark desert plain, herded by mountains, is dominated by the thirteen-story Potala Palace. Set on the highest hill, the 1,000 room palace was once home to the country's secular and spiritual leaders. You can still see the private quarters of the fourteenth Dalai Lama, untouched from the day he escaped the invading Chinese army disguised as a Tibetan soldier.

After years of suppression, religious ceremonies are held here again. Prostrating pilgrims approach the complex clockwise, bowing and praying even before they enter the inner chapels. Many of the faithful tote plastic bags filled with yak-butter used to fuel lamps flickering before the images of their saints. Even though I'm not a Buddhist, I felt that I was standing on sacred ground.

Given the altitude (12,139 feet), the crush of people, and the smoky rooms, hiking up and down the steep stairs was dizzy, thirsty work. I was more than ready for a relaxing cup of tea. Our guides drove us to the entrance of a narrow street edged with whitewashed stone and cement block buildings, many with elaborately decorated iron-work doors. A short walk led to a courtyard, where we were greeted by a smiling grandmother wearing the traditional Tibetan full-length dark dress, a bold striped bangdian (apron) and bright red embroidered boots. Opposite her in the courtyard, the family had gotten a jump start on tea, heating water in a large metal kettle positioned over a "butterfly-fold" solar panel.

Inside, four generations presided over the tea table that was set up in the house's main room. Beds are pushed to the walls during the day, and low banquettes and stools are used for seating. The family offered plates of homemade cookies that looked like fat noodles, toasted barley, fruit, seeds, hard candies and dried yak cheese, which tasted a bit like aged pecorino. Strong, salty, milky black tea was pre-brewed and served from a Chinese-style metal thermos, but our hostess demonstrated making tea the old-fashioned way, in a wooden *Jhandong* churn, with a little help from her grandson.

We learned that tea is called the "water of long life." Red-tinged tea, symbolizing good luck is served at festive occasions. Young men and women traditionally exchanged gifts of tea when they announced their engagement. In Tibetan monasteries, novices are responsible for preparing tea and serving it to monks while they pray. Lamas hold a morning prayer ceremony at which *tsampa* (roasted barley), is mixed with the tea to make gruel. This porridge is sanctified and served as a holy "tea offering."

Tea is still drunk with every meal and enjoyed as comfort food at any time. Once upon a time, people carried a personal tea cup with them wherever they went. The cup was a wooden bowl, but our hosts were proud of their Western-style ceramic cups. Etiquette suggests that guests sip only half the tea in their cups leaving the rest to signal the host that they would like more. It is still considered hospitable to top off visitors' cups every time they take a sip.

After tea we were generously invited to take a closer look at our hosts' home, which included an entire room set up as a religious shrine—complete with holy images and butter lamps. The family embodied the Buddhist precepts of patience, compassion, and respect for all forms of life as they patiently posed for numerous photos and answered the group's many questions. The only question left unanswered is: when can I go back for *bocha*?

"May you be filled with loving kindness.
May you be well.
May you be peaceful and at ease.
May you be happy." —Tibetan Buddhist Blessing

Credits

Acknowledgments

Not one word of this book would have been possible without the love and support of my husband and best friend, Michael. My children, Roman and Teresa, have made me smile throughout the process and our newest baby Mila has the special place of being born along with this book. Thank you to my parents who were "always proud no matter what" I did, and to my brother, a talented writer in his own right, who always challenged me to keep up. I am grateful to my grandparents, who taught me about hard work and what it means to chase a dream, and to my aunts, uncles, and cousins who have provided me with more material than I could write in a lifetime.

Without my new "sisters," Mary Germanotta Duquette and Chrisanne Douglas, I never would have had the courage to embark on this crazy journey. Thank you to Linda Zoeller Anderson for giving me the courage to call myself a "writer." I also extend thanks to Kristi Bates, who has always been quick to offer babysitting, moral support, and friendship.

I thank the writers who have provided me guidance, encouragement, and mentorship—most particularly Babette Donaldson, Frank Hadley Murphy, and Laura Childs. I am grateful to Cynthia Gold, who treated me like a professional right from the beginning, and to Jane Pettigrew who has inspired me to immerse myself in the world of tea. I want to thank the magazine editors who took a chance on me and who taught me how to succeed, in particular Anne Nelson, Justin Shatwell, Valerie Schroth, Alicia Woodward, and Beth Hillson. A particular thanks to William Notte, the Acquisitions Editor at Tuttle, who believed in this project and made it real, and to my editor Jon Steever for his patience, enthusiasm, and restrained, but transformative, editing.

Thank you to those amazing tea writers who contributed to this book. The words you have written have inspired me, made me laugh and made me cry. I must also thank my dedicated illustrators for their beautiful and inspired work: Stephanie Sewhuk-Thomas and Katie Sloss.

Finally, I cannot thank my Tea Pages readers enough for their support and for continuing to read my work. That blog is what brought me to this day.

About the Author

Katrina Ávila Munichiello is a freelance writer, blogger, and tea lover. After nearly a decade working in public health and non-profit administration, she launched a new career as a writer. Specializing in writing about tea, parenting, and food allergies, she has been published in *Yankee Magazine*, *The Boston Globe Magazine*, *Living Without*, among others. Other interests include knitting and crafts, cooking, and, of course, tea. A native of Maine, Katrina, her husband Michael, and their three children now live in Massachusetts.

About the Writers and Artists

Tea Reveries

Frank Hadley Murphy was born in Boston and is the author of the 2008 book, *The Spirit of Tea*. He is the owner of Jade Mountain Tea Company in Santa Fe, New Mexico, and he has served as a judge at a Chinese tea competition and an international tea competition. He lectures nationally and has contributed to *TEA: A Magazine* and *The American Tea Journal*. Murphy graduated from the American Tea Masters Association's tea mastership program and is a senior student of tea master and Taoist priest Roy Fong. He is currently working on his second book, a piece of comedic tea fiction set in New Mexico.

Stephanie Wright is a psychologist and writer living in South Carolina with her three daughters and fellow psychologist and partner Michael. She is the author of *The Witch War Histories, Volume I* which was published in 2004. She and her writing can be found on the web at wrighterly.com, wrighterly.livejournal.com, sixsentences.blogspot.com, and other locations.

The *Outlook* Editor-in-Chief, **Lyman Abbott** (1835–1922), is likely the author of the uncredited essay: "The Spectator on Tea." The son of writer Jacob Abbott, Lyman left his law practice to study theology. He was ordained as a minister in 1860. He became the Editor of the *Illustrated Christian Weekly* in 1870 and later served as Editor-in-Chief of Henry Ward Beecher's *Christian Union*. The latter publication became *The Outlook* in 1893. Lyman Abbott succeeded Beecher as minister at a church in Brooklyn, New York. There were three other editors of *The Outlook* during this period: **Ernest Hamlin Abbott** (1870–1931), **Hamilton Wright Mabie** (1846–1916), and **Francis Rufus Bellamy** (1886–1972).

Peter Anthony Motteux was born in the early 1660s in Rouen, Normandy, France with the name Pierre Antoine Motteux. He left France when the Edict of Nantes was revoked, making Protestantism illegal. He settled in London, England and became an author, playwright, and translator. Motteux is best known for editing a translation of Francois Rabelais's works with Thomas Urqhardt. He was also the editor of England's first magazine *The Gentleman's Journal* from 1692 to 1694. He died in 1718, leaving a wife and three children.

Roy Fong is the founder/proprietor of San Francisco's Imperial Tea Court, the first traditional Chinese teahouse in America. A native of Hong Kong, Mr. Fong was introduced to tea early in life, and has spent many years developing close relations with tea growers and producers in China and Taiwan. He is an ordained Taoist priest and he previously served as Head of Research and Development for the International Tea Masters Association. Fong's writing has been published in *The New York Times*, *Forbes*, *Gourmet*, *TEA: A Magazine*, and other publications, and he has appeared on the National Public Radio program *Talk of the Nation*. He lives with his wife Grace and their two daughters in the San Francisco Bay area. His book, *Great Teas of China*, was published in 2010.

Babette Donaldson is the author of five books in the Emma Lea children's series, including *Emma Lea's Magic Teapot* and *Emma Lea's Tea with Daddy*, as well as the booklet *Family Tea Time*. She has a B.A. in Creative Writing and a B.F.A. in Ceramic Art from San Francisco State University and received her tea certification from the Specialty Tea Institute, the education division of The Tea Council of the United States. She is currently the director of Tea Suite, a nonprofit organization supporting art education. She is co-founder of the International Tea Sippers Society.

Lu T'ung (790–835) was a poet born in northern China and lived a reclusive life, referring to himself as Yü-ch'uan-tzû, the "Philosopher of Jade River." T'ung composed the *Song of Tea* during China's T'ang Dynasty (A.D. 618–907) A great lover of tea, he unexpectedly received a package of Yang-hsien tea from a member of the imperial court. He was overwhelmed by this gift as Yang-hsien was grown solely for use by the emperor. He wrote his poem in honor of the occasion. T'ung died during a mass execution at the capital where he was visiting at the invitation of Emperor Wen Tsung.

Stephen D. Owyoung was born in San Francisco and is a graduate of the University of Hawai'i. He served as a curator of Asian art at museums including the St. Louis Art Museum. He has spent twenty years lecturing on Chinese and Japanese tea and writing about the history, literature and poetry of tea in China.

Kien-Long (also **Qianlong**) (1711–1799) ruled China from 1736–1795, making him one of the longest ruling emperors in history. His given name was Hung-li. In 1795 he abdicated his position to his son so as not to surpass the length of his grandfather's reign. Kien-Long was a great lover of the arts, an essayist, a calligrapher, and a poet. In his lifetime he composed more than 40,000 poems.

Aaron Fisher graduated from university, where he began studying tea and Eastern thought, with a Bachelors degree in anthropology and philosophy. After a decade traveling the world, living in several countries, he settled in Taiwan. Fisher is the senior managing editor of all English publications at Wushing Publications, Ltd. and contributes to *The Art of Tea*. He is also a co-founder and the editor-in-chief of the online magazine *The Leaf*. He has contributed to *Puerh Teapot*, *Enjoying Tea*, *Fresh Cup*, and some smaller publications. In 2008, he helped translate and edit *The Ancient Tea Horse Road* by Sian Yan Yun and his books *Tea Wisdom* and *The Way of Tea* were published in 2009.

SECOND STEEP
Tea Connections

Jodi-Anne Williams-Rogers is a qualified and experienced environmentalist, social development officer and freelance writer living in Johannesburg, South Africa. She has a keen interest in writing, poetry, spirituality, nature and researching South African heritage and life histories of the late 1800s. She has had articles published in *Renaissance Magazine* (Republic of South Africa), *Vision Magazine* (R.S.A.), and *Kindred Spirit Magazine* (U.K.)

Anne Thackeray Ritchie, born in 1837, is the oldest daughter of William Makepeace Thackeray (author of *Vanity Fair*) and Isabella Creach Shawe. Ritchie published a dozen texts and spent her life among some of England's best known authors, including the Brownings, Alfred Lord Tennyson, and the Carlyles, among others. She died in 1919.

Julie L. Carney has worked as an animal control officer, an elected city council member, an online bookseller, and as a volunteer at the Sundance Film Festival. She enjoys writing and photography, and living in the most beautiful part of Upstate New York.

Stephanie Lemmons Wilson enjoys many forms of creative expression including dancing, sewing, tea parties and writing. Find out more about these endeavors at her blog, *Steph's Cup of Tea* (stephcupoftea.blogspot.com).

Louisa May Alcott, born in 1832, was the famous novelist daughter of transcendentalist Amos Bronson Alcott and his wife Abigail May Alcott. She spent much of her life in Massachusetts, most notably in Concord near Henry David Thoreau, Ralph Waldo Emerson, Margaret Fuller, and Nathaniel Hawthorne. The most famous of her thirty books and story collections include *Little Women*, *Little Men*, and *Jo's Boys*. In addition to being an author, Alcott was a suffragette. Alcott died in 1888 at just 55 years of age.

Sir William Robertson Nicoll was born in 1851 in Lumsden, Aberdeenshire and became an ordained minister. He wrote under the pseudonym Claudius Clear. In 1884, he became the editor for Hodder & Stoughton's *The Expositor* and he founded the *British Weekly*, in which "Correspondence of Claudius Clear" was a feature. He is credited with discovering J. M. Barrie who later penned *Peter Pan*. Nicoll died in 1923.

Russell Hires is a single dad living in Tampa, FL, who discovered tea a couple of years ago.

Kirsten Kristensen is the founder and owner of Tea 4 U. She is certified at the highest professional level by the Specialty Tea Institute of Tea USA and is a freelance writer specializing in tea and health topics. Kristensen is also the first Vice President on the board of the Brookdale Community College Alumni Association. In 1998, in Denmark, she published *When Penelope Travels Along,* a practical book about expatriation, cultural adjustment, and assimilation. She is married with two daughters.

Jehiel Keeler Hoyt was born in 1820 and died in 1895. Hoyt was a journalist, the editor of the *New Brunswick Times* (NJ), and was also a compiler of *Hoyt's Cyclopedia of Practical Quotations* in 1881. *The Romance of the Table* was published in 1872 by Times Publishing Co.

Dorothy Ziemann is a married mother of two daughters who works as a pediatric emergency room nurse. She is passionate about knitting, reading, and of course, tea!

THIRD STEEP
Tea Rituals

Sir Edwin Arnold was a poet and journalist who lived in England. He was born in 1832 in Kent, attended Oxford, and became a schoolmaster. He spent seven years in India as a school principal. He became a journalist for the *Daily Telegraph* and a well-regarded poet. His third marriage was to a Japanese woman, Tama Kurokawa, and he spent time living in Japan, leading to the writing of *Seas and Lands* in 1891. He died in 1904.

As the lead writer and editor for *Gongfu Girl* (gongfugirl.com), **Virginia Wright** (aka Cinnabar) has been researching and writing about tea for over two years. Her interest in tea practices is broad, ranging from cave-aged Chinese *pu-erh* to Japanese *Gyokuro* to Turkish *Çay* and beyond, with great focus on the specificity of each culture's traditions. Of course, she enjoys drinking tea as well!

George Robert Gissing was an English novelist born in 1857 in Yorkshire. He was a decorated student, winning the Shakespeare prize in 1875 at Owens College. He was later expelled and spent time in prison for stealing to support a girlfriend. He re-applied himself to a writing career and gained regard in the field. His better-known works include *New Grub Street*, *In the Year of Jubilee*, and *Born in Exile*. By the time of his death in 1903, at the age of 46, he was in his third marriage.

Joseph Rudyard Kipling was born in Bombay, India (then a British colony) in 1865. He was sent to England at age 5 for school, but returned to India at 16 to serve as assistant editor of a local newspaper. Kipling later returned to England and then to the United States after his marriage. In his early 30's he came back to England permanently. He was a very successful author, with such celebrated works as *The Jungle Book* (including the story "Rikki-Tikki Tavi"), *Just So Stories*, and *Kim*. In 1907 he was granted the Nobel Prize in Literature and he was offered the position of British Poet Laureate and knighthood, but he refused both. Kipling had three children, two of whom predeceased him; one died in combat in World War I at age 18. Kipling died in 1936.

At Mr. Kaji Aso's request and with her deep gratitude, **Kate Finnegan** continues his way of tea ceremony at Kaji Aso Studio's tea house, House of Flower Wind. In addition to serving as the Director of Kaji Aso Studio (www.kajiasostudio.com), Finnegan is a painter who has exhibited in Japan, the U.S., and Italy. She is an instructor at Tufts University and the Cambridge Center for Adult Education.

Debbra Summers is fifty-four years old chronologically, nineteen years young at heart, and five foot one and a half. She was born, adopted, and raised in 1960s suburbia. She now lives on a farm near Peterborough in Ontario, Canada with her husband of 30 years, Eric, and their current furry entourage of six cats and an English Bull Terrier named Rosie. She has always loved words and her Gran.

Muriel Harris had a lengthy career in journalism with the *London Daily News*, the *Daily Telegraph*, and *The Manchester Guardian*. She was the first to review George Orwell's work. Harris's first book, *The Seventh Gate*, received a $5,000 prize. Her second book was *The Clinic of Dr. Aicadre*.

FOURTH STEEP

Tea Careers

George Constance, a native of New Orleans, has a B.S. in Geology and worked as a micro-paleontological consultant for over 20 years. He developed his love of tea after meeting his Indian-born wife, Daya. In January 2004 they opened the Indonique Tea & Chai Café which was forced closed by Hurricane Katrina sixteen months later. George and Daya currently reside in Glastonbury, Connecticut. Indonique, now also based in Connecticut, continues to sell tea online.

Dheepa Maturi, a graduate of the University of Chicago Law School, practiced law in a variety of settings—law firms, a public hospital, private practice—before launching her specialty tea brand, Chai, Baby! The Chai, Baby! product line includes all natural, 100% organic, and Fair Trade Certified teas, as well as tea-related gift items.

Thomas J. Lipton was born in Glasgow, Scotland in 1848. His parents ran a grocery store and Lipton left school at 13 to work to support his family. He became a cabin boy at age 16 and picked up odd jobs throughout the United States. In 1870 he came back to Scotland with the hopes of revitalizing the family business. He eventually developed a chain of stores throughout Britain. At age 40 he began his tea business, purchasing tea estates throughout Sri Lanka. He was best known for his phenomenal skills in marketing and his passion for yachting. Lipton died in 1931, at age 83. His tea business continues to be a household name.

Cynthia Gold has been the Tea Sommelier at Swan's Café at The Boston Park Plaza Hotel & Towers since 2004. Gold left her corporate career to pursue her culinary arts education at Johnson & Wales University, graduating Summa Cum Laude. She later attended the Culinary Institute of America in Hyde Park, New York, studying pastry and baking. She has cooked in many restaurants and also owned two of her own: Tea Tray in the Sky, and Elements. Her career and writing has been featured in magazines including *Art Culinaire*, *Boston Magazine*, *Yankee Magazine*, *Imbibe Magazine*, and *Plate Magazine*, among others.

Ahmed Rahim, a native of Iraq, founded Numi with his sister Reem in 1999. They began the business out of Reem's Oakland, California apartment and introduced little known herbs to the United States tea market, including *rooibos*, lemon myrtle, honeybush, and dry desert lime. They have now grown the business to operations in a 25,000 square foot space and continue to make a name for themselves with their high quality products and their commitment to sustainability.

William Gordon Stables was a Scotsman born in 1840. He was a surgeon in the Royal Navy and also wrote adventure fiction for boys and books about animals, health, and history. He composed more than 130 books in his lifetime. He was married in 1874 and died in 1910 at age 69.

Rob Nunally has been the owner of Onomea Tea Company in Hawaii since 2004, when he founded the company with his partner Mike Longo. Nunally is also President of Meta Technologies, a technology sales and solutions company. He graduated from California State University, Hayward's School of Business and Economics with a B.S. in Information Systems. Onomea Tea Company currently has more than 2,200 tea plants and they hope to have three acres of plantings by 2012.

Le Yih was born and raised in Hae-yang, a coastal city in eastern China's Shandong province.

Sebastian Beckwith is the founder of In Pursuit of Tea and is a ranking American tea authority based in New York City. He teaches educational seminars at New York City's China Institute and the Institute of Culinary Education, as well as at museums and other venues. He also leads presentations with the internationally known, integrative health expert Dr. Andrew Weil at Columbia University. He spends several months each year in Asia sourcing teas.

Jane Pettigrew left her career as a language and communications trainer to open her shop, Tea-Time, in Clapham Common, U.K. She has since become a lecturer, writer, and consultant about the world of tea. She has written 13 books on the many and varied aspects of tea, its production, history and culture, and she writes for tea-related magazines and journals. Ms. Pettigrew teaches tea masterclasses and tea tastings, speaks on radio and television, and acts as a consultant to tea companies, new tea businesses, and tableware and teaware companies.

FIFTH STEEP
Tea Travels

Acclaimed filmmaker **Les Blank** has made numerous documentary films since 1960, including *Werner Herzog Eats His Shoe* (1979), *Burden of Dreams* (1982), *Gap-Toothed Women* (1987), and *The Maestro: King of the Cowboy Artists* (1994). *Chulas Fronteras* (1976) and *Garlic Is As Good As Ten Mothers* (1980) have been selected for inclusion in the Library of Congress National Film Registry. Retrospectives of his films have taken place at the Museum of Modern Art in New York, the Walker Art Center in Minneapolis and the Cinémathèque Française in Paris. In 1990, Blank received the American Film Institute's Maya Deren Award for outstanding lifetime achievement, and in 2007 he was the forty-eighth recipient of the Edward MacDowell Medal for outstanding contributions to the field. For more information about Mr. Blank and his films, visit www.lesblank.com.

Gina Leibrecht is a filmmaker and editor living in San Francisco. In 2007 she completed the feature documentary *All in this Tea* with the acclaimed documentary filmmaker Les Blank. Her work has screened in festivals and been broadcast worldwide.

Robert Fortune, born in 1812, was a botanist from Scotland who was responsible for first bringing many of the secrets of tea out of China. As a young man, Fortune worked and trained at Edinburgh's Botanic Gardens. He eventually became London Horticultural Society's collector of Chinese plants and then was hired by the East India Company to sneak into China and bring out as many tea plants and seedlings and as much information about cultivation and production as possible. He brought 20,000 tea plants and seedlings to India's Darjeeling region. He published five books about his travels. Fortune died in 1880.

Eliza Ruhamah Scidmore was a writer, photographer, and geographer born in 1856 in Wisconsin. She was the first female board member of the National Geographic Society. She frequently visited Japan. Scidmore was the original advocate for the planting of the now-famous cherry trees in Washington D.C. She died in 1928.

James Norwood Pratt was born in Winston-Salem, North Carolina, and brought up on land that has been in his family since before the American Revolution. Pratt was educated at Chapel Hill and abroad, and published his first book on tea in 1982. He is one of the world's most widely read authorities on tea and tea lore, thanks to books translated into multiple languages, and numerous columns, articles, and print and TV interviews in U.S. and overseas media. The landmark *James Norwood Pratt's Tea Dictionary* was published in 2009. He appears in several films and the theatrical production of *Okakura* and lives with his wife Valerie Turner in San Francisco.

Laura Childs is the author of ten *Tea Shop Mysteries*. They have been named to the *USA Today* and *New York Times* bestseller lists. For more information, go to www.laurachilds.com.

Brother Anthony of Taizé was born in England in 1942. He has been living in Korea since 1980 and became a citizen in 1994 with the name An Sonjae. He is a professor emeritus at Sogang University, Seoul. He has published many translations of modern Korean literature. He is the co-author of *The Korean Way of Tea* and of *Three Korean Tea Classics*. His home page (http://hompi.sogang.ac.kr/anthony/) is well-known.

Danielle Beaudette, owner of The Cozy Tea Cart, in Brookline, NH, is one of forty in the world who is certified as a Tea Specialist through the Specialty Tea Institute, NY and has completed more than thirty-five tea seminars at the World Tea Expo. She's traveled to China as part of a trade delegation, and to India and Sri Lanka to further her knowledge on the production of tea in these countries.

John Millstead is a police officer in Texas. Prior to that he taught conversational English in China. He was also an international equity trader in Alaska. John has been married to his wife, Anna for over twenty years and they have two wonderful children: J.T. and Marlina.

Stefani Hite is a former public relations/marketing art director turned educator. After several years of teaching and working as a school administrator, Stef and her husband Gary began organizing and leading student exchanges in the firm belief that there is no educational substitute for "being there" and that culture-based travel should be a component of every child's learning experiences.

*Information about **Sir Edwin Arnold** can be found in the "About the Writers: THIRD STEEP: Tea Rituals" section on page 249.*

G. J. Gordon, Esq. was the committee secretary for the Tea Committee established by the British Government in the 1830s to examine the possibility of creating a tea industry in India. Gordon was sent on a mission to China to obtain tea seeds and plants, as well as trained tea makers.

Winnie W. Yu is the Director/Founder of Berkeley, California's Teance. Winnie's passion for tea began at a young age in Hong Kong, an international mecca of local and foreign cuisines. Although fermented *pu-erh* teas were preferred by the old and *Tikuanyins* by the young, Winnie developed a taste for a wide range of teas, from green to black. After moving to the U.S., she was unable to find quality authentic and unblended teas, so she decided to import them herself. After working several years to establish sourcing and infrastructure, Winnie decided to challenge the project further by setting up a new concept of tea—that of a tea tasting program, expertly prepared and education-oriented, to properly introduce tea to the public in the U.S. To this end, Teance was created.

Elizabeth Knight, a former Tea Sommelier at the St. Regis Hotel, is regarded as one of America's foremost authorities on tea and entertaining. Knight is a certified English Tea Master, after studying with Edward Bramah of the Bramah Tea & Coffee Museum and completing the Whittard Tea Course and Examination in London, England. She has published several books on tea and entertaining including *Tea with Friends, Celtic Tea with Friends, Welcome Home,* and *Tea in the City: New York*. Her writing has appeared in *Romantic Homes, Tea & Coffee Asia*, and *TEA: A Magazine* and she speaks all over the country.

The Artists

Katie Sloss has been studying, teaching, and enjoying art at Kaji Aso Studio in Boston for thirty-five years. She also teaches at the Cambridge Center for Adult Education.

Stephane Sewhuk Thomas is a New Hampshire-based artist, former teacher, and mother of three boys.